REVOLUTIONARY AFTEREFFECTS

Revolutionary Aftereffects

Material, Social, and Cultural Legacies of 1917 in Russia Today

EDITED BY MEGAN SWIFT

UNIVERSITY OF TORONTO PRESS
Toronto Buffalo London

ISBN 978-1-4875-2956-7 (cloth)   ISBN 978-1-4875-2958-1 (EPUB)
                                   ISBN 978-1-4875-2957-4 (PDF)

Library and Archives Canada Cataloguing in Publication

Title: Revolutionary aftereffects : material, social, and cultural legacies of 1917
   in Russia today / edited by Megan Swift.
Names: Swift, Megan, 1971– editor.
Description: Includes bibliographical references and index.
Identifiers: Canadiana (print) 20220160619 | Canadiana (ebook) 20220162247 |
   ISBN 9781487529567 (cloth) | ISBN 9781487529581 (EPUB) |
   ISBN 9781487529574 (PDF)
Subjects: LCSH: Russia (Federation) – History – 1991– | LCSH: Russia
   (Federation) – History – Revolution, 1917–1921 – Influence. | LCSH: Russia
   (Federation) – Civilization – 20th century. | LCSH: Russia
   (Federation) – Civilization – 21st century.
Classification: LCC DK510.76.R48 2022 | DDC 947.086–dc23

This book has been published with the help of a grant from the Federation
for the Humanities and Social Sciences, through the Awards to Scholarly
Publications Program, using funds provided by the Social Sciences and
Humanities Research Council of Canada.

We wish to acknowledge the land on which the University of Toronto Press
operates. This land is the traditional territory of the Wendat, the Anishnaabeg,
the Haudenosaunee, the Métis, and the Mississaugas of the Credit First Nation.

University of Toronto Press acknowledges the financial support of the
Government of Canada, the Canada Council for the Arts, and the Ontario Arts
Council, an agency of the Government of Ontario, for its publishing activities.

Canada Council Conseil des Arts
for the Arts   du Canada

ONTARIO ARTS COUNCIL
CONSEIL DES ARTS DE L'ONTARIO
an Ontario government agency
un organisme du gouvernement de l'Ontario

Funded by the   Financé par le
Government   gouvernement
of Canada   du Canada

Contents

Part III: Artistic and Conceptual Aftereffects

REVOLUTIONARY AFTEREFFECTS

Introduction: Reverberations from the Past

MEGAN SWIFT

October 2017 marked a century since the revolutionary events that transformed Russia and legendarily shook the rest of the world. Jubilee moments such as these, indeed Russian and Soviet anniversaries more widely, have performed a pivotal cultural role: they constituted an important calendar of mass festivals of public life that brought together different generations as participants and spectators, and they formed a cycle of occasions that chronicled the longevity of regimes and celebrated the political and cultural symbols crucial to them. Missed, belated, or newly introduced anniversaries cued the public on fluctuations in state policy and the rise and fall of leading cultural figures. From celebrations of the founding of Moscow and St Petersburg, to the birth and death dates of Pushkin and Tolstoy, to military victories, scientific inventions, and civic achievements, imperial, Soviet, and post-socialist anniversaries express(ed) a very broad range of national, cultural, and historical markers, and continue to articulate Russia's sense of its past, present, and path forward.

This volume is concerned with the legacies of 1917 in Russia today, and while the contributing scholars were first prompted to explore this theme on the occasion of the 100th anniversary of 1917, the wider theme of the interplay between 1917 and today continues to be pressing. As Myroslav Shkandrij notes in his recently published monograph, revolutionary turning-points often spark "memory wars" in their aftermath. These memory wars tend to flare around anniversary events, and the disaccord and counter-histories they inspire contribute to the process of consolidating national identity.[1] Thirty years after the fall of the Soviet Union, the revolution looms large – not only because Russians remain divided over whether it arrived forcibly or inevitably, and whether it was a colossally tragic or colossally generative event, but also because the material, social, cultural, scientific, anthropological, geographical, and even moral residues of the revolution remain everywhere in Putin's Russia – now detached, of course, from the political centre that engendered them. This past is indelibly marked on the skin of the nation: some of these traces are fading and barely visible, some are livid scars, and some are so familiar that they appear to be an organic part of the body politic.

This study of revolutionary aftereffects forms part of an emerging discussion in new scholarship about the ways in which Soviet cultural norms and practices inform post-socialist culture more widely.[2] Maria Litovskaya argues that the term "post-Soviet" (rather than another designation that would emphasize a break with the recent past) demonstrates that today's Russians understand themselves by and large as "heirs of the Soviet experience," still sorting through a past that remains mostly "undigested."[3] In the field of demography, Inna Leykin has shown that contemporary policymaking, while ostensibly utilizing neoliberal practices, has in fact absorbed and rearticulated the approaches of the Soviet past.[4] Increasingly, as political scientist Gulnaz Sharafutdinova argues, "cultural and psychological explanations of Russian politics and society [...] focus on mental and attitudinal legacies of the Soviet Union."[5] The current study of 1917, its memorialization and legacy, then, contributes to a larger direction in scholarship that reveals a fundamental, multilayered, and widely dispersed continuity underlying an apparent discourse of discontinuity in post-socialist Russia.[6]

Serguei Oushakine has recently drawn attention to how cultures (or "new" states like post-socialist Russia) inherit a tangible network or "hardscape" of memory places, and how these spaces express the "material legacy of the recent past."[7] A postcolonial approach to the study of socialism prompts us to question the ways, as Oushakine puts it, that "key configurations produced by seven decades of the Soviet way of life" become forms of "intense investment," and also critique, of that recent past.[8] Oushakine's work extends Alexander Etkind's analysis of how this "hardscape" of memory sites takes its place alongside the intangible "softscape" of narratives, texts, and commemorative and cultural rituals.[9] This conceptualization of a past that leaves both hard and soft residues embedded within the present is important for this volume of collected scholarship, which concerns itself with the material as well as the non-material legacies of the revolution. In order to appreciate the wide range of these legacies, this volume includes three parts: material and mnemonic, social and environmental, and artistic and conceptual aftereffects of 1917. The volume encompasses memory and memorialization, city monuments and architecture, gendered practices and norms of family structure, ways of organizing the non-Russian Indigenous cultures that lived alongside the Slavs for centuries into political designations of land and language, land masses delineated as worthy of conservation, and conceptual categories like heroism and violence. The point is that although some revolutionary aftereffects are more direct and evident than others, it is their wide spread and totality that suggest a deep, ongoing cultural phenomenon worthy of extended exploration.

Russia maintains a highly ambiguous relationship with October 1917 as one of its chief "originary narratives."[10] Despite the official ideological repudiation of Marxism-Leninism, Lenin continues to inhabit his centrally located mausoleum, *Pravda* is still publishing (now on-line), and new Mosfilm cinema still begins with the solemn pirouette of the worker and collective farm girl holding a hammer and sickle aloft. More complexly, as Maria Silina's chapter shows, Russia's urban spaces are strewn with revolutionary memorials, spaces, and place names that have become partly or completely detached from their origins, so that the revolution is commemorated through heritage objects that may be ubiquitous yet indecipherable to viewers. Julie Deschepper's chapter highlights the strange contradiction that while most of the revolution-era Constructivist buildings are internationally recognized as having a unique heritage status, the same structures, at home, are neglected and undervalued by Russia's state officials – and are often being kept up instead by young hipster Russians who were born well after the Soviet Union ceased to exist. My own chapter explores why the centenary of the Russian Revolution emerged as a largely silent jubilee that coincided with the first large-scale state commemorations of 1917's most notorious outcome, Stalin's political repressions. My contribution examines the unveiling of the Garden of Memory, in Butovo on the outskirts of Moscow, and the Wall of Sorrow, in the centre of Moscow, in fall 2017, and what these unveilings suggest about how the national past is being mapped, shaped, and distorted by commemorative practice in Russia today.

As this brief overview of some of the work presented in this volume shows, the reverberations of the revolution span outwards very widely and have registered in a broad range of fields, yet scholarly work looking at 1917 in and after 2017 has tended not to reflect this.[11] *Revolutionary Aftereffects* holds, in common with Frederick C. Corney's innovative *Telling October: Memory and the Making of the Bolshevik Revolution* (2004), an interest in how the revolution has been memorialized. While Corney's work is limited to the tenth anniversary of 1917 and the twentieth anniversary of 1905, as well as focusing on the Communist Party's *self*-narration of the revolution through Istpart (the Commission on the History of the October Revolution and the Russian Communist Party), this volume begins by considering how the shaping of the revolutionary narrative has moved forward after 100 years, taking into account the voices of multiple memory agents. Furthermore, the concept of this multi-authored volume is to go *beyond* the issue of memorialization and into the virtually innumerable ways in which the trajectory of the revolution has transformed Russian society and culture. This book includes in one place views from anthropology, art history, cultural history, gender studies, geography, heritage studies, film studies, literary studies, and sociology. It also acknowledges that not all afteraffects of the revolution have had identical trajectories: to borrow Putin's metaphor of the revolution as a time-bomb, the explosion sounded later and the fuse-line ran more circuitously in some areas than in others.[12] An important corrective of this volume is to erase the compartmentalization that so often occurs in Slavic studies between the social sciences and the humanities, allowing a more comprehensive dialogue between the work of scholars in sociology, geography, and anthropology alongside those in cultural studies.

To wit, Jennifer Utrata's contribution examines the stalled gender revolution as an unresolved social legacy of the Russian Revolution that redefined the heart and homes of the nation. While the revolution ushered in truly world-leading advances in gender-progressive legislation and opened domestic doors wide, guiding a flood of women out into the paid labour force, it also retained the residues of more traditional cultural norms whereby, at the end of the workday, women re-entered the domestic door for their "second shift" of unpaid labour as the family's primary caregiver, cook, and housekeeper. A century later, this paradox created by the revolution, in which Russian women were leading the world in gender advances on paper while carrying the burden of emancipation's hidden work at home, continues to have implications for Russia's sky-high divorce rate and the normalization of single motherhood as a family paradigm. Utrata's chapter examines this fallout of 1917 in Putin's Russia, highlighting both the advantages and the challenges of this underlying social contradiction.

David G. Anderson's chapter investigates the resurgence of an ethnographic term seemingly buried with the Soviet past. Putin's use of the term *etnos*, at the Victory Day celebrations in 2017, signalled a return to concepts and categories that shaped nationalities policy after the October Revolution but that were both repudiated and used in disguised form in the following decades of Soviet power. Anderson argues that the persistence of *etnos*-based arguments signals the continued importance of Soviet ethnic governance for post-Soviet statecraft. Like Soviet nationalities policy, national parks policies literally redrew the post-1917 map. Michael W. Tripp's chapter shows that while revolutionary Russia foregrounded modernization and industrialization, it was nonetheless responsible for the creation of a nation-wide (indeed union-wide) system of national parks, as well as for the legislation that is the foundation of environmental protection today. Tripp traces how the revolution delegitimized the preservation of nature as an entity unto itself yet continued to enlarge the scope and territorial extent of the country's protected areas. The establishment of national parks became instrumental in the process of resurrecting environmental consciousness and bolstering the political agendas of Soviet republics – culminating in their independence. This process was repeated within Russia as a mechanism for proclaiming regional autonomy, and now in the Putin era, as Tripp shows, declarations of national park status along the country's peripheries continue to blur the line between the environmental and the political.

One of the key paradoxes at the core of this volume is that, while in the country of its inception the centenary of the Russian Revolution arrived without pomp or circumstance, it was a major topic of interest for academics in North America, Europe, Scandinavia, Southeast Asia, Oceania, and the Global South. Close to forty academic conferences were held in 2017 to discuss the centenary and its meanings, although most of them focused on the revolution's global and transnational impacts – in other words its outcomes abroad rather than at home. This approach treated the Russian Revolution as an export product that reverberated throughout left movements in Europe in the twentieth century and that inspired political resistance to racism and imperialism for the "Black Atlantic," uniting the agendas of the colonial subjects of European empires internationally, as well as of Black Americans.[13] The centenary conference at Columbia University in New York, for instance, foregrounded this notion of revolution as export, exploring issues of the emancipation of women, sexual and gay liberation, internationalism, racial equality, and the rights of ethnic minorities as themes introduced in 1917 that remain topics of urgent debate in, and regarding, Trump-era America.[14]

If these conferences suggested that the Russian Revolution, or at least its legacies, are "everywhere," others took an opposite tack, challenging the very notion of revolution as a conceptual category. At Harvard in the United States and at the University of St Gallen in Switzerland, centenary conferences asked how "revolution" as a concept is to be understood, given the challenges and failures of (every, but especially the Russian) revolution's "rhetoric of emancipation" and "totalizing project[s]."[15] In this scheme, the legitimacy of 1917 is retrospectively challenged not on ideological but on ontological terms. Only one of these international conferences, hosted at University College London (UCL), addressed a theme close to the one that concerns this volume, namely, the importance of the vestiges of revolutionary Russia for Russia today. Although the UCL conference focused on questions of legal tradition, which is largely outside the purview of the present study, it holds in common with our venture a commitment to cross-disciplinarity and inquiry into social and cultural changes in revolutionary ideas as they are carried into Russia's present, and on into its future.[16]

These international gatherings of specialists at academic conferences were not the only scholarly responses to the 1917 centenary. Some fifty scholarly articles were published on the occasion or topic of the revolution's 100th jubilee in journals outside of Russia between 2016 and 2018, by historians, economists, political scientists, literary scholars, and others. The vast majority of these focused on the outcomes of the revolution for the rest of the world: only about one-fifth explored the meaning of the revolution for Russia and Russians. These academic books, articles, and special journal editions highlighted the lessons of the revolution and its impact and called for a rethinking of its legacies. Yet when scholars in Europe, North America, and the Global South wrote about the revolution in 2017, the lion's share of their works were dedicated to an old agenda. Recognizing the global significance of the Russian Revolution, they became defences of or diatribes against global socialist movements and were concerned with whether Marxist-inspired leftist political systems can be considered to have exhausted themselves, were never viable, or, conversely, why Russia's revolution remains an inspiration for governments and oppositions around the globe, especially for the Global South and especially in light of recent crises of capitalism.[17] Michael David-Fox put it well by positing, in his article "Toward a Life Cycle Analysis of the Russian Revolution," that the global impact of communism has overshadowed inquiry into the unfolding trajectory of the revolution itself.[18]

In fact the question of the legitimacy of socialism as a system of government would not be a particularly pressing one for today's specialists in Russian studies and completely misses the point, made by Ilya Kalinin in 2017, that "Perhaps nothing bares the irony of history as much as the fact of the revolution's jubilee."[19] Several scholars specializing in Russia, including those gathered in the present volume, have tended to direct their investigations of the 1917 centenary to the complicated meaning and relevance of the revolution for Russia today. In articles of 2017 and 2018, Sheila Fitzpatrick and Olga Malinova both suggested that Putin, despite being the leader of New Russia and a product of old (Soviet) Russia, would not manage to reconcile the discourses of Russia's past and present. In these and other articles looking at the 1917 centenary, the revolution was described as "embarrassing" for Putin, although "uncomfortable" would probably be closer to the mark.[20] As the Swiss scholar Korine Amacher wrote, "In effect, how is [Putin] to commemorate an event opposed to everything he stands for: stability, traditions, authority and respect for the State?"[21] Kalinin summarized the situation concisely, saying that fall 2017 placed the Putin state in the awkward position of having to address "events that they would rather forget about." Kalinin argues that the Russian state's fear of a revolutionary threat has created the need to safeguard the "revolutionary spectre" from entering the "social consciousness" and therefore blocks the very process of "historical reflection" upon the revolution itself.[22] That crucial process of historical reflection is taking place, instead, in volumes such as the present one.

1917 was more controversial than ever in 2017. The only real consensus was that there was no agreement on the meaning of this landmark event, but also no sense of reconciliation with the past. It is worth keeping in mind, however, that there was never a single or static narrative of the revolution even during Soviet times; rather, the discourse around the revolution kept evolving and transforming.[23] In Russia, in the absence of a unifying state – or public – position on the revolution and with no focalizing event to commemorate its centenary, the 1917 jubilee was met with a diffuse response from academics and media commentators. Some thirty academic conferences were held in 2017 in the Russian Federation on the topic of the Russian February and October Revolutions. Tellingly, the February Revolution was reconsidered as a "conspiracy and coup" rather than as a legitimate revolutionary event, and in *Pravda*, the actors of February 1917 were compared to the Putin oppositionists on Bolotnaia Square in the mass opposition demonstrations of 2011 and the "For Free Elections" protests of 2012. This retrospective reinterpretation turned the February Revolution into what was termed the "first coloured revolution."[24]

Another new approach of 2017, perhaps counter-intuitively for an event that ushered in state atheism, was to view the revolution through the lens of its religious themes or spiritual outcomes, or in conferences hosted by Russian Orthodox organizations.[25] The position of the Russian Orthodox Church, that the revolution was unequivocally a national tragedy, dovetails in intriguing ways with that of the current Russian government. Margarete Zimmermann has recently explored the ways in which the policies of both church and state refute revolution and any possibility of a repetition of the events of 1917.[26]

To sum up, what characterized most of the scholarly responses to the 1917 centenary both inside and outside of Russia, in articles and conferences, was the instrumentalization of the revolution and its outcomes to serve other agendas. Rarely was the revolution considered on its own terms, and rarely in terms of how it has shaped culture in Russia today – although this is the aim of the present volume.

As Elena Baraban points out in her contribution, the lack of agreement on the meaning and outcomes of the revolution may be a positive sign. She suggests that it may be more productive to view the "coexistence of celebratory, appreciative, negative, and mixed responses to the revolution" as a sign of "society's willingness to engage in a mature discussion of its history." Baraban argues that, in the works of bestselling novelist Boris Akunin (Grigori Chkhartishvili), it is precisely the failure of heroism as a discursive category, the negation of the revolution as a heroic event, and the inability of the revolution to produce heroes that allows the possibility of plural and individual responses to 1917. Whether the mixed responses to 1917 that we saw at the revolution's centenary signal healthy pluralism or a chaotic lack of consensus remains a question to be determined in the years to come. The final word in this introduction, as in the volume, goes to Mark Lipovetsky, who suggests that the root cause for the ambiguity and dissension over the revolution originates in a late-Soviet narrative of revolutionary violence that led to the diminishment and, perhaps, the erasure of the revolution "completely." Lipovetsky focuses on films and television productions from the 1960s until the present day that challenge the emancipatory meaning of 1917, replacing it with various narratives of violence, and posits "that the revolution still constitutes a foundational trauma for contemporary elites, cultural and political alike."

It is precisely this foundational trauma and the inability of contemporary state narratives to come to terms with it that creates the silence and ambiguity that we observed from the Russian state on the occasion of the revolution's centenary. The work of this volume is to illuminate the paradoxes and challenges at work in finding a narrative that can accommodate the painful, contradictory, and ambiguous reverberations of the revolutionary past. It is clear that the revolution's aftereffects did not stop dead with the fall of communism in 1991. Those ten days that shook the world, in John Reed's famous phrase, have become ten decades that shaped today's Russia.

July 2021

One month after completing this introduction we selected the cover art for the volume. Ukrainian artist Daria Marchenko's 2015 portrait of Russian president Vladimir Putin, crafted from bullet casings that she had collected in the Donbas region, seemed to visually capture the sense that the face of Russia today has been fashioned out of a violent conflagration of the past in ways that are both discernible and not immediately evident. When Russia invaded sovereign Ukraine in February 2022, setting off a humanitarian disaster, our selection of Marchenko's work, which she called "The Face of War," seemed prescient. Although the present volume does not concern the war in Ukraine, it underlines how important a specialist knowledge of the past has become for understanding Russia's present. Marchenko's stirring portrait also reminds us that the task of the artist, like that of the scholar, is to sort through the empty casings, the littered outcomes of ugly actions, and shape them into a form that elevates human endeavours.

April 2022

NOTES

1 Shkandrij, *Revolutionary Ukraine, 1917–2017*, 1–7.
2 See for instance Satter, *It Was a Long Time Ago, and It Never Happened Anyway*; Sorokin, "Post-sovetskii chelovek razocharoval bol'she chem sovetskii"; Arkhangelski, "Maining konflikta i katastrofy"; and Oushakine, "'We're Nostalgic but We're Not Crazy.'"
3 Litovskaya, "The Function of the Soviet Experience in Post-Soviet Discourse," 15.
4 See Leykin, "The History and Afterlife of Soviet Demography."
5 Sharafutdinova, "Was There a 'Simple Soviet' Person?," 175.
6 For our purposes "1917" is used metonymously to designate the revolution above and beyond just the calendar year 1917.
7 Oushakine, "Postcolonial Estrangements," 286.
8 Ibid., 308.
9 Etkind, "Hard and Soft in Cultural Memory," 40, 56.
10 Oushakine, "Postcolonial Estrangements," 308. The year 1917, of course, included both a February and an October Revolution. While the former toppled the tsar and brought in a provisional government, it was during the latter that the Bolsheviks seized power and began to implement the decrees, reforms, laws, and cultural policies that would characterize the Soviet period, 1917–1991. In this volume "the revolution" will refer to the October Revolution unless otherwise specified.

11 The books that emerged to mark 100 years since 1917 mostly harked "back to the beginning," offering new perspectives on revolutionary Russia, or imagining alternative outcomes. *Centenary of the Russian Revolution: 1917–2017*, a 2018 volume put out by prominent historians in Spain, provides a detailed historiography of how the revolution has been interpreted but does not include reflections on the centenary's meaning. That task is broached in two chapters (of seventeen) of the 2019 volume *Circles of the Russian Revolution: Internal and International Consequences of the Year 1917 in Russia*. See Kolonitsky and Matskevich, "Idle Memory? The 1917 Anniversary in Russia," 202–19, and Malinova, "A Quiet Jubilee: Practices of the Political Commemoration of the Centenary of the 1917 Revolution(s) in Russia," 220–41, both in Adamski and Gajosj, eds, *Circles of the Russian Revolution*.

12 Putin referred to the time-bomb in his first television interview, in December 1991 with St Petersburg Channel 5. See https://ok.ru /putinpravo/topic/70537868156928.

13 "The Red and the Black – the Russian Revolution and the Black Atlantic," held at the University of Central Lancashire in Preston, UK, from 13–15 October 2017.

14 "Agitation for Freedom: Revolution and Its Avant-Garde," held at Columbia University in New York on 1 December 2017.

15 "Red Century: What Do We Make of Revolution?," a graduate conference held at Harvard University in Cambridge, Massachusetts, from 31 March to 1 April 2017, and "One Hundred Years That Shook the World: Failures, Legacies and Futures of the Russian Revolution," University of St Gallen, Switzerland (5–7 October 2017).

16 "Russia's Revolutionary Century: 1917–2017," held at University College London, London, UK, 4–5 November 2017.

17 These works include: Joaquín Aparicio, "Lo posible se hizo real. La Revolución de octubre cien años después" [The Possible Became Real. The October Revolution One Hundred Years Later], *Sociología Histórica* 8, (2017): 41–63; Wilson do Nascimento Barbosa, "One Hundred Years of Learning: The Russian Revolution of 1917," *Agrarian South: Journal of Political Economy* 6, 2 (2017): 221–36; Peter J. Boettke, "A Legacy of Lies and Lost Souls: The Russian Revolution at One Hundred Years," *The Independent Review* 22, 2 (2017): 191–7; Bruno Bosteels, "State or Commune: Viewing the October Revolution from the Land of Zapata," *Constellations* 24, 4 (2017): 570–9; Anthony Gronowicz, "The Global Significance of the Russian Revolution: Imperialism and the Socialist Resistance," *Journal of Labor and Society* 20, 3 (2017): 349–72; Minqi Li, "Barbarism or Socialism: 1917–2017–2050 (?)," *Agrarian South: Journal of Political Economy* 6, 2 (2017):

263–86; Artemy Magun, "The Intellectual Heritage of the 1917 Revolution: Reflection and Negativity," *Constellations* 24, 4 (2017): 580–93; Roger D. Marwick, "Violence to Velvet: Revolutions – 1917 to 2017," *Slavic Review* 76, 3 (2017): 600–9; Sean Sayers, "Reflections on the Centenary of the Russian Revolution," *International Critical Thought* 8, 3 (2018): 257–65.

18 David-Fox, "Toward a Life Cycle Analysis of the Russian Revolution."

19 Kalinin, "2017-yi: Prizrak revoliutsii."

20 Fitzpatrick, "Celebrating (or Not) the Russian Revolution"; and Malinova, "The Embarrassing Centenary: Reinterpretation of the 1917 Revolution in the Official Historical Narrative of Post-Soviet Russia (1991–2017)." See also Amacher, "L'embarrassante mémoire de la Révolution russe."

21 "En effet, comment commémorer un événement qui s'oppose à tout ce qu'il prône: La stabilité, les traditions, l'autorité, le respect de l'État?" (my translation), in Amacher, "L'embarrassante mémoire de la Révolution russe."

22 Kalinin, "2017-yi: Prizrak revoliutsii."

23 In the 1938 *History of the USSR, Short Course*, the revolution was credited with moving Russia from "backwardness to progress"; whereas in the history textbook put out for the fiftieth anniversary in 1967 the importance of the revolution lay in "initiating a socialist transformation of the world." By 1989, a critical distance from the revolution and especially its Stalinist outcomes was permitted: "The creation of the Soviet political system was an achievement [...] But here the deformities were great. Socialist democracy and openness were needlessly curbed, socialist legality was broken." See Shestakov, *Istoriia SSSR. Kratkii kurs*, 3; Berkhin, *Istoriia SSSR*, 3; and Korablev, *Istoriia SSSR*, 351. Fascinatingly, Director of the Russian State Archive of Socio-Political History Andrei Sorokin amalgamates the arguments of the 1967 and 1989 textbooks in his preface to the 2017 exhibition catalogue *1917: Kod revoliutsii. 1917 The Code of Revolution*, 3.

24 "Fevral'skaia revoliutsiia 1917 i 'put' Fevralia': Nerealizovannyi potentsial, mesto i znachenie v istorii Rossii" [The February Revolution 1917 and the "Path of February": Its Unrealized Potential, Place and Meaning in the History of Russia], a conference organized by Memorial and held in Moscow on 15 March 2017. See also Petr Multaluli, "Istorik: Fevral'skaia revoliutsiia – eto pervyi Maidan."

25 For instance, "Religiia i Russkaia revoliutsiia" [Religion and the Russian Revolution], a conference held at the Russian Academy of National Economy and Public Administration (RANEPA), 26–8 October 2017; and "Dukhovnye itogi revoliutsii v Rossii: Kollektivnyi chelovek i tragediia lichnosti" [Spiritual Outcomes of the Revolution in Russia: The Collective

Person and the Tragedy of Individuality], organized by the Transfiguration Brotherhood in Moscow Oblast, Istra Region, 8–9 November 2017.
26 Zimmermann, "Never Again! Remembering October 1917 in the Contemporary Russian Orthodox Church."

REFERENCES

Amacher, Korine. "L'embarrassante mémoire de la Révolution russe." *La Vie des idées*, 14 April 2017: http://www.laviedesidees.fr/La-memoire -encombrante-de-la-Revolution-russe.html. Accessed 17 November 2018.

Arkhangelski, Andrei. "Maining konflikta i katastrofy. Chem putin-skii chelovek otlichaetsia ot sovetskogo," Moskovski Tsentr Karnegi, 2 February 2018, at http://carnegie.ru/commentary/75408. Accessed 28 January 2020.

Berkhin, I. *Istoriia SSSR: Epokha sotsializma. Uchebnoe posobie dlia srednei shkoly.* Moscow: Izdatel'stvo "Prosveshchenie," 1967.

David-Fox, Michael. "Toward a Life Cycle Analysis of the Russian Revolution." *Kritika: Explorations in Russian and Eurasian History* 18, 4 (2017): 741–83.

Etkind, Alexander. "Hard and Soft in Cultural Memory: Political Mourning in Russia and Germany." *Grey Room* 16, Memory/History/Democracy (Summer 2004): 36–59.

Fitzpatrick, Sheila. "Celebrating (or Not) the Russian Revolution." *Journal of Contemporary History* 52, 4 (2017): 816–31.

Kalinin, Ilya. "2017-yi: Prizrak revoliutsii." *Neprikosnovennyi zapas,* and on polit.ru: https://polit.ru/article/2017/11/09/revolution/, published 9 November 2017. Accessed 19 January 2019.

Kolonitsky, Boris, and Mariya Matskevich. "Idle Memory? The 1917 Anniversary in Russia." In *Circles of the Russian Revolution: Internal and International Consequences of the Year 1917 in Russia,* edited by Lukasz Adamski and Bartlomiej Gajosi, 202–19. London and New York: Routledge, 2019.

Korablev, Iu.I. *Istoriia SSSR: Uchebnik dlia desiatogo klassa srednei shkoly.* Moscow: "Prosveshchenie," 1989.

Leykin, Inna. "The History and Afterlife of Soviet Demography: The Socialist Roots of Post-Soviet Neoliberalism." *Slavic Review* 78, 1 (Spring 2019): 149–72.

Litovskaya, Maria. "The Function of the Soviet Experience in Post-Soviet Discourse." In *Russia's New Fin de Siècle: Contemporary Culture between Past and Present,* edited by Birgit Beumers, Ellen Thomas, Melanie Marshall, and Tom Newman, 13–28. Bristol and Chicago: Intellect, 2013.

Malinova, Olga. "The Embarrassing Centenary: Reinterpretation of the 1917 Revolution in the Official Historical Narrative of Post-Soviet Russia (1991–2017)." *Nationalities Papers* Vol. 46, No. 2, 2018: 272–89.

– "A Quiet Jubilee: Practices of the Political Commemoration of the Centenary of the 1917 Revolution(s) in Russia." In *Circles of the Russian Revolution: Internal and International Consequences of the Year 1917 in Russia,* edited by Lukasz Adamski and Bartlomiej Gajosj, 220–41. London and New York: Routledge, 2019.

Multaluli, Petr. "Istorik: Fevral'skaia revoliutsiia – eto pervyi Maidan" [Historian: The February Revolution Is the First Maidan]. Pravda.ru, 3 February 2017: https://www.pravda.ru/news/society/03-02-2017 /1323845-multatuli-0/. Accessed 3 August 2017.

Oushakine, Serguei A. "Postcolonial Estrangements: Claiming a Space between Stalin and Hitler." In *Rites of Place: Public Commemoration in Russia and Eastern Europe,* edited by Julie A. Buckler and Emily D. Johnson, 285–315. Evanston, IL: Northwestern University Press, 2013.

– "'We're Nostalgic but We're Not Crazy': Retrofitting the Past in Russia." *The Russian Review* 66, 3 (July 2007): 451–82.

Satter, David. *It Was a Long Time Ago, and It Never Happened Anyway: Russia and the Communist Past.* New Haven, CT: Yale University Press, 2011.

Sharafutdinova, Gulnaz. "Was There a 'Simple Soviet' Person? Debating the Politics and Sociology of 'Homo Sovieticus.'" *Slavic Review* 78, 1 (Spring 2019): 173–95.

Shestakov, A.V. *Istoriia SSSR. Kratkii kurs. Uchebnik dlia 3-go I 4-go klassov.* Moscow: Gos. Uch-ped. Izd. Narkomprosa RSFSR, 1938.

Shkandrij, Myroslav. *Revolutionary Ukraine, 1917–2017. History's Flashpoints and Today's Memory Wars.* London and New York: Routledge, 2020.

Sorokin, Andrei. *1917: Kod revoliutsii. 1917 The Code of Revolution.* Moscow: Gosudarstvennyi tsentral'nyi muzei sovremennoi istorii, 2017.

Sorokin, Vladimir. "Post-sovetskii chelovek razocharoval bol'she chem sovetskii." *Kommersant.ru,* 17August 2015, at https://www.kommersant.ru /doc/2786007. Accessed 28 January 2020.

Zimmermann, Margarete. "Never Again! Remembering October 1917 in the Contemporary Russian Orthodox Church." *Scando-Slavica* 64, 1 (2018): 95–106: https://doi.org/10.1080/00806765.2018.1449435. Accessed 19 January 2019.

PART I

Material and Mnemonic Aftereffects

1 The Silent Jubilee, the Blank Space: Spatial and Commemorative Practice around the 1917 Centenary

MEGAN SWIFT

In a concept of time organized around revolutions, it was clear what had to be retained from the past in order to prepare the future. It was clear as well what parts must be suppressed, forgotten, and destroyed if need be.

Pierre Nora, "Reasons for the Current Upsurge in Memory" (2007)

What was most notable about the centenary of the Russian Revolution was the absence of state commemoration for this controversial but cornerstone event of the national past. The seventy-four Soviet years of Russian history have presented a challenge to state memory politics in post-socialist Russia, providing on the one hand the Second World War victory that is marked with the most prominent state holiday (9 May) under Putin, and on the other hand requiring distance from 7 November, the anniversary of the revolution.[1] Almost thirty years after the fall of communism, Russians remain split over the meaning, role, and legacy of 1917. At the same time, the state's most unifying commemorative date, the 9 May anniversary of victory, has emerged as a point of dissension between Russia and other European nations, who contest Russia's monolithic internal narrative of Soviet victory. This chapter examines commemorative practice and the state use of public rituals, celebrations, and spaces in the process of selecting and mapping the Russian national past in post-Soviet Russia. Returning to the documents of the Planning Committee for the revolution's centenary, from May 2015, I examine the state's failed attempt to memorialize 1917 using a tribute to national reconciliation, and posit that a complex series of mnemonic substitutions were made in the blank space around 1917, including the first two major state monuments to the victims of Stalinist repression. Yet here the discourse of memorialization was rerouted into a narrative of religious persecution of Russian Orthodox believers, rather than paying tribute to victims of a mass terror. One hundred years after the fact, 1917 is a divisive and unarticulated event that still has not settled into place on the memory map of the national past.

The post-socialist period has been characterized, according to Serguei Oushakine, by the push and pull of dismantling and/or reinvesting in the "structures, conventions and forms" of the Soviet period – and anniversary celebrations are no exception.[2] Whereas under Yeltsin the state distanced itself from mass Soviet-style holiday demonstrations, under Putin this practice was selectively revived and the sixtieth-anniversary celebrations of Victory Day in 2005 became Russia's largest post-Soviet national holiday.[3] Putin invited more than fifty world leaders to attend a military parade in Moscow and in his speech at the formal reception called the Second World War the "most tragic" but at the same time "most heroic" event of the last century.[4] The Russian president termed Victory Day a "sacred day" and "our closest, sincerest and most truly national holiday."[5] This position stands in stark contrast to the revolution's fiftieth-anniversary celebrations in 1967, when the Second World War victory was *not* used to constitute proof of 1917's necessity and legitimacy. At that time, an emphasis was put on socialist Russia's "great emancipatory mission" as a shining example inspiring other socialist revolutions around the globe and leading the way for the fall of the colonial system. The importance of the Second World War victory, in 1967, was that it bolstered the international authority of the Soviet Union and hence its ability to fulfil its international mission.[6] But in May 2005, Foreign Minister Sergey Lavrov's article "Lessons of the Great Victory," published in *Diplomat*, made clear that the "lesson" to be emphasized was "the central, decisive role of the people of our country in the achievement of Victory."[7] The anniversary offered a guidepost for interpreting the national past and articulating a path towards the future. But while that guidepost represented a gathering point for collective national pride *inside* Russia, it became a disputed jubilee in the wider European community and in particular for new European Union members Estonia, Lithuania, Latvia, and Poland. For the leaders of these nations, two of whom refused to attend the sixtieth-anniversary celebrations, the Victory Day jubilee highlighted the contested memory politics surrounding the Second World War. Victory Day for the Baltics and Poland signified not a "master narrative" of Russia as the "heroic liberator of Europe" but rather a "humiliation" and the "loss of independence [and] identity."[8] Latvia's president, Vaira Vīķe-Freiberga, who did attend the Moscow celebrations, publicly called for a process of coming to terms with the past that would allow the Russian state to express regret over the annexation of the Baltic states and Poland enacted through the Molotov-Ribbentrop Pact and the "occupation of the Baltic states for 50 years."[9] This was not the position taken by the Russian state, however, and the seventieth-anniversary celebrations of Victory Day in 2015 continued in the same key as 2005, with Lavrov calling the jubilee "the Great Victory" that "will forever remain a source of pride and a foundation for bringing up the new generation in the spirit of patriotism."[10]

In contrast, post-Soviet commemoration of the 7 November Anniversary of the Great October Socialist Revolution involved a forced identity shift when the holiday was renamed the Day of Reconciliation and Accord by Yeltsin in 1996, and then overwritten in 2005 when Putin moved the state holiday, now named the Day of People's Unity, to 4 November, leaving 7 November as a resonant but no longer relevant page on the calendar.[11] In preparation for the 1917 centenary, the Ministry of Culture under Vladimir Medinsky handed jubilee planning over to the Russian Historical Society and other interested academic societies, so that the questions of the revolution's meaning and relevance in Russia today were dealt with not in state celebrations but in conferences, round-tables, museum and archival exhibits, gallery events, academic books, and the media. The result was a "museumification" of the revolution as an event of the past to be studied, viewed, and discussed in artistic and scholarly settings rather than in state-organized commemorations.[12] If, to paraphrase Maurice Halbwachs, the construction of the collective memory of the past takes place by selecting those events that resonate with the present, then the centenary events sent a message that the revolution resonated as an artifact of the past but not as a ritual relevant to the present.[13]

To put it another way, when it came to Victory Day, on 9 May 2017 the state performances of commemoration – the parade on Red Square, the artillery salute, the international guests – resacralized the narrative of victory, while the centenary events of fall 2017 worked to distance and desacralize October 1917. Scholars like Frederick C. Corney have argued that since 1991 this process of desacralization has increased the equation of the revolution with Stalin's "criminal state," but Sergei Naryshkin, Russia's director of foreign intelligence, who also served on the 1917 centenary organizing committee, has made the opposite claim, positing that the revolution "has stopped dividing and conflicting our citizens."[14] A Levada Center poll taken in March 2017, however, suggests that Naryshkin is wrong: the results reveal a widespread failure to come to terms with the revolution as a painful and unresolved trauma of the past, and a true lack of cohesion regarding the legacy and meaning of 1917.

Russians remain closely divided over whether "Russia should move forward and not dwell on what happened in 1917" (34 per cent), "Russia needs to learn more about the period, in order to avoid repeating its mistakes" (44 per cent), or "Studying the past is not harmful, but is not relevant to Russia's present needs" (20 per cent). The numbers of those who believe that the revolution played a "mostly negative" role in Russia's history has remained quite stable between 1996 under Yeltsin (21 per cent), and 2017 under Putin (25 per cent). A slightly larger but still minority group believe that the revolution played a "mostly positive" role (38 per cent) – and this has grown since 1996, when only 28 per cent felt "mostly positive." The public is even more closely divided on whether the revolution "caused serious harm to Russian culture." In March 2017, 49 per cent believed that it had, while 41 per cent believed that it hadn't.[15] If we proceed from an understanding of anniversaries as public rituals that "affirm common beliefs and ideals" and "create emotional solidarity," then clearly the revolution remains an undecided question, an event for which there is no widespread consensus of meaning – and the events surrounding the 100th anniversary did not help to establish accord.[16]

Examining the 2015 planning documents for the jubilee year, an even more complex narrative emerges. In the transcript of remarks at a round table where the concept of the 1917 jubilee was presented, Minister of Culture Vladimir Medinsky referred to a "living continuity" (zhivaia preemstvennost') running through imperial, Soviet, and post-socialist Russia.[17] The Soviet period, he said, had "great achievements," and today's generation should see the "strength of the human spirit and the heroism of our precursors" in those achievements.[18] But there was also a tragic aspect to the events of the past. For Medinsky that tragedy lies not in Stalin's crimes but in the fact of Russians being divided as a result of the revolution. Today's generation should not understand the past in terms of right and wrong (Medinsky says "not guilty" and "guilty ones"), or Reds and Whites, but rather in terms of two sides who both wanted Russia to flourish but who understood the means to that goal differently. The importance of the past, says Medinsky, is in teaching Russians not to let internal divisions grow. Therefore, the state called for a monument to reconciliation (pamiatnik primireniia) in Crimea, which after the controversial referendum of 2014 had returned home to what he calls its "native harbour," and where the civil war ended in 1920.[19]

This Monument to Reconciliation was one of a mere three memorial projects advanced by the Russian Historical Society to mark the jubilee year. The other two included a set of artistic memorial stamps and an

Figure 1.1. Design for the Monument to National Reconciliation (Sevastopol, Russia)

exhibit called "To the Memory of the Fallen. February. Tragedy. 1917," to be hosted on 18 February 2017 by the Imperial Orthodox Palestinian Society and the Fund of L. Nobel.[20] This last event was undertaken on exactly the date specified, and turned out to be an academic conference, film, and exhibit called "To the memory of the fallen *for belief in Jesus*" (my emphasis) presided over by Patriarch Kirill of Moscow and All Russia, the head of the Russian Orthodox Church.[21] The Monument to National Reconciliation, the final commemorative project marking the centenary of 1917, was to be unveiled on 4 November, Putin's Day of People's Unity, underlining the narrative of historical continuity and national concord. The planned location for this Monument to National Reconciliation, originally Kerch, was moved to Sevastopol.

The design showed a twenty-five-metre column, flanked by an officer of the Red Army and an officer of the White Army. At the top, overseeing both, is a golden figure of the Motherland (figure 1.1). As late as June 2017, just four months before the planned unveiling, construction of the monument was impeded by the protests of a nationalist activist group, "Sut' vremeni" (The Essence of Time), who objected to the fact that the residents of Sevastopol had not been consulted and did not support the construction of the monument.[22] As of 8 November 2017, a square had been prepared, but the monument still had not been constructed, much less unveiled, supposedly in honour of the revolution's centenary.[23] Memorialization of 1917, planned as a tribute to reconciliation with the past, became, literally, a blank space.

This contradiction draws attention to the reasons why Victory Day, also a commemoration of the Soviet past, has emerged as the Putin state's touchstone for memory politics. The narrative around Victory Day still fits seamlessly inside an understanding of the past that Nietzsche, and after him Paul Ricoeur, called monumental history. Monumental history requires that "great moments ... form links in one single chain."[24] This kind of history demands that "entire large parts" of the national past be "forgotten, scorned and washed away."[25] Victory Day has become a conduit for the kind of patriotic nationalism that, Lev Gudkov argues, "serves [...] the centralist and repressive social structure" of the Putin state.[26] Inside Russia, Victory Day has proven resistant to the kinds of challenges and subaltern histories that have developed in the countries of the former Soviet Union, persistently maintaining a "taboo [against] rational analysis."[27] In addition to the challenge mounted against a monolithic understanding of Victory brought to bear by Baltic and Polish national leaders during the sixtieth anniversary of 9 May in 2005, Belarus has, since the late 1980s, also increasingly insisted on a self-narrated war history that counters the one imposed on it by official Soviet culture. This alternative account recodifies the myth of a unified Soviet partisan resistance as an "enforced heroism," instead placing the Belarusian people in the impossible borderland "between Hitler and Stalin."[28]

Putin's Victory Day narrative, however, remains impervious to these challenges. While policymaking has indeed metamorphosized over Putin's terms of office, becoming more critical of feminist and queer activism after the 2012 Pussy Riot arrests, and insisting upon an increasingly anti-Western patriotism in the wake of the For Fair Elections campaign and war with Ukraine, Putin's utilization of Victory Day as a gathering point for patriotic pride has remained remarkably consistent over his terms of office beginning in 2000. In a 2015 speech in the run-up to the seventieth anniversary of 9 May, Sergey Lavrov called the jubilee "the Great Victory" that "will forever remain a source of pride and a foundation for bringing up the new generation in the spirit of patriotism."[29] In the same speech Lavrov referred to the "generation of winners" who had freed Europe and "bor[ne] the brunt of the war."[30] A similar line was taken in the history textbook for public schools published in 2007. In this textbook's manual for teachers, the USSR in 1945 is defined as a "giant superpower that [...] was the victor in the most cruel of all wars."[31] The textbook refers to the annexation of the Baltics in one sentence, saying that, "During the process of defining post-war borders, many territories in Europe fell back to the Soviet Union ... [k SSSR otoshli]"[32] Whereas the 1994 Dolutsky textbook, written under Yeltsin, acknowledges the secret protocol attached to the September 1939 Soviet-German agreement "On Friendship and the Border," which allowed the Soviet Union to absorb Lithuania within its territory, the 2016 Torkunov textbook refers to the agreement but not the secret protocol.[33] Victory Day, not 7 November and not even 4 November, is the day that expresses Russian national unity. Tellingly, the citizens of Sevastopol wanted, instead of the Monument to Reconciliation bringing Red and White together, a monument to the local heroes of the Second World War.[34] As Gudkov points out, "Victory" has become embedded within the very "structures of Russian self-determination," although the "Victory" narrative replaced the idea of Russia as the harbinger of international socialism after the fiftieth-anniversary celebrations in 1967.[35] At 100, the state narrative for the centenary of the revolution, showing that the divisions stemming from 1917 had been overcome, clearly did not resonate. National unity is not understood as a legacy of the revolution.

While Victory Day has become a symbol of national superiority for Putin-era Russia, it is simultaneously a holiday that is the only surviving "totem" of the Soviet past, a fact that presents its own complexities.[36] While Corney argues that a "modern state can really sustain only one successful foundation myth," forcing October to recede as "Victory" thrives, in fact the 1917 centenary drew attention to the difficulty of uncoupling these two events of the national past.[37] As Stephen Lovell has shown, the Great Patriotic War was framed at the time and in the late Soviet years as the "delayed culmination of the revolution," a proof of the legitimacy of 1917.[38] Victory was conjoined to October as a foundation myth for Soviet citizens, for whom "the war was conceptually inextricable from the broader Soviet revolutionary project."[39] Therefore, for the Russian Federation, as successor state of the Soviet Union, to celebrate victory while remaining silent about 1917 requires an act of selective forgetting. Ilya Kalinin, for one, has noted the ambiguous position of the Putin state, which has been forced to balance between the "political rejection of the socialist regime and the symbolic appropriation of the Soviet past."[40] This remodelling of the national past becomes even more intriguing in light of the first two prominent state-sponsored memorializations of Stalinist terror, which took place at the very moment that the 1917 jubilee was *not* being celebrated.

Figure 1.2. The unveiling ceremony of the Garden of Memory at the Butovo
Firing Range (28 September 2017)

The Garden of Memory (*Sad pamiati*), a memorial monument at the
Butovo firing range where some 20,765 victims of the Stalinist terror
were executed between 1936 and 1938, was unveiled on 27 September
2017 (figure 1.2). On 30 October 2017, the Monument to the Victims of
Political Repression (*Pamiatnik zhertvam politicheskikh repressii*), Georgy
Frangulyan's Wall of Sorrow (*Stena skorbi*), was opened in the centre of
Moscow (figure 1.3).[41] Until the year of the 1917 centenary, memorialization of the Stalinist terror had been consigned largely to the realm
of personal memory and unsanctioned gathering. In 2015 the Perm-
36 Memorial Centre of the History of Political Repression, a museum
housed in the only fully preserved Gulag camp in the territory of the former USSR, was closed and its NGO defunded as a foreign agency.[42] The
annual "Return of Names" gathering to honour victims of the Stalinist
terror by doing a reading of their names outside former Soviet political
police headquarters in Moscow, an event requiring some twelve hours,
had always been and remained an unofficial event organized by the
families of victims and state-harassed societies such as Memorial.[43]

Yet when these first state-sponsored memorialization projects finally
did come to fruition, their unveiling ceremonies and the visual imagery of the monuments themselves only led to more questions about
the semiotics of commemoration of the national past under Putin. The
unveiling ceremony for the Garden of Memory at the Butovo firing
range was presided over by Metropolitan Iuvenalii and a small group of

Figure 1.3. Walls inscribed with the names of victims of political repression at Butovo (September 2017). Photograph by Alekander R. Karanik, courtesy of Wikimedia. Used under a CC-BY-SA license

officials from the Russian Orthodox Church.[44] The Butovo firing range itself, along with the Kommunarka site of mass execution, had been purchased by the Russian Orthodox Church in 1995, a church built "on the blood" of the victims, and the "killing fields" fenced off and designated as a sacred space.[45] At the Garden of Memory, a 300-metre- (984-feet-)long, 3-metre- (6.5-feet-)tall granite wall was erected that inscribes the names of victims.[46] In Butovo these are listed chronologically by the day of execution, in alphabetical order, followed by the year of the victim's birth (figure 1.3). The Garden of Memory is indeed set in a garden, with a path for visitors along the memorial wall, which is paralleled on the opposite side by a raised bank. This landscape forces viewers to walk in a long column beside the wall, imitating the spatial practices of a funeral procession.

At the 30 October unveiling of the Wall of Sorrow, President Putin was joined by Patriarch Kirill of Moscow and All Russia, the head of the Russian Orthodox Church. The Wall of Sorrow itself is a dark bronze arced wall 30 metres (100 feet) long and 6.1 metres (20 feet) high. Unlike the Butovo wall, it does not inscribe names but rather represents victims as hooded, anonymous figures. Scratched into the wall like graffiti is the word "remember" in Russian, English, French, Spanish, and eighteen other languages (including all fifteen official languages of the former Soviet republics) (figure 1.5). While Frangulyan himself has likened the shape of the wall to the scythe of the Grim Reaper, the cloaked, elongated figures with bent heads recall depictions of saints in holy icons, and the two cut out "side doors" in the wall (also shaped like human figures) are positioned like the deacons' doors in the iconostasis of a Russian Orthodox Church (figure 1.4).[47] Indeed the central role of Patriarch Kirill and Metropolitan Iuvenalii at these high-profile opening ceremonies of fall 2017, as well as the exclusive use of Russian Orthodox crosses and prayers, misrepresents the Stalinist terror – a multi-faith and multi-ethnic purge that was, moreover, framed in the language of class war at the time – as a memorialization of victims of religious persecution.[48] Patriarch Kirill's declaration, in December 2016, that the 1917 centenary should be met with sincere prayers seems to have been extended onto the centenary's substitute commemoration as well. If Russian Orthodox believers account for approximately 41 per cent of the faith landscape in Russia as of 2012, then the 2017 commemorations of victims of political repression leave out the other 59 per cent of the faith map – the Jewish, Muslim, Buddhist, and atheist believers, as well as the practitioners of Russia's less traditional religions, whose rights were restricted by a 1997 law that replaced the 1990 "Freedom of Faiths" statute making all religions equal under the law.[49] Thus the two new memorials to victims of Stalinist repression, offered up to the public in lieu of the missed centenary and framed by the traditions and imagery of Russian Orthodoxy, threaten to distort the practice of memory and memorialization altogether.[50] In November 2018, further attempts to dominate the narrative of the national past included efforts to ban the "Last Address" campaign in St Petersburg and other cities.[51] Inspired by the *stolpersteine* projects that inscribe the names of Holocaust victims on cobblestones throughout cities in Germany, the "Last Address" project is a grassroots initiative that places small memorial plaques on buildings where terror victims were arrested. The signature silver plaques, with the name, arrest, execution, and rehabilitation date printed on the right and a square cut-out on the left, recall a passport page with the picture cut out. Restrictions on the mounting of

Figure 1.4. Georgy Frangulyan's Wall of Sorrow Memorial to the Victims of Political Repression, unveiled 30 October 2017. B_Veronika_A/Shutterstock.com

Figure 1.5. The wall on the left inscribes the word "Remember" in twenty-two languages. B_Veronika_A/Shutterstock.com

these small memorials to everyday victims suggests an ongoing battle against a self-narrated history of the terror by ordinary citizens. The appearance in 2015 of the non-governmental group "The Immortal [Prison] Hut" (*Bessmertnyi barak*) in opposition to the state-sponsored "The Immortal Regiment," a patriotic society that carries photographs of family members who served in the Great Patriotic War in Victory Day parades, suggests another field of engagement in this battle.[52] The massive Wall of Sorrow stakes a major claim for the state and the church as legitimate speakers for the Soviet past. But the Wall of Sorrow is not just about coopting the memorialization of Stalinist repressions; it is a barrier that can shield the state from the necessity of addressing the revolution. As Ilya Kalinin has argued, the "battle with revolutionary threat" is "not only the discursive but also the ontological centre of Putinist politics."[53] Since the 100th anniversary of the revolution put authorities in the uncomfortable position of having to talk "about events that they would rather forget about," the unveiling of the Wall of Sorrow provided a welcome change of narrative.[54]

In October 2017, instead of an attempt to address the authentic complexities of the national past, the Putin state offered a series of mnemonic substitutions: the historically distanced 4 November holiday for the contested 7 November anniversary; a monument acknowledging a traumatic legacy of the revolution instead of acknowledging the revolution itself; and a commemoration of the victims of political repression framed as, instead, religious repression of Orthodox believers. These substitutions shore up Serguei Oushakine's premise that post-socialist commemorative practices have aimed "not so much at rescuing people and events from oblivion. Rather, these mnemonic practices are structured by a desire to contain and distance the traumatic past." In other words, the massive scale of the tragedy (estimated at somewhere between 700,000 and 1.2 million victims in 1937 alone), the blurred line between victim and perpetrator (Russia's security organs point out that the secret police itself was subjected to ruthless purges), and the fact that it was a crime perpetrated by the state against its own people are "contained and distanced" by reframing the terror, at least for the purposes of public discourse, as an act of religious suppression.[55]

In a 2004 article on memorialization of the Stalinist terror, Alexander Etkind distinguished between the individually produced "soft memory" products like "documents, narratives and literature" that had, until then, comprised the lion's share of terror commemoration in Russia and the "hardening" of memory into state-sponsored "sculptures, obelisks, memorials [and] historical places."[56] As Etkind has argued, a state can assert its own dissimilarity, its own transformation, "[b]y building monuments to its former victims [...] Every such monument affirms the difference between the current state and the former one."[57] Thus, by side-stepping the enormity and complexity of the terror, the Putin state unwittingly reveals its ambiguous sense of distinction from the former Soviet regimes and leaves itself vulnerable to criticism about the continued presence of political repression and prison camps in Russia.

How, then, should we understand the state's 2017 selective amnesia about 1917? If, as Wulf Kansteiner tells us, the difference between history and memory is that history attempts to give an objective rendering of the past with emotional distance from the subject matter, while memory continues to link to current cultural discourse and resists a cool examination from various perspectives, then it appears that state attempts to relegate the revolution to the realm of history in honour of the 1917 centenary resulted, instead, in an upsurge of the complexity and subjectivity that characterize memory.[58]

If we proceed from an understanding of anniversaries as public rituals that "affirm common beliefs and ideals" and "create emotional solidarity," then it would seem that the revolution remains an undecided question.[59] As I have argued, a unifying position on 1917 continues to elude both the Russian state and the Russian public, and while the state has been willing to stake a claim in what Russian academician A.V. Torkunov terms the "universal importance" of the Russian Revolution, it has done so while attempting simultaneously to depoliticize the discourse around revolutionary events.[60] This depoliticization, however, conflicts with the fact that to celebrate, or not celebrate, the jubilee is politicized. While the Communist Party is the keeper of the officially outmoded ideology, the Putin state is the unwilling heir of the anniversary itself.[61]

In her 2018 article on the increasingly strong link between church and state discourse, Margarete Zimmermann argues that the state-proposed position on the revolution, of "unity and reconciliation," follows the course set by the Russian Orthodox Church.[62] According to Olga Malinova, the reason that this idea of reconciliation with the Soviet past did not resonate with the Russian public in 2017 is because it harked back to Boris Yeltsin's feeble and inadequate "Day of Reconciliation and Accord," built on the smouldering ashes of 7 November. For Malinova the only tenable position on the revolution will have to be a national "working-through of a great, tragic, criminal event of the past."[63] But so far this "working through the trauma" approach has been applied only to Stalinist crimes, and only as crimes against martyrs for the faith.

Clearly 1917 remains a contentious issue even more than a century after the fact. Yet the anniversary's status as a productive memory place may, in fact, emerge precisely from its competing meanings and contradictions over those one hundred years. The function of the anniversary in Soviet as well as post-Soviet times has consistently gone beyond its apparent purpose of marking a date. Indeed, anniversary making was employed in Soviet times for diverse objectives, including securing scarce economic resources, to the point that the Committee of People's Commissars had to routinely chastise local committees for zealous and arbitrary use of jubilees.[64] Another significant use of the anniversary was to signal a shift in cultural policy, making anniversaries part of a common semiotic code used in the discourse between state and citizen. St Petersburg's 250th anniversary was (and could be) celebrated on a four-year delay, in 1957, and signalled a crucial change that permitted acknowledgment of Leningrad's special contribution to the war effort.[65] As a rule, a discordant, contentious anniversary meant an important one. One has only to think of Pushkin anniversary events from 1887 to 1949, when the writer was at times claimed or repudiated by the state, and when it could not be finally decided whether to celebrate his life or death.[66] The People's Commissariat of Posts and Telegraph utilized the seventy-fifth anniversary of Dostoevsky's death in 1956 to issue a postage stamp that signalled his full rehabilitation as a "great Soviet writer" after decades of non-anniversaries signalling Dostoevsky's exclusion from the pantheon of literary greats.

Indeed, even Victory Day has not had a monolithic meaning but has been constructed and reconstructed according to various political and cultural exigencies. In 1947, Stalin "downgraded" Victory Day to a working holiday, a policy that Krushchev maintained after 1953 and Brezhnev finally changed by making 9 May a non-working holiday in 1965.[67] As Pierre Nora tells us, *lieux de mémoire* exhibit a "capacity for metamorphosis, an endless recycling of their meaning, and an unpredictable proliferation of their ramifications."[68] The state silence surrounding the 1917 centenary signals that 1917 has been consigned not to the dustbin of history, to borrow Trotsky's famous phrase, but rather to the larger recycling bin of cultural production. This silent centenary has simply added one more layer to the production of its meaning and legacy.

NOTES

1 Much has been written about post-Soviet commemoration of the Second World War. See, for instance, Kirschenbaum, "Introduction. World War II in Soviet and Post-Soviet Memory"; Elizabeth A. Wood, "Performing Memory: Vladimir Putin and the Celebration of World War II in Russia";

Norris, "Memory for Sale: Victory Day 2010 and Russian Remembrance"; and Lovell, "Introduction. World War II and the Remaking of the Soviet Union," in *Shadow of War, Russia and the USSR, 1941 to the Present*, 2–19.

2 Oushakine, "Postcolonial Estrangements," 308.

3 On this see, Ločmele, Procevska, and Zelče, "Celebrations, Commemorative Dates and Related Rituals."

4 Vladimir Putin, "Speech by the President of Russia at a Formal Reception Dedicated to the 60th Anniversary of Victory," The State Kremlin Palace, Moscow, 9 May 2005. http://en.kremlin.ru/events/president/transcripts/22960. Accessed 1 August 2017. All translations from Russian are mine unless otherwise noted.

5 Ibid.; and Vladimir Putin, "Speech by the President of Russia at the Military Parade in Honour of the 60th Anniversary of Victory in the Great Patriotic War," Red Square, Moscow, 9 May 2005. http://en.kremlin.ru/events/president/transcripts/22959. Accessed 1 August 2017.

6 Berkhin, *Istoriia SSSR*, 3–5; Trukhanovskii, ed., *Istoriia mezhdunarodnykh otnoshenii i vneshnei politiki SSSR, 1917–1967 v trekh tomakh*, 5–8.

7 Lavrov, "Uroki velikoi pobedy." All translations from Russian are mine unless otherwise noted.

8 Mälksoo, "The Memory Politics of Becoming European," 664–5.

9 Ibid., 665.

10 Lavrov, "Remarks by Foreign Minister Sergey Lavrov at a Gathering for the 70th Anniversary of Victory in the Great Patriotic War, Moscow, May 5, 2015."

11 For a more detailed synopsis of the evolution of the November holiday, see Elena Baraban's chapter, "The Hero and the Revolution in the Works of Boris Akunin and Akunin-Chkhartishvili," in this volume.

12 Putin, Decree of the President of the Russian Federation "On the Preparation and Carrying Out of Measures Dedicated to the 100th Anniversary of the Revolution of 1917 in Russia."

13 While Maurice Halbwachs (1877–1945) is the first modern theorist of collective memory, scholars like Buckler and Johnson have cautioned that "[t]heorists of cultural memory no longer subscribe to [his] belief that collective memory 'evolves according to its own laws, and any individual remembrances that may penetrate are transformed within a totality of having no personal consciousness.'" Quoted from Maurice Halbwachs, *The Collective Memory*, trans. F.I. and V.Y. Ditter (New York: Harper and Row, 1980). See Buckler and Johnson, "Introduction," in *Rites of Place*, 9.

14 Corney "'Twentieth-Century Apocalypse' or a 'Grimace of Pain'?" 316–17. See the Gusman interview with Naryshkin, "Sergei Naryshkin," at https://historyrussia.org/proekty/100-letie-revolyutsii-1917-goda/sergej-naryshkin-revolyutsionnye-sobytiya-1917-goda-bolshe-ne-raskalyvayut-obshchestvo.html. Accessed 8 May 2018.

15 Levada-Center, "The October Revolution."
16 Ločmele, Procevska, and Zelče, "Celebrations, Commemorative Dates and Related Rituals," 110.
17 Transcript of the public talk by Minister Medinsky, who presented the 100th Anniversary concept, 20 May 2015, in *Odnako*, http://www.odnako .org/blogs/navstrechu-100-letiyu-revolyucii-zveno-v-istoricheskoy -preemstvennosti-epoha-gigantskih-dostizheniy-i-platforma/. The transcript is from a round-table called "100 let Velikoi rossiiskoi revoliutsii: Osmyslenie vo imia konsolidatsii" [100 Years since the Great Russian Revolution: Trying to Give Meaning in the Name of Consolidation] at the Moscow Museum of the Contemporary History of Russia. Accessed 8 May 2018.
18 Ibid.
19 Ibid.
20 The Imperial Orthodox Palestine Society is an academic society dedicated to the study of the Middle East. It was renamed the Russian Palestine Society during the Soviet period but has reclaimed its prerevolutionary title; see http://www.ippo.ru. The fund of L. Nobel supports the Russian Ludwig Nobel Prize [Rossiskaia premiia Ludviga Nobelia], which was established in the late nineteenth century by Swedish engineer, businessman, and humanitarian Ludwig Nobel (older brother of Alfred Nobel who established the Nobel Prize). Putin revived the prize in 2006. It is awarded to "significant persons of today for outstanding professional achievements and unconditional merits to humankind." See http:// ludvignobel.ru.
21 See Putin, Decree of the President of the Russian Federation "On the Preparation and Carrying Out of Measures Dedicated to the 100th Anniversary of the Revolution of 1917;" and https://historyrussia .org/images/documents/sostavorgkomitet.pdf.
22 See the article of 14 June 2017: Sizikov, "Pamiatnik primireniia narod ne primirit: Otkrytoe pis'mo" [The Monument to Reconciliation is not reconciling the people: An open letter]. Accessed 15 May 2018. The activists were part of the Sevastopol chapter of "Sut' vremeni," an internet-based group and self-described "left-patriotic organization" that was founded in 2011 with the goal of opposing ongoing cultural projects aimed at "de-Sovietization" and "de-Stalinization." Their website can be found at: https://eot.su/welcome. Their open letter opposing the 2017 "Monument to Reconciliation," addressed to Sevastopol regional governor Dmitry Ovsianikov and other municipal representatives, can be read here: https://eot.su/tags/sevastopol. Accessed 15 November 2019.
23 See "Skandal'nyi pamiatnik primireniia v Sevastopole stal bratskoi mogiloi biudzhetnykh millionov" [The Scandalous Monument to Reconciliation in

Sevastopol Has Become a Mass Grave for Budgetary Millions], at http://obyektiv.press/analitika/skandalnyj-pamyatnik-primireniya -v-sevastopole-stal-bratskoj-mogiloj-byudzhetnykh-millionov. Accessed 18 April 2018. The monument was unveiled some three and a half years later, on 22 April 2021.

24 Friedrich Nietzsche, *Unfashionable Observations*, quoted in Ricoeur, *Memory, History, Forgetting*, 290.

25 Ibid, 290.

26 Gudkov, "The Fetters of Victory."

27 Ibid.

28 Oushakine, "Postcolonial Estrangements," 301.

29 Lavrov, "Remarks by Foreign Minister Sergey Lavrov at a Gathering for the 70th Anniversary of Victory in the Great Patriotic War, Moscow, May 5, 2015."

30 Ibid.

31 Filippov, *Noveishchaia istoriia Rossii 1945–2006*, 6.

32 Ibid., 10.

33 Dolutskii, *Otechestvennaia istoriia XX vek*, 407; Torkunov, *Istoriia Rossii*, 4.

34 Sizikov, "Pamiatnik primireniia narod ne primirit."

35 Gudkov, "The Fetters of Victory"; and in this volume, see Megan Swift, "Introduction: Reverberations from the Past," 20.

36 Corney, "The Vanishing Traces of October," 337.

37 Ibid.

38 Lovell, *Shadow of War*, 4.

39 Weiner, *Making Sense of War*, 7–8.

40 Kalinin, "2017-yi: prizrak revoliutsii."

41 The date is significant since 30 October is the Day of Remembrance of the Victims of Political Repressions. It has been celebrated since the demise of the Soviet Union in 1991. Frangulyan is the creator of other memorial and monumental sculptures, including ones to Soviet writers Isaac Babel and Joseph Brodsky. His work is found in Moscow and other cities all over Russia, as well as in Italy, Belgium, and Jerusalem.

42 In September 2015 Perm-36 lost its appeal for being categorized as a "foreign agent." See http://www.themoscowtimes.com/news/article /perm-36-ngo-loses-appeal-against-foreign-agent-label/535733.html. Accessed 1 November 2018.

43 Young, "Historical Memory of the Gulag (3): Contested Memory." Accessed 15 October 2017.

44 Iuvenalii is the Metropolitan Krutitsky and Kolomensky, a prestigious position that holds the responsibility of directing the Moscow Patriarchate in periods between patriarchal elections.

45 Comer, "Uncovering Violent Narratives," 168.

46 Ibid., 168. The Vietnam Veterans Memorial is slightly higher (3.1 metres, or 10 feet), but is shorter in length – about 75 metres long, or 246 feet. Since it inscribes more than twice as many names as at the Butovo site (58,320), the script for each name is smaller.

47 The likeness to the imagery of Russian Orthodox iconography was noted by human rights group The Moscow Helsinki Group. See "Predlagat' obshchestvu prostit' prestuplenie gosudarstva protiv chelovechnosti ne imeet prava nikto!" [No One Has the Right to Propose That Society Forgive the Crime of the Government against Humanity]. 15 December 2017. https://mhg.ru/predlagat-obshchestvu-prostit-prestupleniya -gosudarstva-protiv-chelovechnosti-ne-imeet-prava-nikto. Accessed 1 November 2017.

48 Even before the high-profile unveilings of monuments in fall 2017, scholars and critics were calling attention to the potential usurpation of the memory of Stalinist repression by the Russian Orthodox Church. See, for instance, Etkind, "Hard and Soft in Cultural Memory," and Sarah J. Young's blog post, "Historical Memory of the Gulag (3): Contested Memory." Accessed 15 October 2017.

49 These less traditional religions and denominations are required to undergo special registration procedures. The 1997 law also limits the scope of activities in which they can lawfully engage. See Davis, "The Russian Orthodox Church and the Future of Russia," 660–1. On the percentage of Russians who consider themselves Russian Orthodox believers see "Religions in Russia: A new framework," 22 December 2012: http:// www.pravmir.com/religions-in-russia-a-new-framework/. Accessed 1 November 2018.

50 Religious scholar Daniel Payne asserts that the ROC and Putin's Foreign Ministry under Sergei Lavrov have engaged in parallel national expansionist projects. In the church's case, this refers to the reclamation of territories held in Stockholm, Copenhagen, Paris, Nice, Cannes, Biarritz, San Remo, Florence, Vienna, and Baden-Baden; church and state have also jointly expressed a mission to unite Russians living inside and outside of Russia. See Payne, "Spiritual Security, the Russian Orthodox Church, and the Russian Foreign Ministry," 717–18.

51 See Kizyma, "Skandal s zapretom tablichek 'Poslednego adresa' doshel do Putina" [The Scandal of the Ban of "Last Address" Tablets Has Reached Putin]. Accessed 22 December 2018.

52 "Immortal Regiment" parades take place in honour of Victory Day not only in Russia but in diaspora communities as well. Regarding such parades in Canada see https://www.rbth.com/international/2017/05/09 /over-1500-toronto-residents-march-in-the-immortal-regiment_759511.

Accessed 15 November 2019. "The Immortal Prison Hut" was founded in 2015 by activist Andrei Shalaev in order to "preserve the memory of repressions in the USSR." Like the "Immortal Regiment," the group also displays photographs, in this case of those arrested and sent to prison camps. The group's site can be found at https://bessmertnybarak.ru/about/. Accessed 15 November 2019.

53 Kalinin, "2017-yi: prizrak revoliutsii."

54 Ibid.

55 Oushakine, "Postcolonial Estrangements," 286. Antony Kalashnikov notes in his review article of scholarship produced on the collective memory of Stalinism since 2000 that Russian books on the Stalinist past "focus [...] largely on the memory of the Great Patriotic War rather than on the memory of Stalinism proper." See Kalashnikov, "Stalinist Crimes and the Ethics of Memory," 599.

56 At that time, Etkind wrote that "One who is not dedicated to pursuing the issue will be hard pressed to find a monument, a cemetery, or a museum devoted to the memory of the Soviet terror." Etkind, "Hard and Soft in Cultural Memory," 37, 41.

57 Ibid, 41.

58 Kansteiner, quoted in Muižnieks, *Geopolitics of History*, 8.

59 Ločmele, Procevska, and Zelče, "Celebrations, Commemorative Dates and Related Rituals," 110.

60 Torkunov, "The Universal Importance of the Russian Revolution of 1917." Torkunov claims that 2,000 books supported by the Russian Academy of Sciences were "timed" to come out in the centenary year.

61 Currently the Communist Party holds 43 seats out of 450 in the State Duma.

62 Margarete Zimmermann, "Never Again!," 95.

63 Malinova, "The Embarrassing Centenary," 24.

64 Emily Johnson points out that "both at the end of the 1920s and in April 1941, the Council of People's Commissars [Sovnarkom] issued decrees intended to curtail what it called 'a bacchanalia of jubilee-celebrating.'" See the decree of 10 April 1941 preserved in archives of the Executive Committee of the Leningrad City Soviet: TsGA, SPb, f. 7384, op. 29, ed. Khr. 711, l. 235. Quoted in Johnson, "Jubilation Deferred," 91.

65 Johnson, "Jubilation Deferred," 82.

66 On the Pushkin anniversaries of the twentieth century and particularly under Stalin, see Stephanie Sandler, *Commemorating Pushkin: Russia's Myth of a National Poet* (Stanford, CA: Stanford University Press, 2004), and Karen Petrone, *Life Has Become More Joyous, Comrades: Celebrations in the Time of Stalin* (Bloomington, IN: Indiana University Press, 2000). See also Jonathan Brooks Platt's book, *Greetings, Pushkin! Stalinist Cultural Politics*

and the Russian National Bard (Pittsburgh: Pittsburgh University Press, 2016), specifically dedicated to this jubilee: https://www.amazon.com /Greetings-Pushkin-Stalinist-Cultural-Politics/dp/0822964155/ref=sr_1_3 ?ie=UTF8&qid=1544641870&sr=8-3&keywords=platt+jonathan.
67 Norris, "Memory for Sale," 206–9. See also Wolfe, "Past as Present, Myth, or History? Discourses of Time and the Great Fatherland War," 262.
68 Nora, "Between Memory and History," 12.

REFERENCES

Berkhin, I. *Istoriia SSSR: Epokha sotsializma. Uchebnoe posobie dlia srednei shkoly.* Moscow: Izdatel'stvo "Prosveshchenie," 1967.
Buckler, Julie, and Emily D. Johnson. "Introduction." In *Rites of Place: Public Commemoration in Russia and Eastern Europe,* edited by Julie A. Buckler and Emily D. Johnson, 3–12. Evanston, Ill: Northwestern University Press, 2013.
Comer, Margaret. "Uncovering Violent Narratives: The Heritage of Stalinist Repression in Russia since 1991." In *Heritage of Death: Landscapes of Emotion, Memory and Practice,* edited by M. Frihammar and H. Silverman, 164–77. London: Taylor and Francis, 2017.
Corney, Frederick C. "'Twentieth-Century Apocalypse' or a 'Grimace of Pain'? The Vanishing Traces of October." In *Russian Culture in War and Revolution, 1914–22, Book 2: Political Culture, Identities, Mentalities, and Memory,* edited by Murray Frame, Boris Kolonitskii, Steven G. Marks, and Melissa K. Stockdale, 313–39. Bloomington, IN: Slavica, 2014.
Davis, Derek H. "The Russian Orthodox Church and the Future of Russia." *Journal of Church and State* 44, 4 (Autumn 2002): 657–70.
Dolutskii, Igor'. *Otechestvennaia istoriia, XX vek: Uchebnik dlia X klassa srednei shkoly.* Moscow: Mnemozina, 1994.
Engelhardt, Tom. *The End of Victory Culture, Cold War America and the Disillusioning of a Generation.* New York: HarperCollins, 1995.
Etkind, Alexander. "Hard and Soft in Cultural Memory: Political Mourning in Russia and Germany." *Grey Room,* 16, Memory/History/Democracy (Summer 2004): 36–59.
Filippov, A.V. *Noveishchaia istoriia Rossii 1945–2006. Kniga dlia uchitelia.* Moscow: "Prosveshchenie," 2007. http://yanko.lib.ru/books/hist/pilippov -history_dlya_uchit.pdf.
Gudkov, Lev. "The Fetters of Victory." *Eurozine* (3 May 2005). https://www .eurozine.com/the-fetters-of-victory/.
Gusman, Mikhail. "Sergei Naryshkin: Revoliutsionnye sobytiia 1917 goda bol'she ne raskalyvaiut obshchestvoj." https://historyrussia.org/proekty /100-letie-revolyutsii-1917-goda/sergej-naryshkin-revolyutsionnye

-sobytiya-1917-goda-bolshe-ne-raskalyvayut-obshchestvo.html. Accessed
8 May 2018.

Johnson, Emily D. "Jubilation Deferred: The Belated Commemoration of the
250th Anniversary of St. Petersburg/Leningrad." In *Rites of Place: Public
Commemoration in Russia and Eastern Europe,* edited by Julie A. Buckler and
Emily D. Johnson, 81–102. Evanston, Ill: Northwestern University Press, 2013.

Kalashnikov, Antony. "Stalinist Crimes and the Ethics of Memory." *Kritika:
Explorations in Russian and Eurasian History* 19, 3 (Summer 2018): 599–626.

Kalinin, Ilya. "2017-yi: prizrak revoliutsii." *Neprikosnovennyi zapas* and on
polit.ru: https://polit.ru/article/2017/11/09/revolution. 9 November 2017.

Kirschenbaum, Lisa. "Introduction. World War II in Soviet and Post-Soviet
Memory." *The Soviet and Post-Soviet Review* 38, 2 (January 2011): 97–103.

Kizyma, Roman. "Skandal s zapretom tablichek 'Poslednego adresa' doshel
do Putina" [The Scandal of the Ban of "Last Address" Tablets Has Reached
Putin]. 12 December 2018. RKB.ru: https://www.rbc.ru/spb_sz/12/12/2018
/5c10b16a9a7947e59db2f953. Accessed 22 December 2018.

Lavrov, Sergey. "Uroki velikoi pobedy." *Diplomat* (mai 2005). http://www
.mid.ru/foreign_policy/news/-/asset_publisher/cKNonkJE02Bw/content
/id/441036. Accessed 2 August 2017.

– "Remarks by Foreign Minister Sergey Lavrov at a Gathering for the
70th Anniversary of Victory in the Great Patriotic War, Moscow." 5 May
2015. Website of the Embassy of the Russian Federation in Washington, DC.
http://www.russianembassy.org/article/remarks-by-foreign-minister
-sergey-lavrov-at-a-gathering-for-the-70th-anniversary-of-victory. Accessed
1 August 2017.

Levada-Center. "The October Revolution." https://www.levada.ru/en/2017
/04/21/the-october-revolution/. Accessed 3 August 2017.

Ločmele, Klinta, Olga Procevska, and Vita Zelče. "Celebrations, Commemorative
Dates and Related Rituals: Soviet Experience, Its Transformation and
Contemporary Victory Day Celebrations in Russia and Latvia." In *The
Geopolitics of History in Latvian-Russian Relations,* edited by Nils Muižnieks,
109–38. Riga: Academic Press of the University of Latvia, 2011.

Lovell, Stephen. *Shadow of War: Russia and the USSR, 1941 to the Present.*
Chichester: Wiley-Blackwell, 2010.

Malinova, Olga. "The Embarrassing Centenary: Reinterpretation of the 1917
Revolution in the Official Historical Narrative of Post-Soviet Russia
(1991–2017)." *Revolutionary Russia* 31, 1 (2018): 24–45.

Mälksoo, Maria. "The Memory Politics of Becoming European: The East
European Subalterns and the Collective Memory of Europe." *European
Journal of International Relations* 15, 4 (2009): 653–80. http://journals
.sagepub.com.ezproxy.library.uvic.ca/doi/abs/10.1177/1354066109345049.
Accessed 1 August 2017.

Medinsky, Vladimir. "100 let Velikoi rossiiskoi revoliutsii: Osmyslenie vo imia konsolidatsii." *Odnako* (20 May 2015). http://www.odnako.org/blogs /navstrechu-100-letiyu-revolyucii-zveno-v-istoricheskoy-preemstvennosti -epoha-gigantskih-dostizheniy-i-platforma/. Accessed 8 May 2018.

Muižnieks, Nils, ed. *The Geopolitics of History in Latvian-Russian Relations.* Riga: Academic Press of the University of Latvia, 2011.

Nora, Pierre. "Between Memory and History: Les Lieux de Memoire." Translated by Marc Roudebush. *Representations* 26, Special Issue: Memory and Counter-Memory (Spring 1989): 7–24.

– *Realms of Memory, Rethinking the French Past.* Vol. 1. Trans. Arthur Goldhammer. New York: Columbia University Press, 1996.

– "Reasons for the Current Upsurge in Memory." *Eurozine,* 8 October 2007. http://www.eurozine.com/articles/2002-04-19-nora-en.html. Accessed 15 May 2018.

Norris, Stephen M. "Memory for Sale: Victory Day 2010 and Russian Remembrance." *The Soviet and Post-Soviet Review* 38, 2 (January 2011): 201–29.

Oushakine, Serguei Alex. "Postcolonial Estrangements: Claiming a Space between Stalin and Hitler." In *Rites of Place: Public Commemoration in Russia and Eastern Europe,* edited by Julie A. Buckler and Emily D. Johnson, 285–314. Evanston, Ill: Northwestern University Press, 2013.

Payne, Daniel P. "Spiritual Security, the Russian Orthodox Church, and the Russian Foreign Ministry: Collaboration or Cooptation?" *Journal of Church and State* 52, 4 (Autumn 2010): 712–27

Petrone, Karen. "Moscow's First World War Memorial and Ninety Years of Contested Memory." In *Rites of Place: Public Commemoration in Russia and Eastern Europe,* edited by Julie A. Buckler and Emily D. Johnson, 241–60. Evanston, Ill: Northwestern University Press, 2013.

Putin, Vladimir. Decree of the President of the Russian Federation, "On the Preparation and Carrying Out of Measures Dedicated to the 100th anniversary of the Revolution of 1917 in Russia," 19 December 2016: https://historyrussia.org/images/documents/0001201612200017.pdf. Accessed 16 April 2018.

Ricoeur, Paul. *Memory, History, Forgetting.* Translated by Kathleen Blamey and David Pellauer. Chicago: University of Chicago Press, 2006,

Sizikov, Kirill. "Pamiatnik primireniia narod ne primirit: Otkrytoe pis'mo." https://regnum.ru/news/2287988.html. Accessed 8 May 2018.

Torkunov, A.V. *Istoriia Rossii: 10 klass: Uchebnik dlia obshcheobrazovatel'nykh organizatsii. V trekh chastakh. Chast' 2.* Moscow: Prosveshchenie, 2016.

– "The Universal Importance of the Russian Revolution of 1917." *Herald of the Russian Academy of Sciences* 88, 3 (2018): 159–62.

Trukhanovskii, V.G., ed. *Istoriia mezhdunarodnykh otnoshenii i vneshnei politiki SSSR, 1917–1967 v trekh tomakh.* Vol. 1. Moscow: Izdatel'stvo "Mezhdunarodnye otnosheniia," 1967.

Weiner, Amir. *Making Sense of War: The Second World War and the Fate of the Bolshevik Revolution*. Princeton, NJ: Princeton University Press, 2001.

Wolfe, Thomas. "Past as Present, Myth, or History? Discourses of Time and the Great Fatherland War." In *The Politics of Memory in Postwar Europe*, edited by Richard Ned Lebow, Wulf Kansteiner, and Claudio Fogu, 249–83. Durham, NC: Duke University Press, 2006.

Wood, Elizabeth A. "Performing Memory: Vladimir Putin and the Celebration of World War II in Russia." *The Soviet and Post-Soviet Review* 38, 2 (January 2011): 172–200.

Wood, Nancy. *Vectors of Memory: Legacies of Trauma in Postwar Europe*. New York and Oxford: Berg, 1999.

Young, Sarah. "Historical Memory of the Gulag (3): Contested Memory." Post of 17 September 2015. http://sarahjyoung.com/site/. Accessed 15 October 2017.

Zimmermann, Margarete. "Never Again! Remembering October 1917 in the Contemporary Russian Orthodox Church." *Scando-Slavica* 64, 1 (2018): 95–106.

2 Gentrification, Post-Tourism, and Trauma: Uses of the 1917 Revolution's Memory Places in 2017 Russia

MARIA SILINA

City centres in the former Russian Soviet Federative Socialist Republic (RSFSR) were formed *en masse* by the 1960s, when the commemorative culture of communism reached its peak.[1] Today, Russians live inside an impressive network of commemorative infrastructure created in the late Soviet Union. Here plaques, monuments, and museums dedicated to Bolshevik heroes are ubiquitous. These artifacts undergo annual cleaning and renovation, and are reutilized as the venue for everyday civic rituals like marriage ceremonies. Some of them simply remain untouched and unnoticed elements of the urban landscape for years. Beginning in 1965, the USSR became increasingly engaged in an emerging global heritage network with the creation of the International Council on Monuments and Sites (ICOMOS) and the All-Russian Society for the Protection of Historical and Cultural Monuments (VOOPIK, *Vserossiiskoe obshchestvo okhrany pamiatnikov istorii i kultury*). Since then, an appreciable network of communist heritage sites has been created and still serves as a basis for inventories of heritage objects in Russia. Today, this omnipresence of ideological objects representing solely Bolshevik party values poses a problem for heritage management.

In official databases, one can find many communist places of memory, such as the Moscow hospital building where, according to a catalogue, "on 23 April 1922, Vladimir Lenin underwent surgical removal of a bullet."[2] This building, constructed in 1830–40, could have been added to the heritage database because of its age value; instead, it was legitimized as a communist site of memory. Today, real estate agents make use of this dual value, because once a building has acquired a formal protected status as a Bolshevik landmark its market value increases, even though the history behind it is contested. As this article will show, Russia is colonized by communist heritage objects that have lost their commemorative value. They still play a significant role in such urban development strategies as gentrification and what is called the post-tourist agenda, but they also reveal the necessity of finding a way to rethink the communist origin of heritage infrastructure. In this text, I will use the concept of gentrification to signify the process of renovation for the sake of bourgeoisification of impoverished neighbourhoods and landmarks that have lost their glamour. Today, the modernization of urban areas builds on the valorization of historic monuments as tourist attractions. The emphasis on mass tourism as the prime consumer of historic places is reflected in the concept of post-communist tourism ("post-tourism") that will also be used here.

In contemporary scholarship, heritage is traditionally seen as the product of a rupture, be it political, cultural, or merely temporal.[3] It is typically some radical political change or considerable shift in the symbolic, spatial, and conceptual perception of history that paves the way for a concept of a legacy that is supposed to be saved, restored, and celebrated. This is notably the case with communist heritage studies that treat communism and the communist past in the context of allochronism, division, and neglect.[4] Without contesting the power of metaphoric gestures (the "collapse" of the USSR and of the Berlin Wall in 1989, the demolition of monuments to underline the ending of the epoch, and so on), I will show that in many cases the rupture is only symbolic, while memorial communist objects remain intact and reused for decades. Some of them are inscribed into an authorized heritage discourse (AHD); others acquire commemorative and cultural value with time and can be considered as intangible heritage sites and a part of the cityscape.[5] The emphasis on this under-recognized communist urban memorabilia allows us to problematize the limits of ideology in public spaces in post-communist countries and to address the question of heritage communities in contemporary Russia.[6] This is why it is especially tempting to consider the revolutionary and communist legacy as a part of current heritage production or, more precisely, a post-tourist and gentrification paradigm offered by the growing body of critical heritage studies.[7]

In Russia, strategies for treating the Soviet legacy are paradoxical and part of a double bind. This became especially evident after the activities of 2017, the centennial anniversary of the 1917 revolution. Contemporary discourse on the 1917 revolution and its representation in public space is mutually nourished by two patterns. First, there are motives of victory, inspired by the almost century-long Soviet historiography of Bolshevik leadership in the revolution. The victorious narrative – honouring Bolshevik civil war heroes or promoting Vladimir Lenin's image – remains visible in the gentrification and post-tourist agenda. The second concept is one of trauma, inherited from the dissident and anti-communist tradition of the 1960s. The trauma pattern can be seen in the linking of the 1917 revolution to the Stalinist repressions of the 1930s. In attempts to amalgamate these two contradictory narratives, the Russian Ministry of Culture has included the concept of the nation's reconciliation in its policy on public Soviet history. It has already been shown that commemorative activities for the 1917 revolution conform to the victorious-traumatic pattern of the Great Patriotic War as a highly traumatic event that was, ultimately, successful.[8] This chapter strives to contribute to these debates, directly focusing on attitudes towards the 1917 revolution demonstrated in public spaces, through a critical heritage-studies lens. As I will show, the Bolshevik-inspired narration of the victorious revolution, paired with the dramatic overtones of traumatic experience, has created blind spots in commemoration traditions, as well as numerous broken references and alienated spaces of collective memory in contemporary Russia.

The aim of this chapter is twofold. It seeks to address uses of communist heritage regarded as cultural production; but it also intends to analyse the outcomes of the double-bind message of the victorious-traumatic experience of the 1917 revolution common in today's Russia. To do this, I will first address the 1917 centennial anniversary activities that summarize the current state of the Soviet legacy in Russia. Like Mark Lipovetsky in his filmic analysis in this volume, I argue that current treatment of the communist legacy has late-Soviet origins. This includes the Bolshevik-dominated historiography of the 1917 revolution, as well as a late-Soviet dissident tradition of equating the revolution, socialism, and Stalinism. In the next section, I will scrutinize modes of production and uses of the communist and post-communist commemorative network and sites of memory in today's Russia. I will demonstrate that the majority of such places and symbols are used in a post-tourism and gentrification paradigm to celebrate victorious images of Soviet history. Finally, I will examine the production of dark and traumatic memory after the communist period. As I will show, the unfinished process of de-Stalinization has led to weak heritage communities as well as the poor development of trauma studies and dark history narratives in contemporary Russia. As a result, this chapter will demonstrate that the impressive commemorative infrastructure left by the Soviet Union incorporates many misleading allusions that make contemporary Russian cities unique and chaotic spaces, full of references to complex and even self-contradictory memories.

**The 100th Anniversary of the 1917 Revolution(s)
and Late-Soviet Narratives**

In 2013, the term "Great Russian Revolution of 1917–1922" (*Velikaia Ros-
siiskaia revoliutsiia*) was introduced as part of a "single concept of history" by a commission composed of high-ranking federal functionaries
and ministers of education and culture.[9] This term has been widely
used since then, and in reference to all commemorative activities during the 2017 anniversary.[10] Yet it remains highly problematic because it
amalgamates not only the overthrowing of imperial power in February
1917 and the Bolshevik uprising in late October 1917 but also the civil
war under the label "the revolution." This time span, from 1917 to 1922,
is supposed to hide and neutralize the events of the civil war in order to
further the idea of a revolution as a great affair leading to the nation's
reconciliation. Such views are promoted by leading Russian officials,
including President Vladimir Putin and Minister of Culture Vladimir
Medinsky.[11] As early as 2015, Medinsky proposed erecting a monument
to reconciliation in the Crimean city of Kerch, a peninsula notorious
for brutal civil war battles but also for its annexation by the Russian
Federation in 2014. Remarkably, Crimean communities firmly opposed
the idea, as discussed in Megan Swift's chapter in this volume. Despite
several attempts and official claims of Russian authorities to promote
such an unveiling by November 2017, at the last moment the project
was rejected.[12]

   In 2017, major efforts to celebrate the 100th anniversary were directed
towards a winner-driven history of 1917 told from the point of view of
the Bolsheviks. The majority of the events concentrated on the October
Revolution, on Lenin narratives, and on the heroic myth of 1917, despite
the official concept of the Great Russian Revolution of 1917–22.[13] These
narratives were nourished by a decades-long iconography of the 1917
revolution. Indeed, from the very beginning, the politics of the Bolsheviks were aimed at dividing socialist parties and promoting their own
individual profile by radicalizing any differences and downplaying
the similarities.[14] In the first years after the revolutions, the emphasis
was put on the fractional debates of Bolsheviks and Mensheviks, as
well as on the disputes about proximity to other socialist parties. Beginning in the late 1920s, key figures of the October Revolution such as
Leon Trotsky, Grigory Zinoviev, and Lev Kamenev were deprived of
their place in the political pantheon and repressed. Still, some of these
disgraced figures had been publicly acknowledged during the tenth
anniversary of the October Revolution in 1927, even though in negative
light. For example, paintings dedicated to the attempted assassination

of Lenin by socialist-democrats in 1918 and to the overall struggle for power were commissioned and exhibited during the 1927 celebrations.[15] By the mid-1930s, the number of promoted revolutionaries had dramatically dropped: only the single heroic figures of Vladimir Lenin, Felix Dzerzhinsky, and Joseph Stalin were represented in public spaces.[16] With the de-Stalinization of 1956, Soviet scholars started reintegrating into the historical narrative the 1917 February Revolution, the impact of other socialist and non-socialist parties, and other topics that had been silenced during Stalin's time.[17] This process was, however, slowed by the re-Stalinization of the 1960s.[18] The perestroika era saw a short revival of interest in other leaders and participants in the revolution. *Ogonek* magazine featured anti-Stalinist Fedor Raskolnikov, but he failed to become as popular as the Bolshevik figures that were promoted during the 1930s and the 1950s.[19] Others, like Leon Trotsky or Nikolai Bukharin, entered the public domain, but not as autonomous participants of the 1917 revolution. Still, they have been presented as failed rivals and opponents of those in power. In 2017 Leon Trotsky was once again depicted as an evil force and the anti-hero of the revolution in the prime-time TV series *Trotsky*.[20]

Today the history of the 1917 revolution in Russia is militaristic, class-dividing ("Reds" and "Whites"), and, in most cases, Lenin-centric. In 2017, large shows in federal museums followed the main official program. The *1917 – The Code of Revolution* exhibition in the Museum for Contemporary Russian History in Moscow, an exhibition at the Museum of Political History in St Petersburg, as well as the art history exposition *Someone1917* (*Nekto1917*) at the Tretyakov Gallery in Moscow were among the most publicized. All of them concentrated on a Bolshevik-led course of the October Revolution. Sometimes the communist-oriented narratives in contemporary museums are particularly striking in their emphasis on the Soviet interpretation of history. For instance, in 2017, a local museum of Frunze, a Bolshevik civil war commander, celebrated the ninety-ninth anniversary of the victory over Czech legionaries. The activities included the battle's reconstruction and a meeting in front of the Bolshevik victims' memorial.[21] In another local museum, in Samara, curators presented a detailed chronology of the 1917 October Revolution as it would have been presented in the Soviet Union.[22] The show featured portraits of Felix Dzerzhinsky and Vladimir Lenin, as well as images of victorious Bolsheviks, diligently following the narrative drawn from the coffee table books published in the late 1960s for the fiftieth anniversary of the October Revolution.[23] The only real difference from the late-Soviet narrative could be seen in the addition of portraits of Joseph Stalin.

They were banned during the 1960s and the 1980s, and were rehabilitated only recently.

The Lenin-centric image of the revolution spread globally, and the substitution of revolutionary events by a sole figure is sometimes striking. In February 2017, a date that presumes commemorative activities towards the imperial overthrow, a local museum of Lenin in Podolsk, established in 1937, launched a series of open talks and guided tours dedicated to Lenin, "who lived with his family in Podolsk for a brief period of time."[24] Even the Moscow Darwin Museum of Biology promoted its exposition by featuring a bear fur that was seen by Lenin at the agricultural fair in Moscow in 1923.[25] It is worth mentioning that today the Lenin-centric image of the revolution is associated not only with official culture but also with nonconformism and anti-communism. Indeed, already by the 1970s, images of Lenin have served as a nonconformist artistic practice and, since the 1990s, as a source for metaphoric iconoclasm.[26] Lenin's portraits were used as an instrument to recontextualize political and artistic reality by playing with the idea of ideological overproduction of the images. The absurdity of this omnipresence, exposed in nonconformist works, served as an amplification of the everyday experiences of Soviet citizens. Today, the Soviet Union no longer exists, and the overproduction of ideological goods has become history. Still, the tradition of metaphoric iconoclasm is alive. Shows at Davidson College in the United States, as well as the project *My First Lenin* at the Moscow Biennale of Contemporary Art, prove the popularity of kitsch narratives in the contemporary art market.[27] The critical gestures of Soviet nonconformist artists were commodified for their recognizable cold war-era symbolism. A Lenin-centric narration, be it an official or a nonconformist one, overshadows the complexity of the revolutionary legacy in the USSR. It blocks any opportunity to discuss how and why Lenin actually became the only symbol of the revolution.

Another pattern, which I would term post-dissident, provides a trauma narrative to contemporary authorities, most notably the Ministry of Culture, in their anniversary activities. This pattern had begun by the 1960s and is still developing, being widely disseminated in an authorized discourse on the revolutionary legacy. It comprises the direct linking of the revolution, the victims of political terror, and communist ideology. Before the late 1960s, Soviet dissidents hoped to reform the governmental system by means of Marxism and socialism, but after 1968 they gradually turned away from communism as a prospective political ideology and started to regard Stalinism and communism as synonyms. Since the 1960s the dichotomy of Stalinism and civic society has been exemplified in the activities of Soviet dissidents, who have been the object of various studies of anti-Stalinism/anti-communism.[28] The most important figure to make this connection was Alexander Solzhenitsyn in his 1973 book *Arkhipelag Gulag* (*Gulag Archipelago*), where he openly expressed his anti-Stalinist and anti-communist beliefs.

This connection received its full expression during the perestroika era, when the second wave of de-Stalinization occurred.[29] In 1987, the popular Soviet magazine *Ogonek*, which initiated and stimulated public debates on the revolution and its legacy, bound together victims of repression and the 1917 revolution.[30] It wasn't until 1989, however, as Korine Amacher notes, that the anti-revolutionary aspirations came to the surface, and socialism, the Russian Revolution(s), Stalinism, communism, and Soviet culture were finally equated.[31] Indeed, as Frederick C. Corney observes, already in the 1990s as well as in 2007, the year of the ninetieth anniversary of the 1917 revolution, "Russia ... was the center of world anti-Communism," thanks to the fact that "Russian [*Rossiiskie*] authorities in 1992 have not only repudiated the socialist choice in 1917 but have also reassured the world that communism on this planet has been buried and will not be resurrected."[32]

The tie between the socialist revolution and Stalinist repressions was officially made in 2017. The year marked both the hundredth anniversary of the Russian Revolution and the eightieth anniversary of Stalinist repressions in Russia.[33] All possible traumatic experiences of the 1917–22 revolution were destined to be expressed by activities commemorating the Great Purge. A number of the 2017 memorial openings are good examples of the popularity of the neo-dissident agenda of equating the socialist revolution and mass killings. As Megan Swift discusses in the previous chapter, in 2017 the Butovo firing range on the outskirts of Moscow, which was active from 1934 to 1953 and where at least 20,760 people were killed, was turned into an authorized commemorative place. The new memorial Garden of Memory was opened there in September 2017. As with any anniversary-linked opening, the Butovo memorial contains a number of problematic messages. Since the 1990s, the commemorative actions there have been tightly connected to the Russian Orthodox Church that took over ownership of the property in 1995, despite the fact that victims of the Great Purge were of various national, cultural, and religious backgrounds. The monument itself was patterned after Maya Lin's famous Vietnam Veterans Memorial in Washington, DC. This site has since served as a prototype for war memorials globally, but has been criticized for its absence of context and its openly aestheticized form.[34] As a result, the Garden of Memory in Butovo is a straightforwardly pro-Russian and pro-Christian site of memory, although it was designed to be neutral. A grass-roots memorial place was thus replaced by an authorized narrative: victims are honoured as dominantly Russian Christian martyrs. More than that, the steadfast support of the government in designing and managing this memorial poses another sensitive problem. As I will show in the section on the dark past, the official position on repressions does not exclude strong support for the secret services, and this creates a highly dissonant memory politics.

As early as the 1960s, Alexander Solzhenitsyn demonstrated that anti-Stalinism and anti-communism can easily come together with nationalistic and paternalistic aspirations and an elitist cultural agenda in Russia. Indeed, these anti-Bolshevist, anti-communist, anti-Soviet beliefs also contained a very powerful and positive message to Russian society: pre-revolutionary times became a kind of paradise lost for the Russian cultural landscape. Since the 1960s, anti-communist and pro-state beliefs are embodied in a cry for lost spirituality violated by Bolshevik anti-religious propaganda, as well as for the fine culture of the aristocracy that was shattered by the uneducated masses. Cultural activities championed by the dissident movement were strongly influenced by Christian culture and even adopted its vocabulary, acquiring a strong conservative and anti-egalitarian character. Hence, restoration of religious traditions and churches as well as reappraisal of pre-revolutionary heritage were regarded as spiritual service.[35] In the 2017 celebrations, these aspirations are clearly seen in mourning for the collapsed Russian empire and the royal family that embodied the most valued virtues such as piety and being highly cultured. Thus, the Hermitage Museum launched an exhibition on the revolution in 2017 that emphasized the tragedy of the crushing of imperial Russian culture by barbaric Bolsheviks. A number of exhibitions throughout Russia were equally dedicated to the fate of the Romanov dynasty. Large shows at federal museums drew an image of a traumatic past that should never be repeated.[36] As we shall see in the next section, positive images of lost but regained culture are also widely promoted in touristic and modernized public spaces as non-political and/or non-communist urban heritage objects.

Tourism and the Gentrification of the Revolutionary Legacy

The current agenda related to the communist legacy in Russia is accompanied by fierce political debates. Nevertheless, the majority of commemorative actions to reframe communist sites of memory can be understood in the context of post-tourism and gentrification. Modernization of communist places follows two main patterns.[37] The first strategy seeks to replace communist and revolutionary content with pre-revolutionary material. The other instrumentalizes cold war-era symbols to engage people in nostalgia and/or Red tourism activities.[38]

The most straightforward is the gentrification of prominent communist places in the nation's capital for the sake of attracting more visitors. Some top Soviet-era public spaces are being remade as locations of glorious history. Today, museum activists of the still-numerous Lenin museums and sites of memory openly declare their interest in tourist visitation. Under a Red tourism stream, Lenin-related sites like the city of Ulianovsk and Gorki Leninskie (the birth and death places, respectively, of the revolutionary leader) are popular among tourists from China who can benefit from visa-exempted tours in Russia.[39] In 2017, the former Lenin Museum in Vladivostok launched a show on Vladimir Lenin to mark the 1917 revolution and to attract "foreign tourists who show enduring interest in a 'red legacy.'" [40] In fact, this small museum initially had nothing to do with Lenin sites of memory, and its opening was considered part of an all-Union trend to create as many Lenin museums as possible. Today the communist industry of imagined sites associated with Lenin has found its development in tourist-oriented activities. The Vladivostok exhibition combined cold war-era narratives with a straightforward depoliticization of these propaganda images by turning them into kitsch and exotic artifacts. The same China-focused profile was explicit at the *Rulevie Revoliutsii* (*Rulers of Revolution*) exhibition at the State Museum of Oriental Art, which opened in Moscow in September 2017. It features dozens of Sino-Soviet, Mongolian, and Korean artifacts from the 1950s and provides no critical or historical distance, as if the wide Soviet-Asian communist collaborations under the guidance of Stalin and Mao were still happening.

Urban landmarks from the Stalin era are also at the centre of modernization and gentrification. Indeed, in years past many architectural highlights of Soviet culture have been restored. These include the Moscow Leisure Park (1928), the Vera Mukhina monument *Worker and Collective Farm Woman* (1937; also known as *The Worker and the Kolkhoz Woman*), as well as underground stations of the early 1950s and the Moscow Agricultural Exhibition ensemble (VDNKh, 1939–54). These celebrated representative ensembles, created in Stalin's time, are some of the most important sources of the usable past.[41] Efforts are made to inscribe these complexes into the logic of tourist behaviour and economic profit. Paradoxically, it is their image of the imperial grandeur of Stalin's era that makes them economically attractive and consumable.

The modernization of the VDNKh reveals multiple problems with the contemporary integration of Stalin-era objects into the modernized city.

The VDNKh was built in the late 1930s to demonstrate the advantages of collectivization, a forced consolidation of individual peasant households into collective farms during the early 1930s. Since 1958 it has housed a completely different narrative, promoting Soviet successes in the aircraft industry using the visual lexicon of cold war confrontation. In 2014, after decades of neglect following the collapse of the USSR in 1991, municipal authorities moved forward with plans to restore the exhibition. Today the 1950s Stalinist design is being revived, with multiple errors and excesses.[42] Now, as in the 1950s, visitors can learn about the revolution and the Soviet Union from the multi-figured sculptures and mosaics inspired by the Stalinist version of history. For instance, the Povolzhie pavilion candidly follows a Stalin-centric version of the 1917 revolution. It puts emphasis on the Povolzhie region as the key location of revolutionary victories by Bolsheviks. The ongoing modernization has already endangered the authenticity of the ensemble. Indeed, it could serve as a very powerful site of memory for the Soviet peasantry in commemoration of violent collectivization, repeated hunger in the 1930s and 1950s, and ruinous policies in environment and agriculture. Instead, it is turned into a place of socialist nostalgia and post-Soviet prosperity, attracting billions of rubles and the unreserved support of President Vladimir Putin.[43] The current general director of the exhibition, Ekaterina Pronicheva, emphasizes the double nature of the complex – its non-ideological character as a modernized city park and its status as a magnificent symbol of the Soviet past.[44] The idea of the non-ideological character of the urban park, modernized and visitor-friendly, completely overshadows its past and the role of the VDNKh as a site of memory.[45] The exhibition's status as the most prominent locus in Moscow is ensured for years to come with an ambitious extension of its territory and the construction of objects described in the press with superlatives, such as Europe's biggest oceanarium and largest skating rink. This is how a potential site of memory has turned into a gentrified park with a rich history.

In the same way, old communist content is being replaced by new that includes positive references to the pre-revolutionary era.[46] A post-dissident reading of history implies the idea of class division, cultural degradation of the post-revolutionary period, and straightforward competition between Reds and Whites; (uneducated) people and the aristocracy. In post-Soviet Russia, this formed a powerful narrative of the spiritual and cultural role of the intelligentsia and culture workers who opposed Party propaganda. These class-driven, uncritical aspirations found their home in ideas of religion and spirituality that were repressed after the revolution and embodied in the figure of Nicholas II.

The tsar and his family symbolize all positive features: morality, religious rigour, spirituality, aristocratic origin, and high education. The symbolic message of restoring historic justice with the reconstruction of places of tsarist and former imperial power is so strong that it can replace literally everything. The beginning of this movement was marked in the Yeltsin era by the rebuilding of the gigantic Cathedral of Christ the Saviour in Moscow (1995–2000) and the ceremonial burial of the Romanov family in the Church of Sts Peter and Paul in St Petersburg (1998); and since the 2000s this restoration has become more intense. In 2012, a grass-roots commemorative action, "Forgive us, Tsar," was launched to mark the ninety-fourth anniversary of the killing of Emperor Nicholas and his family in 1918.[47] The Moscow monument-obelisk to outstanding thinkers and personalities in the struggle for the liberation of workers was opened in 1918. It was, in turn, remade out of the 1914 monument to the Russian rulers of the Romanov family to mark the 300th anniversary of the dynasty. For a long time, it was one of the few memorials from the revolutionary era that survived in the nation's capital. In 2014, in honour of the 400th anniversary of Romanov rule, it was again remade into a monument to the Russian rulers.[48]

The next example shows that the process of decontextualization has always been very intense and always without critical distance. The Ipatiev house in Yekaterinburg where the Russian tsar and his family were killed was already made into a museum in the 1920s. At that time, the bullet-torn wall against which the tsar and his family were killed was reconstructed and turned into a tourist attraction. Later, in the 1930s, authorities completely hid this exhibition. Further, the whole house was demolished in the 1970s to erase any trace of this site of memory. Today, municipal authorities use another powerful but very straightforward narrative of the imperial grandeur of tsarist Russia and grief for its loss: in 2003 a church was built on the site, and the whole history of the communist memorial activities was convoluted and silenced.

At a more basic level, all former museums dedicated to revolutionary history are transformed into period rooms showcasing pre-revolutionary everyday life and promoting family values. The efforts to reshape and renuance ideological sites of memory are not new, as the tendency was already apparent during the Khrushchev thaw. As Jason Read Morton notes, already in the 1960s the museum (of Vasili Chapaev) in Cheboksary was part of a larger effort to reinvigorate the Soviet family as one way of keeping the revolutionary flame alive. Hence, "Not only did the House-museum showcase the domestic atmosphere of the Chapaev family and emphasize the fact that the house itself was built by Vasilii Ivanovich and his father and brothers, it displayed several objects made by Chapaev himself."[49] As the author witnessed, this account was still in effect in 2013. The process of a further de-ideologization of specifically communist places intensified soon after 1991. The transformation of revolutionary sites of memory into pre-revolutionary culture shrines included much from typical Soviet narratives. The elegance of the pre-revolutionary aristocratic lifestyle was mixed with the grandeur of Soviet heroism.[50] Revolutionary leaders and Bolshevik heroes of the civil and Great Patriotic Wars are now used to promote a de-communized local history, folklore, and portrait of the everyday life of the region.

Examples of this practice are ubiquitous. The Lenin Museum in Samara turned its memorial rooms into an old school ethnographical exhibition. A Bolshevik and Stalin-associated exhibition in the St Petersburg apartment museum of the Alliluevs, the family of the first wife of Joseph Stalin and "old Bolsheviks," follows the same aim. It displays the family's life as representative of the pre-revolutionary lifestyle. According to the director of Gorki Leninskie, the death place of Lenin, the museum is proud to work today as a "multi-profile, absolutely non-ideological object." [51] It seems the museum workers do not find any contradiction in these beliefs and their intensive work with Chinese visitors who hunt for Red tourism attractions. In 2017, some of the Vasily Chapaev museums in Cheboksary and in Balakovo became the topic of a municipal meeting to consider their restoration.[52] As one local functionary claimed, the Chapaev Museum is more important than the strawberry festival that is promoted as the tourist brand of the region.[53]

As the Russian case shows, politically charged legacies can be de-ideologized through the bureaucratization of heritage management. As today's Russia is an official heir to the Soviet Union, monuments and other objects are parcelled out between federal and municipal authorities or are relocated to private institutions. Only some communist objects become a matter of public debate and thus push heritage production further. This is the case of the eponym of Vadim Podbelsky, who participated in the suppression of anti-Bolshevik riots in Yaroslavl and Tambov. His name was given to a Moscow metro station in 1990. Following a wave of protests, in 2014, the name was changed to Bulvar Rokossovskogo (Rokossovsky Boulevard) after a hero of the Great Patriotic War. Another example is the Moscow metro station Voikovskaya, named after the alleged organizer of the assassination of the tsar in 1918, Petr Voikov. For decades it has come under constant fire from protesters who want it renamed, but this has not yet been done.

As a general rule, monuments are just being restored, as in the case of the Stepan Khalturin monument built in 1923 in Viatka. It underwent restoration in 1965 and 2005.[54] The Dzerzhinsky monument in front of the Moscow Institute of Higher Economics also undergoes regular renovation.[55] And the same is true for the Viktor Nogin bust on the Kitai-gorod, a revolutionary after whom this metro station was named from 1971 until 1990. In the early 1930s, he was criticized for being supportive of a democratic coalition in 1917, but he had been "lucky" to die before the Great Purge began. Because of the lack of revolutionary leaders worth commemorating in the 1960s, Nogin was rehabilitated and honoured.[56] The toponym is a typical example of a site of memory named after a Bolshevik activist whose biography went unnoticed by heritage communities and remains unproblematized today, and is therefore simply left intact. Other eponyms underwent successful integration into the city fabric and lost their initial cultural meaning. As contemporaries noticed in the 1920s, some of the newly appearing toponyms sounded ridiculous: streets were named after Leo Tolstoy and Maxim Gorky, even though people could still remember that these noted writers were sceptical of and publicly criticized the Bolsheviks.[57] Today, these toponyms have completely lost any trace of their communist origin.

The Traumatic Past and Its Uses

With the dominance of a Bolshevik-driven history of the 1917 uprisings, no commemorative strategy for public spaces has been elaborated for topics such as the multiple forces of the 1917 uprising, the civil war, the collectivization campaign of 1928–31, mass hunger, dissident culture, and national conflicts. Today, virtually no trace of the February Revolution or other socialist parties is visible in Russian cities.[58] The Mars field memorial in Petrograd (St Petersburg) was built soon after February 1917 and was dedicated to its victims, marking the fulfilment of the Russian Revolution; now it is associated with Bolshevism.[59] The same is true for a project of the Museum of Revolution that was carried out before October 1917.[60] The museum was thought to exhibit the history of Russian revolutionaries of the late nineteenth century, including activities of the *Narodnaia Volia* (People's Will) organization that successfully assassinated Alexander II in 1881, and was not related to the Bolshevik Party. Even heritage protection that saw a rise in prerevolutionary times was later considered to be exclusively an achievement of Bolshevik cultural policy.[61]

Other important commemorative activities, such as *prazdniki svobody* (Days of Freedom) in honour of the overthrow of the empire, were celebrated only until 1929.[62] Some places are still dedicated to more unorthodox revolutionaries, but their biographies are forgotten and their role in the revolution remains under-recognized. This is the case for Vladimir Milutin, who was a Menshevik, an opponent of the Bolsheviks. He was briefly a commissar of agriculture and headed the statistics department of the Soviet government. Like many other politicians, he was subjected to repressions in 1937. A small Moscow park was named after him in 1932. The change was proposed by the All-Union Organization of Cooperative Manufacturing, and it has kept this name through all these years. It is still called Milutin Park, although all memories of the personality have vanished. Another example is even more striking. In 1956, a Moscow region station and a village were named after Cadet (Constitutional Democratic) party member Fedor Kokoshkin, who was one of the first victims of the Bolsheviks. The controller general of the Russian Provisional Government, he was violently killed in January 1918 when the Bolsheviks still struggled for power. This crime became one of the most discussed events of the era.[63] Neither in the 1950s nor today has the story behind the place ever been problematized.

Especially preoccupying are the efforts of the Ministry of Culture to orchestrate anniversary events to encourage the silencing of the civil war (1917–the 1920s), as well as various peasants' and civil riots. The anti-Bolshevik riots of 1918–21 in Tambov, Narym, Samara, Saratov region, and western Siberia were stigmatized during the Soviet era as counter-revolutionary and anti-patriotic, believed to have been inspired by foreign *interventy* (interveners). They were rehabilitated by Boris Yeltsin in 1996, but the majority of these sites of memory are still waiting to be recognized.[64] An alternative commemorative day in honour of victims of the Red Terror was even established in the late 1970s among dissidents, but it did not last into the post-Soviet era.[65] Some monuments were erected to commemorate peasant riots, but they have since been reframed as non-political symbols. Hence, *Tambovsky muzhik* (Tambov peasant), a statue in Tambov, was erected as a monument to all peasant victims of the civil war, but it was quickly rebranded to advertise locally produced products. The remembrance of the dark past appeared to be less needed than a positively charged brand, and the traumatic experience was completely replaced by commercial needs.[66] Locations of mass killings during the civil war had always been a matter of rumours in many Russian towns, but very few of them were officially recognized as sites of memory.[67] This is a striking contrast to the scrupulous commemorative efforts of the Bolsheviks.[68] Not only places but heritage communities are also scarcely represented today. Only some national and cultural minorities have claimed their right to commemorate the violence in the revolution and civil war. Today the Cossacks are the most vocal in expressing the memory of cultural and political censure and are the most explicit in their anti-communist sentiments.[69] This does not contradict the fact that other intercultural and international commemorative projects are blocked. As Yaroslav Goloubinov has shown, all attempts by the Czech Republic to centre the tombs and burial places of soldiers according to the convention signed by Boris Yeltsin in the 2000s have met fierce opposition. The local authorities and community still regard foreign legionnaires who found themselves in Russia in the turmoil of the First World War as invaders and enemies of Russian sovereignty.[70]

Even more problematic is the valorization of sites of memory that emerged during Stalin's time. As in Germany and other countries that exercised state terror or were subjects of cross-repressions and annexation, as literally all eastern-European countries were, the narration of terror always contains plenty of contradictions and ambiguities. The dark past is only partly represented in Holocaust-type memorials. It implies a drama realized by a particular group in a limited period of time, like the state secret services' terror directed against innocent victims. In Russia, popular grass-roots initiatives such as *Poslednyi Adres* (Last Address) and *Eto priamo zdes'* (It Happened Right Here) follow German analogues – the *Stolpersteine* and *Topographie des Terrors* projects. The Solovki detention camp may be the most studied case. Formerly witness to thousands of prisoners, Solovki Island is now a popular tourist pilgrimage destination.[71] As many visitors to dark sites have noted, information is very scarce, and some former Gulag barracks are still being used for different civic purposes.[72] Indeed, when compared to communist commemorative initiatives to emphasize the pre-revolutionary dark past supported by meticulous research that included oral histories, contemporary efforts to reshape or simply replace the Soviet remembrance infrastructure are statistically insignificant.[73] More than that, frequent activities in honour of the Soviet secret services run parallel to the commemorative measures of the Great Purge. With the presidency of Vladimir Putin, a former high-ranking KGB officer, this organization, responsible for unlawful repressions since the late 1910s, acquired heightened visibility. The unveiling of new monuments and memorial plaques in honour of secret service officers as well as the annual celebration of the foundation of the secret service enjoy the full support of the Russian government and the president.[74] This support partly explains the poor development of heritage studies in the country, especially of its trauma and dark past segments.[75]

Another key to the limited visibility of dark past memoirs is the unfinished process of de-Stalinization in Russia. The signs of the under-recognized impact of the repressions can be traced back to the 1960s. Since then, a lot of memorial plaques have been installed to honour disgraced politicians and artists in the course of de-Stalinization. All of them, including the ones dedicated to the executed leading civil war military figure Mikhail Tukhachevsky, the tortured world-renowned theatre director Vsevolod Meyerhold, and many others, bear no information on the reasons for their death. In contemporary public spaces, the mention of atrocities is also avoided in almost all personal plaques of victims of the Great Purge. This is the case with Nikolai Nekrasov (Golgofsky), an engineer, a member of the Cadet (Constitutional Democratic) party, and in 1917 the minister of road transport and finances in the Constituent Assembly. In 1930, he was accused of anti-revolutionary activities and sent to a forced-labour camp at the White Sea–Baltic Canal construction site to work as an engineer, and was even released in 1933. In 1939, though a highly skilled worker at the Moscow-Volga canal project in Dmitrov, Nekrasov was again arrested and accused of sabotage. He was executed in 1940. In honour of the sixtieth anniversary of the Moscow-Volga canal launch in 1997, a memorial plaque was installed at his house in Dmitrov that mentioned none of the repressions against him.[76] It should be noted that the city Dmitrov is one of the few places in Russia that made visible its own dark history. The local museum dedicated a part of its exposition to the Dmitrovlag, the camp that was built in 1932 to provide a working force for the Moscow-Volga canal.[77] Some buildings used by prisoners retained their initial function, such as the House of Culture. This episode of semi-silenced and semi-revealed truths explicitly demonstrates the limitations of the remembrance of the dark past in contemporary Russian cities.

The move to hide a difficult past comes not only from the state. Family members, too, prefer not to mention the fact of repressions. This is the case with Nikolai Gorbunov, a secretary of the Soviet Academy of Sciences, who was killed in 1938. A plaque was installed by his son in 2001 that did not disclose the reason for his father's death. A plaque for famous Silver Age thinker and Solovki camp prisoner Pavel Florensky was installed in Moscow in 1997 in commemoration of his passing. It too contains no indication of Florensky's tragic end. As these examples show, avoiding any mention of repressions is a fairly standard practice of the authorized post-Soviet discourse on Stalinism.

Another prevalent tendency is creating a new object of commemoration that has no historical roots rather than valorizing a pre-existing one that could highlight real victims or their heirs. This is the case of the Moscow Monument to the Victims of Political Repression, a project that was initially born among dissidents in the 1970s. In 2016, the Russian federal government seized on the initiative that had been unfulfilled all those years due to lack of funding. In 2017, the unveiling of the monument, The Wall of Sorrow, literally became the culmination of the scant 1917 anniversary celebrations.[78] The Wall, unveiled by Russian president Vladimir Putin and Patriarch Kirill on 30 October, the annual Day of Remembrance of the Victims of Political Repressions, is a typical example of overshadowing real and innumerable sites of memory. Indeed, in the USSR, while there was an impressive network of museums of tsarist exile, showcasing the atrocities of the pre-revolutionary authorities and the heroism of future Bolshevik leaders, by 1930 there was a new gulag system of forced labour camps – numbering more than 30,000 – throughout the vast territory of the USSR, including at the former places of imperial exile.[79] In Russia today, the Solvychegorsky and Narymsky museums still exhibit the everyday life of tsarist prisoners, while almost none of them were reprofiled as sites of memory of Soviet banishment. For instance, the *Vologodskaia ssylka* (Vologda exile) museum was opened in 1937 as a museum dedicated to Stalin's exile during the tsarist period. After de-Stalinization in the mid-1950s, it functioned as a display of Bolshevik exile, and after 1969 as the museum-house of Maria Ulianova, a younger sister of Vladimir Lenin and a revolutionary activist. As was discussed in the previous section, the rededication of the museum to Lenin's relatives clearly followed the tendency to reshape revolutionary discourse towards family values. Today, one can find a memorial plaque dedicated to Stalin, who lived there, as well as a wax figure of the young *vozhd* (leader) in the exposition. Even though visitors are invited to participate in a survey on their attitude towards Stalin, this participatory action feels purely decorative and insufficient. Still, schoolchildren could find out much more about tsarist exile and everyday life in pre-revolutionary Russia than about the various Gulag camps situated in Vologda in the Soviet era. The same goes for Russian penitentiaries and their museumification. Thus, no account of the Soviet period is seen in the Peter and Paul prison in St Petersburg where Dostoevsky and Lenin were famously held. Another place, the museum at Gorokhovaya 2 is dedicated to the secret services, but its functioning as a detention site is barely mentioned. Tellingly, one of the preserved confinement cells is a memorial prison room where

Lenin was held in detention; thus, it is directly bound to legitimized communist memorabilia.[80]

All other types of representation of the dark past, such as the Communist Party legacy that left myriad visual symbols of its power incorporated in everyday life, are not recognized as a matter of memorial and/or critical valorization. The question remains acute: do Russians need to preserve communist memorials and sites of memory, especially those reserved for politicians and prominent party members? Institutionally, Soviet political mass sculpture is now stored in the sole park of communist statues – Muzeon in Moscow.[81] The park follows the example of other European sites of disgraced political sculpture, such as Memento Park in Budapest, Hungary. Others, like a depository of socialist realist paintings, Rosizo, regard paintings as exotic and consumable objects. But the vast majority of party-affiliated and communist-legitimized memorabilia still inhabit Russian public spaces. According to statistics, most of the Lenin monuments preserved in Russia are in the nation's capital – 103 statues in Moscow.[82] Today some activists are trying to raise their voices against the demolition of openly ideological and politicized heritage objects that have no artistic and/or cultural value, as is often the case with mass-copied communist memorabilia. This is the case in the city of Korolev, formerly called Kalinin after Mikhail Kalinin, a Soviet politician of the 1930s. The major stakeholder is the Communist Party, which enthusiastically applies to restore or rename this or that communist site of memory and which proposed bringing back a sculpture bust of Kalinin to a local park. The inquiry gave Korolev activists the impetus to work in the archives in order to restore the history of this park and the city name.[83] The local community hasn't achieved any consensus on the case. However, such initiatives pose a question on how to achieve a balance between heritage expertise, communal nostalgia, and the contested memory of the political regime that underlines complex post-Soviet urban identities.[84] So far, the solution is straightforward and simple. Authorities, both local and federal, tend to create new commemorative infrastructure to replace an older example. This happened to a Moscow residential building that was classified as historically significant in the Soviet era because Mikhail Kalinin had lodged there in the 1910s. Recently, the city authorities have launched a municipal program encouraging chosen street artists to paint on the facades and to depict distinguished people connected to Russian culture. This is how a building "where Mikhail Kalinin lived" now bears a portrait of world-famous composer Igor Stravinsky, who emigrated from Russia in 1914 and never lived in Moscow, let alone in the house.

In Korolev, there is no tangible link to Mikhail Kalinin; the city was renamed after him completely arbitrarily. Today, Moscow authorities follow the same strategy to create new sites of memory and produce misleading and thus "imagined" public spaces that still bear myriad "broken" and non-existent references.

Conclusion

This chapter demonstrates several of the most common uses of the rich communist and revolutionary legacy in today's Russia. It comprises a double-bind narrative of a victorious revolution that left traumatic memories. The success of the revolution embodies militaristic images of the victories in the civil war, heroic secret service activities, and the Great Patriotic War mobilization patterns. The post-tourist paradigm offers a de-politicized and modernized image of the communist past. It includes Red tourism and kitsch attractions for international tourists and pre-revolutionary images of everyday life substituted in almost all expositions of former revolutionary local museums for domestic tourism. Gentrification strategies for Moscow communist landmarks offer another means with which to celebrate the Soviet past. The "dark past" heritage has in turn acquired only limited development. The civil war and Gulag sites of memory, as well as tsarist exile museums, remained untouched by historical and museological re-exposition.

As I have shown above, while communist commemorative heritage is one of the most developed and sophisticated networks in the Soviet Union, it still waits to be studied in its entirety. Communist heritage had also acquired a wide dissemination due to meticulous expertise that strove to label every historic location as a Soviet site of memory. The most important question is still open: how should the Communist Party memorial sites that were systematically developed throughout the seventy years of the Soviet period be treated when the communist legitimization of these places is dead? Some of them have no initial historic reference but did become local sites because the generations have been using them through all these years. Today, some of them are part of urban identity, while others remain unnoticed and ignored. Yet others are being replaced by new commemorative objects unrelated to the site. If the official heritage experts are tightly connected to the commercial interests of urban developers, non-governmental activists still experience difficulties and limitations in recognizing the cultural value of monuments. Keeping in mind the complexity and coherence of the Soviet heritage infrastructure, experts today are challenged to find a balanced approach towards existing communist objects that includes both post-Soviet nostalgia *and* recognition of a dark past.

NOTES

1 A complete analysis of communist commemorative infrastructure is still lacking. Recent scholarship is extensive though fragmentary: see Buckler and Johnson, eds, *Rites of Place*; Tolstoi, ed., *Khudozhestvennaia zhizhn' Sovetskoi Rossii: 1917–1932*; Velikanova, *The Public Perception of the Cult of Lenin*, 149–62; Rozanov and Reviakin, *Arhitektura muzeev V.I. Lenina*; Voronov, *Sovetskaia monumentalnaia skulptura, 1960–1980*. The holistic approach to cultural development under the Bolsheviks is analysed in numerous books on Soviet cultural revolution: see Pavliuchenkov, *Partiia, revoliutsiia, iskusstvo, 1917–1927 gg*; Kim, *Kulturnaia revolutsia v SSSR, 1917–1965*; Arnoldov, *Sotsialism i kulturnaia revolutsia*.
2 Resolution on heritage zones in Moscow, 20 December 1999, with additions from 3 October 2017; Moscow Municipal Government: http://docs.cntd.ru/document/901751725.
3 Tunbridge and Ashworth, *Dissonant Heritage*, 6–8, 20–33.
4 Faulenbach, *"Transformationen" der Erinnerungskulturen in Europa nach 1989*; Challand, "1989, Contested Memories and the Shifting Cognitive Maps of Europe."
5 On the AHD see Laurajane Smith, *The Uses of Heritage*, 29; and Laurajane Smith, "'Intangible Heritage."
6 The *Faro Convention* defines heritage communities as groups "of people who value specific aspects of cultural heritage which they wish, within the framework of public action, to sustain and transmit to future generations." Treaty No. 199, Faro Convention, 2005 (ratified 2011), article 2.b, *Council of Europe Framework Convention on the Value of Cultural Heritage for Society*: https://www.coe.int/en/web/conventions/full-list/-/conventions/treaty/199.
7 On heritage as cultural production see Kirshenblatt-Gimblett, "Theorizing Heritage"; Appadurai, "The Production of Locality."
8 Amacher, "L'embarrassante mémoire de la Révolution russe"; Boltunova, "'Prishla beda otkuda ne zhdali'"; Goloubinov, "Un champ de bataille mémoriel," 70.
9 Ekaterina Kravtsova, "Debate Rages over State History Textbooks," 23 April 2013, *The Moscow Times*: https://www.themoscowtimes.com/2013/04/25/debate-rages-over-state-history-textbooks-a23630.
10 Amacher, "L'embarrassante mémoire." For official resolutions on the 100th anniversary see the *Russian Historical Society*: http://rushistory.org/proekty/100-letie-revolyutsii-1917-goda.html. The anniversary initiative corresponds to those of renaming and replacing the October Revolution Day, 7 November, by a Day of Reconciliation and Accord in 1996 and then ultimately in 2005 by a Day of National Unity. See Corney, "'Twentieth-Century Apocalypse' or a 'Grimace of Pain'?," 315; Guzman, interview with Sergei Naryshkin, "Sergei Naryshkin: Revoliutsionnie sobytiia 1917."

11 A transcript of the public talk by Minister Medinsky who presented the
    100th anniversary concept, 20 May 2015, *Odnako*: http://www.odnako
    .org/blogs/navstrechu-100-letiyu-revolyucii-zveno-v-istoricheskoy
    -preemstvennosti-epoha-gigantskih-dostizheniy-i-platforma/. For a
    helpful overview of the anniversary celebrations and its blind spots
    see Kolonitskii and Matskevich, "Unberechenbare Vergangenheit in
    ungewissen Zeiten."

12 "Kulminaciia soglasiia i primireniia ne sostoialas iz-za suti vremeni,"
    26 November 2017, *Informer, Krymskii novostonoi portal*: http://ruinformer
    .com/page/kulminacija-soglasija-i-primirenija-ne-sostojalas-iz-za-suti
    -vremeni.

13 For a list of the main events and a list of local events honouring
    the 100th anniversary of the 1917 revolution see: "Plan osnovnykh
    meropriiatii, sviazannykh so 100-letiem revoliutsii 1917 goda v Rossii,"
    23 January 2017, *The Russian Historical Society*: http://rushistory.org
    /images/documents/plan100letrevolution.pdf, and http://rushistory
    .org/images/documents/region-plan-revolution100.pdf.

14 Engelstein, *Russia in Flames*, 226–30; Kolonitskii, "Kulturnaia gegemoniia
    sotsialistov v Rossiiskoi revoliutsii 1917 goda." See also "Peredovaia.
    XX s'ezd KPSS i zadachi issledovania istorii partii," 6–7.

15 The painting by V.P. Andersen, *Liquidation of the Uprising of the Left-Wing
    Party of Socialist-Revolutionaries in 1918*, displayed at the tenth exhibition of
    the Association of Artists of Revolutionary Russia (AKhRR) in honour of
    the tenth anniversary of the Red Army in 1928, in AKhRR, *Tenth Exhibition*,
    144. See also: Tolkachev *Assassination of Vladimir Lenin*, early 1930s,
    reproduced in Lelevich, "Lenin v izobrazitel'nom iskusstve," 19.

16 Yunge, *Revolutsionery na pensii*.

17 See also: "Peredovaia. Ob izuchenee istorii istoricheskoi nauki";
    "Peredovaia. XX s'ezd KPSS i zadachi issledovania istorii partii"; Ganelin,
    Sovetskie istoriki, 125–6.

18 Jones, *Myth, Memory, Trauma*, 212–57.

19 The debates over his biography were initiated in the popular weekly
    illustrated magazine *Ogonek*: Polikarpov, "Fedor Raskolnikov," 4–7, with
    follow-up in later issues: for example, Chaikin, "Istoria dla vsekh odna,"
    6–7; "Pochta Ogonka," 31; "Pochta Ogonka, slovo chitatelia," 6, etc.

20 Oliver Carroll, "Russian State-Run TV Marks Revolution's Centenary with
    Surprise Series Recounting Rise and Fall of Leon Trotsky," 16 October 2017,
    The Independent: http://www.independent.co.uk/news/world/europe
    /russian-revolution-centenary-leon-trotsky-biopic-channel-one-ussr
    -bolshevik-marxist-joseph-stalin-a8002636.html.

21 Many Russian local museums run their sites through popular national
    social networks, where I have drawn the announcement of the Samara

Frunze Museum published on 5 October 2017: https://vk.com
/club124838584.

22 See the full description of the exhibition, "Faces of the XX Century.
Hundred Years of the Russian Revolution of 1917," on the official website
of the Samara Museum: http://www.artmus.ru/exhibitions/id-195.html.

23 See, for example, albums of that period such as *Iskusstvo, rozhdennoe
Oktiabrem* (Moscow: Sovetskii khudozhnik, 1967).

24 "Sotrudniki muzeia v Podolske predstaviat v fevrale tsikl program pro
Lenina," 9 February 2017, *Riamo Podolsk*: https://podolskriamo.ru
/article/42567/sotrudniki-muzeya-v-podolske-predstavyat-v-fevrale
-tsikl-programm-pro-lenina.xl.

25 Stanislav Kuptsov, "Darvinovskii muzei pokazhet shkuru unikalnogo
medvedya, kotoruiu videl Lenin," 11 February 2017, *Metro*: http://www
.metronews.ru/novosti/moscow/reviews/darvinovskiy-muzey
-pokazhet-shkuru-unikalnogo-medvedya-kotoruyu-videl-lenin-1216597/.

26 Balina, Condee, and Dobrenko, eds, *Endquote: Sots-Art Literature and Soviet
Grand Style*. See also on late Soviet history and Lenin images: Gamboni,
The Destruction of Art, 51–90; on Lenin's cult: Scherrer, "L'érosion de
l'image de Lénine"; TJ Smith, "The Collapse of the Lenin Personality Cult
in Soviet Russia, 1985–1995."

27 On theoretization of kitsch in heritage production see Atkinson, "Kitsch
Geographies and the Everyday Spaces of Social Memory." It's tempting
to mention that Soviet art production that once was coined as kitsch (and
juxtaposed to genuine abstract art) by Clement Greenberg in the late 1930s,
after the 1970s was radically contextualized and changed its connotations
in art projects of nonconformist Soviet artists. On the changing attitude
towards Soviet images in the 2000s, see: Dobrenko, "O sovetskikh
suzhetakh v zapadnoi slavistike," 30–1.

28 The most notable example of the anti-liberal agenda of Soviet dissidents is
the 1978 Solzhenitsyn Harvard Commencement Speech. See also Horvath,
The Legacy of Soviet Dissent.

29 Sherlock, *Historical Narratives in the Soviet Union and Post-Soviet Russia*, 69.

30 See for example, Bykov, "Po pravu pamiati," 6–7, on Bolshevik
revolutionaries who died during the Great Purge; "'Deti Arbata,'
Pisma Anatoliu Rybakovu," 4–5, for readers' feedback on the legacy
of repressions; Donkov and Nikonov, "Yan Rudzutak," 10–11, on Yan
Rudzutak repressed in 1937, and many more.

31 Amacher, "Révolutions et révolutionnaires en Russie."

32 Corney, "'Twentieth-Century Apocalypse,'" 313.

33 *State Policy Concept* on immortalizing the memory of victims of political
repressions, 15 August 2015, No 1561-p.

34 Foss, "Ambiguity as Persuasion."

35 Likhachev, "Pamiatniki kultury – vsenarodnoe dostoianie"; Petrianov-
    Sokolov, "Pamiat eto sovest" [Memory Is Conscience]; Likhachev,
    "Dostoinstvo kultury" [Dignity of Culture]. The article in *Ogonek* on
    the Moscow Church of Christ the Saviour, demolished in 1931, was
    emblematically called "Exploded Conscience": Mikosha, "Tiazhkii put'
    prozrenia." On the history of the heritage movement in the USSR, see
    Kelly, "The Shock of the Old."
36 Janeke, "Revolution im Museum 1917–2017," 335, 338. The same appeal
    to not repeat the tragic events of the 1917 revolution, as well as a
    proclamation of the united and reconciled nation, was pronounced by
    Vladimir Putin, who addressed the upcoming anniversary in his annual
    speech on 1 December 2016, *Nevskie Novosti St. Petersburg*: https://nevnov
    .ru/471658-putin-napomnil-o-godovshchine-oktyabrskoi-revolyucii
    -1917-goda.
37 On heritization as gentrification see Gravari-Barbas, ed., *Habiter le
    patrimoine: Enjeux – approches – vécu*. On the post-Soviet development
    of entertaining and consumer-oriented culture in Russian museums
    see Mazaev, "Transformatsia istoriko-kulturnogo i khudozhestvennogo
    muzeia v postsovetskoi Rossii."
38 On the origins of the phenomenon of Red tourism see: Li, Hu, and Zhang,
    "Red Tourism"; and for a bibliographical overview on Red tourism in
    Eastern Europe, Light, "Gazing on Communism." In Russia, for a case
    study of Ivanovo's architecture as heritage asset, Timofeev, "From 'Red
    Manchester' to 'Red Disneyland.'"
39 "Turoperatory rasschityvaiut na vsplesk interesa kitaiskikh turistov k
    Rossii v 2017 godu," *Infox*, 14 February 2017: http://www.infox.ru
    /tourism/russia/2017/02/14/Turopyeratoryy_rassc.phtml.
40 "Stoletie revoliucii muzei Arseneva otmetil vystavkoi o Lenine," *Vostok
    Media*, 3 March 2017: http://www.vostokmedia.com/r2/03-03-2017
    /n318330.html.
41 The term "usable past" was coined by American historian Van Wyck
    Brooks in his 1918 essay, "On Creating a Usable Past," *The Dial* (11 April
    1918): 337–41.
42 "Zajavlenie Obshestvennogo dvizheniia 'Arkhnadzor' VDNkH –
    dostoprimechatelnaia i neohraniaemaia territoriia," *Arkhnadzor*,
    13 May 2015: http://www.archnadzor.ru/2015/05/13/vdnh
    -dostoprimechatelnaya-i-neohranyaemaya-territoriya/.
43 Pierre Sautreuil, "Russian Communist Park Restored amid Wave of
    Nostalgia," *L'Agence France-Presse*, 22 August 2014: http://news.yahoo
    .com/russian-communist-park-restored-amid-wave-nostalgia-055424770
    .html; "Vladimir Putin visited VDNKh," *Kremlin*, 4 August 2015: http://
    kremlin.ru/events/president/news/50094.

44 Panel *VDNKh Collection: Unique Heritage and Opportunities for Development* at the Moscow Urban Forum in December 2014.
45 Silina, "Chto sluchilos s VSkHV?" [What Has Happened to the Moscow Agricultural Ensemble?].
46 The most explicit example of reconnecting communist sites of memory to traditional culture is China: Madsen, "From Socialist Ideology to Cultural Heritage."
47 "'Prosti nas, Gosudar,' massovoe pokaianie vdol rossiiskikh i ukrainskikh dorog," *Uroki istorii*, 30 July 2012: http://urokiistorii.ru/article/51333.
48 See counter-actions and performances against the Obelisk removal: "Unichtozhenie Stely Svobody."
49 Morton, "The Creation of a 'People's Hero,'" 111.
50 Hartzok, "Children of Chapaev," 19–20; Morton, "The Creation of a 'People's Hero,'" 107–8.
51 An interview with the Suzdal local museum director: "Turist poshel drugoi," *TV-Mig*, 19 February 2017: https://tv-mig.ru/news/eksklyuziv/turist-poshyel-drugoy/.
52 Naila Galimova, "V cheboksarskom skvere V.I. Chapaeva ustanoviat edunstvennii v mire bronevik 'Cherep,'" *Komsomolskaia Pravda Kazan*, 12 December 2017: https://www.kazan.kp.ru/online/news/2960726/.
53 Aleksei Pismennii, "Deputat predlozhil provodit v Saratovskoi oblasti festival 'Rok nad Volgoi,'" *Versia Saratov*, 13 December 2017: https://nversia.ru/news/view/id/119357/; see also "Komandir na likhom kone," *Moskovskii Komsomolets Ufa*, 22 October 2014: http://ufa.mk.ru/articles/2014/10/22/komandir-na-likhom-kone.html. The efforts to promote Chapaev are especially vocal if we compare them to the de-communisation both on federal and local levels in the former Soviet republics that geopolitically were once close to Russia, such as Ukraine, Azerbaijan, et cetera. In 1925, in Ukrainian Podilsk (former Kotovsk) in Odessa region, a mausoleum for a mummy of a killed Bolshevik military hero, Grigorii Kotovsky, was created. The Kotovsky mausoleum was demolished by the German forces during the Great Patriotic War in 1941 and restored by the Soviet authorities in 1965. Today, the Bolshevik hero of the civil war era is not welcomed by Ukrainians in the time of de-communisation. Equally, a popular myth during the communist period, the story of twenty-six Baku commissars as martyrs, is now reframed as its opposite. The monument to the commissars (1958) and a pantheon (1968) over their burial place (1920) were demolished in 2009 as they are now considered to have been predators with national interests inspired by foreign forces. The rest were buried in the city cemetery accompanied by multi-ethnic and multi-confessional rituals.

54 "Pamiatnik Khalturinu: 'Tikhii' jubilei," blog post, 10 September 2013: http://kasanof.livejournal.com/82562.html.

55 A recent student project at the Higher School of Economics in Moscow that problematizes the presence of his image in Russian public spaces today: "Pamiatnik Dzerzhinskomu v Vyshke, chto dalshe?," *Dezherzhinsky*: http://dzerzhinsky.tilda.ws/.

56 Engelstein, *Russia in Flames*, 198–9.

57 Alexander Zhirkevich, journal entry, 25 July 1920, in A.V. Zhirkevich, "Potrevozhennie teni ... Simbirskii dnevnik" (Moscow: Eterna-print, 2007), Prozhito: http://prozhito.org/notes?date=%221920-01-01%22 &diaries=%5B30%5D.

58 Makarkin, "Deiateli Fevralia 1917-go v istoricheskoi pamiati sovremennoi Rossii."

59 Kolonitskii, *Simvoly vlasti i borba za vlast'*, 45–54.

60 On the museum of revolution see: Sarkisian, "Fevralskie istoki Gosudarstvennogo muzeia Revoliutsii." See also: Petrone, "The Great War and the Civil War."

61 Razgon, "Okhrana istoricheskikh pamiatnikov v dorevolutsionnoi Rossii (1861–1917 gg.)." See also Susan Smith, "Cultural Heritage and 'the People's Property,'" 403–23.

62 Kolonitskii, *Simvoly vlasti*, 36–47.

63 Gotie, *Moi zametki*, 105–6; Benua, *Dnevnik, 1916–1918*, 648.

64 For a useful overview on rehabilitation laws in Russia see: Doklad Komissii pri Prezidente Rossiiskoi Federatsii po reabilitatsii zhertv politicheskikh repressii o khode ispolneniia Zakona Rossiiskoi Federatsii, "O reabilitatsii zhertv politicheskikh repressii."

65 Entry from 16 March 1977, *Khronika tekuchikh sobytii*.

66 See news on the unveiling: "V Tambove otkryt pamiatnik russkomu muzhiku," *Regnum*, 4 November 2007: https://regnum.ru/news/909752 .html. The message of the monument was transformed within years; see one of the local sites that promotes cultural tourism in Tambov region: "Pamiatnik Tambovskomu muzhiku," *Tambovia*: http://tambovia.ru /pamjatnik_tambovskomu_muzhiku.html.

67 On rumours about civil war mass shooting places in Izhevsk: "V Izhevske ustanovleno mesto massovykh rasstrelov v 1918 godu," a transcript of the Radio Svoboda broadcast on 13 July 2008: https://www.svoboda.org /a/456004.html; in Rybinsk, Gessat-Anstett, *Une Atlantide russe*, 109–17.

68 The first mention of the White terror was very well documented already in the 1920s: Rafienko, "Istoriko-revoliutsionnie muzei v 1920-e gody," 84. There are a number of sites of memory of the White guards' terror, exemplified at the museum on Mudiug Island, as well as of the so-called Barge of Death (*barzha smerti*), but no mention of concentration camps

created by the Bolsheviks during the civil war, as for example a camp near Syrzan.

69 "Khranit kulturu." Private initiatives in the 1960s developed into so-called *narodnie musei* (people's museums) and local history museums like the Albazinsky local history museum in Amur region (1967); numerous Cossacks' museums in Orenburg region; and private museums of anti-Bolshevik resistance. For the latter, see Andrew Higgins, "Putin-Era Taboo: Telling Why Some Soviets Aided Nazis," *New York Times*, 21 June 2017: https://www.nytimes.com/2017/06/21/world/europe/vladimir-putin -russia-vladimirmelikhov.html.

70 Goloubinov, "Un champ de bataille mémoriel," 65–6, 69.

71 Comer, "Uncovering Violent Narratives."

72 Karl Schlögel, "Museumswelten im Umbruch," 20, 22.

73 By 1989 all museums had a revolution section following the concept that was set already at the 1931 Soviet Museum Congress. See also Kim, ed., *Kulturnaia zhizn' v SSSR, 1928–1941*, 258, 287.

74 Forest and Johnson, "Unraveling the Threads of History." This process started immediately after 1999 and took on wider coverage in the course of celebration of the Day of the State Security of the Russian Federation on 20 December, unveiling monuments and memorial plaques.

75 On heritage expertise and Russian public spaces, see Silina, "Obschestvennoe dostoianie kak travma." On the traumatic past in Russia, Etkind, *Warped Mourning*.

76 Inventory of Memorials and Monuments to Victims of Political Repression created by the Sakharov Centre: https://www.sakharov-center.ru/asfcd /pam/?t=pam&id=1183&pic=1.

77 Sungurov, "… I nareche ego Dmitrov."

78 On the unveiling of the Wall of Sorrow, see also Megan Swift's chapter in this volume.

79 Introduction to the Map of Gulag Camps created by the Memorial Society: http://www.memo.ru/history/nkvd/gulag/maps/pre.htm.

80 For a useful overview on the heritage status of Soviet prisons, see Reznikova, "Tiurmy Peterburga – Petrograda – Leningrada"; on the symbolic significance of prisons during the February revolution see Kolonitskii, *Simvoly vlasti*, 30–5.

81 Rukhina, *Muzeon. Park of Arts*.

82 See statistics on surviving Lenin monuments: http://leninstatues.ru /skolko. According to the data from 2016, 6,000 monuments survived in Russia (compared to 7,000 in 1991).

83 Mironova, "Istoriia odnogo skvera."

84 For a recent overview on uses of ideological heritage in order to shape contemporary urban identity in former communist countries, see Young

and Kaczmarek, "The Socialist Past and Postsocialist Urban Identity in Central and Eastern Europe"; and Paskaleva and Cooper, "Forming Post-Socialist Urban Identities through Small-Scale Heritage-Based Regeneration."

REFERENCES

AkHRR, *Tenth Exhibition*. Cat. Moscow: AkHRR, 1928.
Amacher, Korine. "Révolutions et révolutionnaires en Russie. Entre rejet et obsession." *Revue d'études comparatives Est-Ouest* 45, 2 (2014): 129–73.
– "L'embarrassante mémoire de la Révolution russe." *La Vie des idées*, 14 avril 2017: http://www.laviedesidees.fr/La-memoire-encombrante-de-la-Revolution-russe.html.
Appadurai, Arjun. "The Production of Locality." In *Counterworks: Managing the Diversity of Knowledge*, edited by Richard Fardon, 204–25. London and New York: Routledge, 1995.
Arnoldov, A.I. *Sotsializm i kulturnaia revoliutsiia: Nekotorye filosofskie problemy kulturnoi revoliutsii*. Moscow: Znanie, 1967.
Atkinson, David. "Kitsch Geographies and the Everyday Spaces of Social Memory." *Environment and Planning* 39 (2007): 521–40.
Balina, Marina, Nancy Condee, and Evgeny Dobrenko. *Endquote: Sots-Art Literature and Soviet Grand Style*. Evanston, IL: Northwestern University Press, 2000.
Benua, Alexander. *Dnevnik, 1916–1918*. Moscow: Zakharov, 2006.
Boltunova, Ekaterina. "'Prishla beda otkuda ne zhdali': Kak voina poglotila revoliutsiu." *Neprikosnovennii zapas* 116, 6 (2017): 109–28.
Buckler, Julie A., and Emily D. Johnson. *Rites of Place: Public Commemoration in Russia and Eastern Europe*. Evanston, IL: Northwestern University Press, 2013.
Bykov, Nikolai. "Po pravu pamiati." *Ogonek* 24 (1987): 6–7.
Chaikin, V. "Istoria dlia vsekh odna." *Ogonek* 33 (1987): 6–7.
Challand, Benoît. "1989, Contested Memories and the Shifting Cognitive Maps of Europe." *European Journal of Social Theory* 12, 3 (2009): 397–408.
Comer, Margaret. "Uncovering Violent Narratives: The Heritage of Stalinist Repression in Russia since 1991." In *Heritage of Death: Landscapes of Emotion, Memory and Practice*, edited by M. Frihammar and H. Silverman, 164–77. London: Routledge, 2017.
Corney, Frederick C. "'Twentieth-Century Apocalypse' or a 'Grimace of Pain'? The Vanishing Traces of October." In *Russian Culture in War and Revolution, 1914–22, Book 2: Political Culture, Identities, Mentalities, and*

Memory, edited by Murray Frame, Boris Kolonitskii, Steven G. Marks, and Melissa K. Stockdale, 313–39. Bloomington, IN: Slavica, 2014.

"'Deti Arbata,' Pisma Anatoliu Rybakovu." *Ogonek* 27 (1987): 4–5.

Dobrenko, Evgeny. "O sovetskikh suzhetakh v zapadnoi slavistike." In *SSSR, Zhizn posle smerti*, edited by I. Gluschenko, B. Kagarlitski, and V. Kurennoi, 27–34. Moscow: Izdatelskii dom Vysshei shkoly ekonomiki, 2012.

Doklad Komissii pri Prezidente Rossiiskoi Federatsii po reabilitatsii zhertv politicheskikh repressii o khode ispolneniia Zakona Rossiiskoi Federatsii. "O reabilitatsii zhertv politicheskikh repressii." 15 February 2000. *Lichnii arkhiv A.N. Yakovleva*: https://alexanderyakovlev.org/personal-archive/articles/7141.

Donkov, Igor', and Aleksandr Nikonov. "Yan Rudzutak." *Ogonek* 36 (1987): 10–11.

Engelstein, Laura. *Russia in Flames: War, Revolution, Civil War, 1914–1921.* Oxford: Oxford University Press, 2017.

Etkind, Alexander. *Warped Mourning: Stories of the Undead in the Land of the Unburied.* Stanford, CA: Stanford University Press, 2013.

Fardon, Richard. *Counterworks: Managing the Diversity of Knowledge.* London and New York: Routledge, 1995.

Faulenbach, Bernd. *"Transformationen" der Erinnerungskulturen in Europa nach 1989.* Essen: Klartext-Verlag, 2006.

Forest, Benjamin, and Juliet Johnson. "Unraveling the Threads of History: Soviet-Era Monuments and Post-Soviet National Identity." *Annals of the Association of American Geographers* 92, 3 (2002): 524–47.

Foss, Sonja K. "Ambiguity as Persuasion: The Vietnam Veterans Memorial." *Communication Quarterly* 34, 3 (1986): 326–40.

Frame, Murray, B.I. Kolonitskii, Steven G. Marks, and Melissa K. Stockdale. *Russian Culture in War and Revolution, 1914–22.* Bloomington, IN: Slavica Publishers, 2014.

Frihammar, M., and H. Silverman. *Heritage of Death: Landscapes of Emotion, Memory and Practice.* London: Routledge, 2017.

Gamboni, Dario. *The Destruction of Art: Iconoclasm and Vandalism since the French Revolution.* London: Reaktion Books: 1997.

Ganelin, R.Sh. *Sovetskie istoriki: O chem oni govorili mezhdu soboi. Stranitsy vospominanii o 1940–1970-h godakh.* St Petersburg: Nestor-Istoriia, 2006.

Gessat-Anstett, Élisabeth. *Une Atlantide russe: Anthropologie de la mémoire en Russie post-soviétique.* Paris: La Découverte, 2007.

Glushchenko, Irina, Boris Kagarlitsky, and Vitalii Kurennoi. *SSSR: Zhizn posle smerti.* Moscow: Izdatelskii dom Vysshei shkoly ekonomiki, 2012.

Goloubinov, Iaroslav. "Un champ de bataille mémoriel: La guerre civile de 1917–1921 à Samara." *Le mouvement social*, 260 (July–September 2017): 53–70.

Gotie, Yuri. *Moi zametki*. Moscow: Terra, 1997.

Gravari-Barbas, Maria, ed. *Habiter le patrimoine: Enjeux – approches – vécu*. Rennes: Presses universitaires de Rennes, 2005.

Guzman, Mikhail. "Sergei Naryshkin: Revoliutsionnie sobytiia 1917 goda bolshe ne raskalyvaiut obshchestvo." Interview, 7 November 2017. *The Russian Historical Society*: http://rushistory.org/proekty/100-letie -revolyutsii-1917-goda/sergej-naryshkin-revolyutsionnye-sobytiya-1917 -goda-bolshe-ne-raskalyvayut-obshchestvo.html.

Hartzok, Justus Grant. "Children of Chapaev: The Russian Civil War Cult and the Creation of Soviet Identity, 1918–1941." PhD diss., University of Iowa, 2009.

Horvath, Robert. *The Legacy of Soviet Dissent: Dissidents, Democratisation and Radical Nationalism in Russia*. London: Routledge, 2005.

Istoriia muzeinogo dela SSSR. Vol. 1. Moscow: Goskultprosvetizdat, 1957.

Janeke, Kristiane. "Revolution im Museum 1917–2017: Heikles Gedenken in Russland." *Osteuropa* 6–8 (2017): 323–41.

Jones, Polly. *Myth, Memory, Trauma: Rethinking the Stalinist Past in the Soviet Union, 1953–70*. New Haven, CT: Yale University Press, 2013.

Kelly, Catriona. "The Shock of the Old: Architectural Preservation in Soviet Russia." *Nations and Nationalism* 24, 1 (2018): 88–109.

"Khranit kulturu." *Ogonek* 40 (1986): 14–15.

Khronika tekuchikh sobytii 44 (1977): http://antology.igrunov.ru/after_75 /periodicals/hronika/hronika-44.html.

Kim, M.P., ed. *Kulturnaia revolutsia v SSSR, 1917–1965*. Moscow: Nauka, 1967.

– *Kulturnaia zhizn v SSSR, 1928–1941: Khronika*. Moscow: Nauka, 1976.

Kirshenblatt-Gimblett, Barbara. "Theorizing Heritage." *Ethnomusicology* 39, 3 (Fall 1995): 367–80.

Kolonitskii, Boris. *Simvoly vlasti i borba za vlast', K izucheniui politicheskoi kultury Rossiiskoi revoliutsii 1917 goda*. St Petersburg: Liki Rossii, 2012.

– "Kulturnaia gegemoniia sotsialistov v Rossiiskoi revoliutsii 1917 goda." *Neprikosnovenni zapas* 116, 6 (2017): 72–87.

Kolonitskii, Boris, and Maria Matskevich. "Unberechenbare Vergangenheit in ungewissen Zeiten: Hundert Jahre Revolution im heutigen Russland." 27 August 2017. *Geschichte der Gegewart*: http://geschichtedergegenwart .ch/unberechenbare-vergangenheit-in-ungewissen-zeiten-hundert-jahre -revolution-im-heutigen-russland/.

Lebedev, P.I. *Iskusstvo, rozhdennoe Oktiabrem*. Moscow: Sovetskii khudozhnik, 1967.

Lelevich, G. "Lenin v izobrazitel'nom iskusstve." *Sovetski Muzei* 1 (1931): 14–22.

Li, Yiping, Zhi Yi Hu, and Chaozhi Zhang. "Red Tourism: Sustaining Communist Identity in a Rapidly Changing China." *Journal of Tourism and Cultural Change* 8, 1–2 (2010): 101–19.

Light, Duncan. "Gazing on Communism: Heritage Tourism and Post-Communist Identities in Germany, Hungary and Romania." *Tourism Geographies: An International Journal of Tourism Space, Place and Environment* 2, 2 (2000): 157–76.

Likhachev, D.S. "Pamiatniki kultury – vsenarodnoe dostoianie." *Istoriia SSSR* 3 (1961): 3–12.

– "Dostoinstvo kultury." *Ogonek* 48 (1986): 10–11.

Madsen, Richard. "From Socialist Ideology to Cultural Heritage: The Changing Basis of Legitimacy in the People's Republic of China." *Anthropology & Medicine* 21, 1 (2014): 58–70.

Makarkin, Aleksei. "Deiateli Fevralia 1917-go v istoricheskoi pamiati sovremennoi Rossii." *Neprikosnovennii zapas* 116, 6 (2017): 129–39.

Mazaev, P. "Transformatsia istoriko-kulturnogo i khudozhestvennogo muzeia v postsovetskoi Rossii." In *SSSR: Zhizn posle smerti*, edited by Irina Gluschenko, Boris Kagarlitsky, and Vitaly Kurennoi, 216–25. Moscow: Izdatelskii dom Vysshei shkoly ekonomiki, 2012.

Mikosha, Vladislav. "Tiazhkii put prozrenia." *Ogonek* 41 (1988): 10–15.

Mironova, Maria. "Istoriia odnogo skvera." *Sputnik*, 21 October 2017: http://in-korolev.ru/novosti/problemy/istoriya-odnogo-skvera.

Morton, Jason Read. "The Creation of a 'People's Hero': Vasilii Ivanovich Chapaev and the Fate of Soviet Popular History." PhD diss., University of California, Berkeley, 2017.

Muzeevedenie: Iz istorii okhrany i ispolzovaniia kulturnogo nasledia RSFSR. Moscow: N/A, 1987.

"Pamiatnik Dzerzhinskomu v Vyshke, chto dalshe?" *Dezherzhinsky*: http://dzerzhinsky.tilda.ws/.

Paskaleva, Krassimira, and Ian Cooper. "Forming Post-Socialist Urban Identities through Small-Scale Heritage-Based Regeneration: A Role for Intangibles?" *Journal of Urban Design* 22, 5 (2017): 670–88.

Pavliuchenkov, A.S. *Partiia, revoliutsiia, iskusstvo, 1917–1927 gg.* Moscow: Mysl, 1985.

"Peredovaia. Ob izuchenee istorii istoricheskoi nauki." *Voprosy istorii* 1 (1956): 3–12.

"Peredovaia. XX s'ezd KPSS i zadachi issledovania istorii partii." *Voprosy istoirii* 3 (1956): 3–12.

Petrianov-Sokolov, I.V. "Pamiat eto sovest'." *Ogonek* 35 (1986): 18–20.

Petrone, Karen. "The Great War and the Civil War." In *Russian Culture in War and Revolution, 1914–22*, edited by Murray Frame, B.I. Kolonitskii, Steven G. Marks, and Melissa K. Stockdale, 259–72. Bloomington, IN: Slavica Publishers, 2014.

"Pochta Ogonka." *Ogonek* 34 (1987): 31.

"Pochta Ogonka, slovo chitatelia." *Ogonek* 11 (1988): 6.

Polikarpov, Vasilii. "Fedor Raskolnikov." *Ogonek* 26 (1987): 4–7.

"'Prosti nas, Gosudar', massovoe pokaianie vdol' rossiiskikh i ukrainskikh dorog." *Uroki istorii*, 30 July 2012: http://urokiistorii.ru/article/51333.

Rafienko, E.N. "Istoriko-revoliutsionnie muzei v 1920-e gody," *Muzeevedenie: Iz istorii okhrany i ispolzovaniia kulturnogo nasledia RSFSR*. Moscow: Ministerstvo kul'tury RSFSR, AN SSSR, NII kul'tury, 1987.

Razgon, A.M. "Okhrana istoricheskikh pamiatnikov v dorevolutsionnoi Rossii (1861–1917 gg.)." In *Istoriia muzeinogo dela SSSR, 73–128.* Moscow: Goskul'tprosvetizdat, 1957.

Reznikova, Olga. "Tiur'my Peterburga – Petrograda – Leningrada." *Uroki istorii*, 3 June 2009: http://urokiistorii.ru/article/227.

Rozanov, E.G., and V.I. Reviakin. *Arkhitektura muzeev V.I. Lenina.* Moscow: Stroiizdat, 1986.

Rukhina, Eva. *Muzeon: Park of Arts.* Moscow: N/A, 2014.

Sarkisian, N.M. "Fevralskie istoki Gosudarstvennogo muzeia Revolutsii: Obschestvo doma-muzeia pamiati bortsov za svobody v marte 1917 – sentiabre 1919 gg." Conference held at the State Museum of Political History of Russia, 2017: http://www.polithistory.ru/papers2017/.

Scherrer, Jutta. "L'érosion de l'image de Lénine." *Actes de la recherche en sciences sociales* 85 (November 1990): 54–69.

Schlögel, Karl. "Museumswelten im Umbruch. Russische Museen nach dem Ende des Sowjetunion." *Transit* 47 (2015): 6–29.

Sherlock, Thomas. *Historical Narratives in the Soviet Union and Post-Soviet Russia: Destroying the Settled Past, Creating an Uncertain Future.* New York: Palgrave Macmillan, 2007.

Silina, Maria. "Chto sluchilos s VSkHV?" *Artguide*, 25 April 2016: http://artguide.com/posts/1022.

– "Obschestvennoe dostoianie kak travma." *Colta*, 21 December 2016: http://www.colta.ru/articles/art/13464.

Smith, Laurajane. *The Uses of Heritage.* Oxford and New York: Routledge, 2006.

– "'Intangible Heritage': A Challenge to the Authorized Heritage Discourse." *Revista d'Etnologia de Catalunya* 40 (2015): 133–42.

Smith, Susan. "Cultural Heritage and 'the People's Property': Museums in Russia, 1914–21." In *Russian Culture in War and Revolution, 1914–22,* edited by Murray Frame, B.I. Kolonitskii, Steven G. Marks, and Melissa K. Stockdale, 403–24. Bloomington, IN: Slavica Publishers, 2014.

Smith, TJ. "The Collapse of the Lenin Personality Cult in Soviet Russia, 1985–1995." *Historian* 60, 2 (1998): 325–43.

"Stoletie revoliutsii 1917-go goda: Ofitsial'nye dokumenty." *The Russian Historical Society*: http://rushistory.org/proekty/100-letie-revolyutsii-1917-goda.html.

Sungurov, Roman. "... i nareche ego Dmitrov." *Nashe Nasledie* 112 (2015): http://www.nasledie-rus.ru/podshivka/11203.php.

Timofeev, Mikhail. "From 'Red Manchester' to 'Red Disneyland': Constructivist Architecture and the Representation of Ivanovo." *Quaestio Rossica* 4, 3 (2016): 72–92.

Tolstoi, V.P. *Khudozhestvennaia zhizn' Sovetskoi Rossii: 1917–1932: Sobytiia, fakty, kommentarii: Sbornik materialov i dokumentov*. Moscow: Galart, 2010.

Tunbridge, J.E., and G. Ashworth. *Dissonant Heritage: The Management of the Past as a Resource in Conflict*. Chichester: John Wiley and Sons, 1996.

"Unichtozhenie Stely Svobody: 7 lektsii o revoliutsionnykh mysliteliakh." *Theory and Practice*, 28 August 2013: https://theoryandpractice.ru/posts/7541-stela-svobody.

Velikanova, Olga. *The Public Perception of the Cult of Lenin Based on Archival Materials*. Lewiston, NY: Edwin Mellen Press, 2001.

Voronov, N.V. *Sovetskaia monumental'naia skulptura 1960–1980*. Moscow: Iskusstvo, 1984.

Young, Craig, and Sylvia Kaczmarek. "The Socialist Past and Postsocialist Urban Identity in Central and Eastern Europe: The Case of Lódz, Poland." *European Urban and Regional Studies* 15, 1 (2008): 53–70.

Yunge, Mark. *Revolutsionery na pensii. Vsesoiuznoe obschestvo politkatorzhan i ssylnopereselentsev, 1921–1935*. Moscow: AIRO-XXI, 2015.

Zhirkevich, A.V. "Potrevozhennie teni ... Simbirskii dnevnik." Moscow: Eterna-print, 2007, Prozhito: http://prozhito.org/notes?date=%221920-01-01%22&diaries=%5B30%5D.

3 Revolutionary Architecture in Russia Today: The Avant-Garde as a Disputed Heritage

JULIE DESCHEPPER

What was once built to testify to a singular and eternal present becomes the symbol and proof of its mutability.

Dylan Trigg, *The Aesthetics of Decay* (2006)

During the fall of 2017, an exhibition organized by the St Petersburg Committee for the Preservation of Historical and Cultural Monuments (KGIOP) was held at the Gallery Rosfoto. The exhibition was called "Revolution and Heritage – Heritage of Revolution" and presented wonderful unpublished photographs of two complementary phenomena during the Bolshevik government's first years of existence: destruction and construction of monuments.[1] On the one hand, unique photographs of ancient monuments were exhibited, especially of churches that were being meticulously destroyed. In contrast, the exhibition included photographs of sculptures of monumental propaganda.[2] More interestingly, it showed a large number of photographs of Leningrad's avant-garde architecture – buildings and ensembles from the 1920s and 1930s. This important presence of avant-garde architecture in an exhibition on Revolution and Heritage in 2017 Russia was as fascinating as it was, we will see, unexpected.

The introductory text of the exhibition was clear about the broader purpose of the event:

There is no doubt that the Great Russian Revolution of 1917 provided an impetus towards shaping the modern architectural image of the city. [...] The aim of the exhibition organizers was not to show the course of events of the Revolution, but rather to represent the impact of those events on the future of the city.[3]

All photographs emphasized the Soviet state's powerful desire to build a socialist society. Avant-garde architecture indeed undeniably shaped the new face of Soviet urbanism and is therefore tightly linked with the so-called socialist cities (*sotsgoroda*). Moreover, avant-garde architecture was revolutionary from an aesthetic, conceptual, and political point of view.

Rejected in the 1930s before being revalued in the 1960s, avant-garde architecture is much more than a legacy of the revolution – it is a cultural heritage of the revolution, but one that is controversial in today's Russia. Values projected onto this heritage, as well as the ways of preserving it, diverge greatly and are often paradoxical. While the KGIOP's exhibition explicitly underlines that the avant-garde is a revolutionary heritage, 100 years after 1917 it appears that the assimilation of these buildings within the national heritage of the Russian Federation, especially in the 2000s, is not readily accepted. In fact, a quick excursion through some of St Petersburg's main avant-garde monuments – the Krasnoe Znamia Factory, the Water Tower of the "Krasnyi Gvozdilschik" Factory, or the residential buildings of Traktornaia ulitsa – makes it hard to believe that these buildings have been registered on the heritage lists since the Soviet period, so worrying is their state of conservation (figure 3.1).[4]

Nevertheless, it is beyond the scope of this chapter to draw a precise portrait of these buildings' conservation state from an aesthetic or architectural point of view, just as it is to denounce the current situation. Rather, I propose to examine the reasons for rejecting, neglecting, abandoning, destroying, restoring, or rebuilding avant-garde monuments in today's Russia (until 2017). While not denying the complexity of the situation, the main argument I develop is that the paradoxical relationship towards avant-garde architecture is actually closely linked to a controversial, ambiguous, and evolutionary attitude towards the October Revolution in Soviet and post-Soviet Russia – one that Korine Amacher has characterized as "rejection and obsession."[5] In other words, the treatment of these material remains of the revolution is still intimately linked with the political uses of the revolutionary period (1917–22) that is a fundamental and yet contested part of Russian history. Therefore, through an analysis of the conception, representation, and policies of avant-garde heritage in Russia, this chapter also contributes to a better understanding of the memory of 1917 today.

For this purpose, after having introduced briefly the "revolutionary component" of avant-garde architecture, I will explore its destiny and designation as heritage. Relying upon a presentation of the current

Figure 3.1. Water Tower of the "Krasnyi Gvozdilschik" Factory (Y.V. Chernikhov, 1930–1). Photograph by the author, 2017

state of several avant-garde buildings and an analysis of the different representations associated with this architecture, this exploration will reveal the close link between the avant-garde and the revolution in contemporary Russia. I will then examine the development of new grass-roots movements that intend to protect and enhance this heritage. I will highlight the motivation of these movements' actors and analyse their different actions through the prism of their representations and uses of the revolutionary past. Finally, I will address the "de-ideologization" of avant-garde architecture on the occasion of the 1917 centenary.

Avant-Garde: A Revolutionary Architecture and Heritage of the Revolution

While the October Revolution is today no longer considered as a historical break but rather as a pivotal year that was part of a complex international and long-term dynamic, it must be said that, with regard to heritage preservation and artistic production, October 1917 was a turning point.[6] As many scholars have shown, the Bolshevik Revolution provoked radical modes of expression and even gave birth to a Soviet aesthetic – to which belonged the architectural productions discussed in this chapter. To better grasp the historical, artistic, and political importance of avant-garde architecture until today, I will give an overview of its development and main characteristics, questions that have been researched in depth by several scholars.[7]

The revolution was "mainly about the development of the arts as ideology," declared Anatoly Lunacharsky, the first commissar of education.[8] In architecture, the Marxist-Leninist ideology was indeed omnipresent in the architectural projects (realized or not) – even though the architects themselves were sometimes not convinced communists. Architecture had to create, or more precisely to "stimulate without decree," new ways of life (novyi byt), echoing Marxist-Leninist theories in daily life. Although some of the buildings were shaped with radical and striking visual forms, some of them were characterized by a more sober aesthetic, reflecting a Marxist aspiration to an "asceticism based on simplicity," sometimes qualified as minimalism.[9] These innovative and experimental architectural creations embodied the will of the Bolshevik and then Soviet government to shape a "new (wo)man" by progressively transforming behaviour and social interactions, goals that could be carried out, thanks to housing standardization and to new inventions.[10] These projects were dedicated to improving the well-being of citizens but also to developing technological and industrial equipment. Examples of such projects include collective housing for workers or students, workers' clubs and other leisure facilities, factories, canteens, and buildings and towers for telecommunications.[11] Beyond the great variation of forms and functions, the sheer number of avant-garde buildings is impressive.[12]

As Catherine Cooke has observed in her study of the Marxist element of Constructivism, the style to which Soviet architectural avant-gardes are often reduced, this architecture had a proactive role to play: at the time it worked as a "social condenser" and "agent of specific social change," carrying a new collective social project.[13] This is why socialist cities, as they were conceived, need to be understood as a "full-fledged urban mechanism."[14] Following Cooke, it must be underlined that these buildings were part of a broader political plan: they were supposed to contribute to the construction of socialism in the literal and figurative senses. This explains why this architecture has been invested with a deep meaning by and for the Soviet regime, a meaning that is still associated with this architecture today. The projection of an idealized, accomplished communist future, sometimes considered as a form of "utopia," could be linked with the project carried out by avant-gardist architects. However, these creations were not supposed to last forever. Rather, they were thought to be part of a process to educate populations in the present.

One must also keep in mind that the construction of these new buildings inevitably led to a campaign of destruction on the new Bolshevik soil, especially of ancient monuments, a controversial and violent phenomenon to which this architecture is still related today. The construction of the House of Government was, for instance, carried out after the destruction of the Church of St Nicholas the Wonderworker on Bersenevka Street.[15] In addition, their construction took place during a terribly difficult period for the Soviet Union: the 1920s were years of civil war and characterized by hesitations in politics and an alarming economic situation.[16] As the Vesnin brothers, leading avant-garde architects, summarized it, "We have to remember that our Soviet architecture developed during a period when we were poor to the last degree."[17] Access to production material of any quality or quantity was indeed a real problem. Inevitably, this influenced the quality (or lack of quality) of these constructions, as well as their ability to survive the passage of time. Furthermore, the living conditions in these experimental buildings, especially in collective habitations, hardly fitted the dream of a transformed society. To put it another way: inhabitants often rejected a new collective way of life as an affront to their traditions, especially of family and private space.[18] In addition, after the decree of 1932 that intended to impose socialist realism in all the arts, the avant-garde was officially violently rejected and was subject to severe and aggressive criticism as a formal, bourgeois, and "imposed foreign architecture."[19] Dom Narkomfin, for example, the apartment block designed for high-ranking employees of the Ministry of Finance, was criticized as too "Corbusianist," a reference to the French architect Le Corbusier.[20] After this troubled period and the rejections to which the the avant-garde was subjected, the 1960s, 1970s, and 1980s represent, by contrast, the apogee of its rehabilitation and, then, heritagization.[21]

In the late 1960s, in a gesture aimed at fixing the architectural damage sustained during the Stalinist years, attention was focused on the restoration of ancient monuments as well as on Soviet architecture broadly speaking. Whereas the turn towards the pre-revolutionary past has been well analysed, the new interest in Soviet buildings is much less well known.[22] However, the desire to have a properly Soviet monumental and architectural heritage, in a country that seemed to associate the lengths of lists of protected monuments with the solidity of its regime, led to compulsive inscription for most monuments and buildings erected on Russian soil during the Soviet period. The architect Georgy Mikhailovich Orlov (1901–1985), while he was first secretary of the Union of Soviet Architects (1963–81), declared in June 1966 during the constitutive meeting of the All-Russian Society for the Protection of Historic and Cultural Monuments (VOOPIK) that:

> It is essential to recall that our cultural heritage is not only constituted of ancient and pre-revolutionary monuments. The best productions of Soviet architecture, which reflect socialist culture and ideology and our lifestyle, need legitimately to be inscribed as cultural heritage and legally protected. This needs to be done urgently because the buildings that characterize our epoch, built by the best Soviet architects such as Shchusev, Fomin, the Vesnin brothers, Ginzburg, etc., are today rebuilt uncontrollably. [...] This must be done for the 50th anniversary of the Soviet state.[23]

Aware of the fundamental importance of the event for the regime, Orlov judiciously referred to the fiftieth anniversary in order to convince his *preservationist* colleagues of the political, cultural, and social role of avant-garde architecture. In addition, he seized the opportunity of the anniversary, if not to launch, at least to promote, the idea of the avant-garde's heritagization. Although Orlov was the only one raising this issue during the meeting, his words strongly highlight the link between celebrating the revolution and the avant-garde's heritagization.

Indeed, in 1967 architecture and heritage experts of the Governmental Inspectorate of Monuments compiled a list of Moscow's Soviet architectural monuments that was then submitted to the architecture committee of VOOPIK.[24] Discourses on and uses of heritage actively helped to legitimize Soviet power during its years of existence, though the appreciation and value of heritage differed from one period to another. Triggering stormy debates, this list dedicated to the Soviet capital was eventually accepted – after revisions – twenty years later. Meanwhile, other cities such as Leningrad and Sverdlovsk (now Yekaterinburg) saw their main avant-garde architectural monuments registered as national heritage during the 1970s.[25]

Further, if in the 1960s this will to protect Soviet heritage depended only on ideological imperatives, in the 1970s and 1980s it relied mostly on historical and scientific motivations. Indeed, the Plenum of the Scientific and Methodic Council of the Ministry of Culture, held in October 1978 to celebrate the sixtieth anniversary of Lenin's decree on the protection of historical and artistic monuments, was clearly testified to the fact that Soviet architecture was already considered as a heritage to be preserved from a scientific point of view. It was indeed dedicated to the "Preservation of urban and architectural monuments of the Soviet era," and gathered together dozens of heritage experts from all over the Soviet Union for the purposes of discussing issues related to Soviet architectural heritage.[26] E.R. Krupnova presented a paper on the "Issues of Restoration of 1920s–1930s Monuments," insisting on the fundamental historical significance of these buildings in Soviet architecture but also in Soviet history.[27] However, the main year for heritagization of avant-garde masterpieces was 1987, when on 23 March several Constructivist monuments were registered, including Dom Melnikov (figure 3.2), Club Zuev Golossov, Dom Narkomfin, Shukhov Tower, Krasnopresnenskii univermag, the Palace of Culture, ZIL (the Likhachev Palace of Culture) by the Vesnin Brothers, Mayakovskaia metro station, Krasnie Vorota, Dinamo stadium, the building that housed the journal *Izvestiia*, and the Planetarium.[28]

Furthermore, in honour of the 100th birthday of the architect Konstantin Melnikov in 1990, seven more monuments were added to the list.[29] From this moment, a considerable number of buildings were registered and officially became an architectural heritage to protect in the USSR.

This page of Soviet heritage history is crucial for grasping the situation in 2017. It explains why most Soviet buildings, and especially avant-garde ones, are still inscribed on heritage lists. In consequence, what is at stake in post-Soviet Russia is not principally *recognizing* these buildings as heritage monuments but rather respecting this official status. In other words, the problem lies in the effective application of the law regarding cultural heritage, which requires the authorities at the local, regional, or federal level responsible for cultural heritage to protect, preserve, restore, and valorize them. But why is their heritage status forgotten, ignored, or simply rejected? Disentangling this complex issue requires reflection on the political, social, and cultural representations that are currently associated with the architectural heritage of the avant-garde.[30]

Figure 3.2. The Melnikov House (today "Melnikov Museum"), Moscow.
Photograph by the author, 2017

Avant-Garde Heritage and the Controversial
Memory of the October Revolution

As previously mentioned, despite their heritage status, most avant-garde buildings have been, after 1991, largely abandoned, neglected, stigmatized, sometimes demolished, or restored with methods often criticized by experts.[31] This phenomenon has stimulated much attention at the national and international levels. It has been clearly identified and denounced, and has led to academic publications since the mid-2000s. Several avant-garde buildings have been included in the World Monuments Watch List, such as the Rusakov Club in 1996 and 2008, the Melnikov House in 2006, and the Dom Narkomfin in 2002, 2004, and 2006. On the latter, John Stubbs – director of the World Monuments Fund – declared that "of all the over 200 architectural conservation projects that the World Monuments Fund is addressing in 86 countries at this time, it is the fate of the Narkomfin Building that worries us the most."[32] Moreover, two international events have played a role in raising awareness about the issue.[33] First, from 17 to 20 April 2006, Moscow hosted the conference "Heritage at Risk – Preservation of the 20th Century Architecture and World Heritage," organized by ICOMOS, Docomomo, and the International Union of Architects.[34] This international event led to the signing of the Moscow Declaration, a short text that publicly denounced the flagrant failure of Russia to protect its modern heritage, especially the avant-garde, and that directly called on Russian authorities, appealing

> to the relevant national and professional organizations to act with urgency to safeguard, protect and prevent from damage twentieth-century properties worthy of listing as monuments as well as monuments and sites that are already included in local and national registers.[35]

During the event and in order to raise a large audience's awareness, several exhibitions were presented at the Shchusev State Museum of Architecture in Moscow, among them *Lost Vanguard* by the photographer Richard Pare and *Repressed Architecture. Preservation of Architectural Avant-Garde in Russia and Germany.*[36] The Heritage at Risk Conference was a turning point – firstly, because it led to the publication of a common academic documentation on avant-garde conservation, and secondly, because it affirmed grass-roots movements in Russia.[37] Yet this initiative seems not to have changed the position of the Russian authorities in charge of preservation. This, however, did not discourage the defenders of Soviet heritage; instead, it encouraged them to act more firmly, frequently, and differently.

Indeed, the internationalization of the avant-garde "issue" kept on going in 2007 at the New York Museum of Modern Art (MOMA), with the new presentation of Pare's exhibition and its accompanying symposium, "Vanguard Lost and Found: Soviet Modernist Architecture between Peril and Preservation."[38] Following this, a special issue of *Future Anterior: Journal of Historic Preservation, History, Theory and Criticism* was dedicated to the "Preservation of Soviet Heritage."[39] The preservation of avant-garde heritage was officially an international problem, not only Russia's. In 2008, a third international event became decisive. Organized by the governmental heritage preservation committees of both Russia and Germany, the "Petersburg dialogue" was held in St Petersburg under the authority of ICOMOS.[40] Experts launched a comparative study of the avant-garde in both countries (for Russia, only in St Petersburg), presented case studies, and developed the idea of a new cooperation in the cultural field through avant-garde preservation and restoration. Three years after the Moscow Declaration, experts again made public appeals to act urgently and denounced the threat that the monuments were under.[41] In 2011, responding to international criticism, Russian heritage authorities recognized that they had an erroneous estimate of the value of these buildings.[42] A report drawn up by the Moscow city management for the protection of architecture (*Moskomarhitektura*) acknowledged that the buildings of this period had been long neglected because of a lack of appreciation for their historical and heritage value.[43]

Consequently, historian of architecture and international modern heritage expert Natalia Dushkina has claimed the necessity of inscribing avant-garde buildings in the World Heritage List of UNESCO (United Nations Educational, Scientific and Cultural Organization). To her, the monuments that must be inscribed are Dom Narkomfin, Club Rusakov, Club Kauchuk, Dom Melnikov, Dom Nikolaev, Shukhov Tower, and Maiakovskaia metro station. In 2017 she presented this list again as one of the only ways to preserve the avant-garde in Russia.[44] In doing so, she stated that an international solution is the only way to preserve Russian national heritage. Thus, although the avant-garde is legally recognized as heritage in the Russian Federation, it was no longer *considered* as heritage by the authorities in charge of its preservation, whereas, at the same time, it has been loudly asserted as having world heritage status by international experts. This chronology of events, actions, and declarations highlights the fact that heritage is never an easily accepted concept but rather varies depending on actors, communities, and political contexts. Indeed, these buildings, after being given the status of heritage and having an international reputation, have been progressively depreciated, and are not even considered as heritage anymore. In other words, this is a de-heritagization process. To grasp the logic at stake, the concept of the "heritagization cycle" proposed by Lucie Morisset is useful, as it allows us to think about the process of heritagization of each object as a non-linear one.[45] Following this framework, the avant-garde has been through different stages that are repeating, oscillating between neglect and re-evaluation, while the category of actors defending one or the other position has inevitably changed.

It must be emphasized that the phenomenon of heritage neglect is neither unique nor specific to Russia.[46] Nevertheless, the number of distinctive buildings abandoned and their lack of preservation make Russia a special case. How can we explain this official lack of preservation of monuments that are considered to have world heritage status? One of the primary causes appears to be the negative ideas today associated with the avant-garde. To capture it, Anke Zalivako proposed a reading grid in 2007 that remained relevant as late as 2017. She evoked four main causes to explain this ambiguous and complex attitude: economic ones, the issue of defamation, the low priority given to the buildings, and a lack of will and knowledge among both the administrative services responsible for cultural heritage in Russia and Russian citizens. The economic dimension seems today to be more important than ever. Although avant-garde buildings suffered in the 1990s after the fall of the Soviet Union, which at the time meant the end of their use and the loss of their socialist identity, the late 1990s and the 2000s have been firmly characterized by a new shape for post-Soviet cities. Destroying ancient or modern buildings often provides an opportunity to build new and higher ones, which is desirable in a nation that is trying to radically "modernize" – and perhaps Westernize – its urban face. Meanwhile public awareness about preservation has been changing slowly. This is, firstly, because of the profile of the international events noted above, as well as the existence of published academic conclusions that cannot be ignored by the professionals in charge of cultural heritage at an official level (although they can be taken into account or not). Secondly, new actors are working hard to raise citizens' awareness, as discussed further below.[47]

While fundamentally agreeing with Zalivako's analysis, I would like to focus on the underlying reasons for the negative assessment that she calls "defamation," and to understand the lack of will of the authorities in charge of preserving the architectural heritage that she describes. If there is undeniably a question of personal aesthetic taste that can be expressed at an official level, the origins of negative valuation are also to be found both in the history of these buildings and in their forms and functions. As Marat Khusnullin, Moscow deputy mayor for construction and urban development, for example, commented on Constructivist residential buildings in 2016, "We are for constructivism, although personally I think these buildings should be left as monuments to what should not be built."[48] As part of a broader international style, the avant-garde was often considered to be non-Russian – though regarded as properly Soviet. Thus, Constructivism as a movement could not contribute to a growing a national discourse on the specificity of the Russian identity, and this is an important cause of its rejection, especially at an official level. Moreover, the fact that this architecture embodies the revolutionary period creates a strong prejudice against it. The rejection of revolutionary monuments in Moscow was analysed by Forest and Johnson in 2002, when they designed a three-categories model of "political status of Soviet-era 'places of memory.'"[49] This model is today quite dated, especially for the monuments considered "disavowed" that actually became "glorified" in 2017. This turn highlights how quickly urban development and the uses of the past are evolving in post-Soviet Russia. Still, Forest and Johnson addressed fundamental issues: to them, monuments that reflected the Russian Revolution were "contested" sites, as they were a "source of conflicts espousing contrasting ideas of national identity."[50] Focusing on statues and museums, they did not discuss architecture, although it, too, especially today, is highly relevant for their analysis. Indeed, the revolutionary component of the avant-garde hardly fits the current narrative of history in Russia, presented as a linear one marked with heroic moments and heroes (above all the Second World War – the Great Patriotic War) and in which the break embodied by the revolutions seems to have been set aside to enhance the modernity and greatness of the Russian empire and the Stalinist period.[51]

According to this logic, the rupture embodied by the 1917 revolution and the unstable period of the Bolshevik seizure of power, as well as the figure of Lenin, remain controversial and seem to have been abandoned to better enhance the state's "greatness." Plus, the idea of a collective life is far removed from the current individualist model of existence. Whereas the avant-garde was considered in the late Soviet period to be a testament to Soviet genius, it is today not representative of the history that the Russian state wants to write about itself, nor of its chosen image to celebrate the nation. "Greatness," as understood in contemporary Russia, is not to be found in buildings that promoted new collective ways of life and that were erected to build socialism. Therefore, the conception of what *makes* heritage has slowly evolved in Russia since Putin first arrived in power. While this "authorized" heritage conception had been in place since the Yeltsin era – as evidenced by the reconstruction of the Church of the Kazan Mother on Red Square in 1993 or the construction of the shiny new Cathedral of Christ the Saviour for the 850th anniversary of Moscow in 1997 – the emphasis on the roots of Great Russia, especially since the nationalist turn observed since 2012, led to a promotion of both religious (i.e., Orthodox) monuments and ones that evoke "greatness" by being tall, imposing, impressive monuments or buildings (for instance, the gigantic monument to Vladimir the Great near Red Square in 2011). Regarding Soviet heritage, the reconstruction in 2009, at the entrance of the parc VDNKh, of the Soviet Pavilion of the

International Exhibition held in 1937 in Paris, used as the pedestal for the world-famous emblem of socialism Vera Mukhina's sculpture *The Worker and the Kolkhoz Woman*, is one of the most striking examples of the use of heritage from the Soviet period to promote a new narrative about Russian grandeur. In the previous chapter, Maria Silina discussed the restoration of these Stalin-era ensembles in terms of a Red tourism agenda and ongoing gentrification process. What is important from the point of view of heritage studies is that this brand-new pavilion has been granted the highest patrimonial status, a protection at the federal level. This status, in turn, tells us much about what is considered to be the heritage of contemporary Russia. Already in 2004, Moscow Mayor Yury Luzhkov summarized this reflection with the fantastic sentence, "in Moscow culture, the concept of the copy is sometimes no less meaningful than that of the original. Because the semantic, historical and cultural 'charge' that such a copy carries can often be even richer and deeper than the original architectural solution."[52] However, from rejection and denial, the avant-garde became the object of renewed interest from a small group of Russian citizens and local authorities in the mid- and late 2000s.

Grass-Roots Movements and the Avant-Garde: New Actors and a Renewed Vision of the Revolutionary Heritage

Tired of witnessing the increasing dilapidation of avant-garde architecture despite their efforts, a small group of avant-garde specialists and admirers started to organize and try to take over regional or local authorities' mission to protect and document these buildings. This increasing concern highlights the link between a new fascination with the avant-garde and a renewed vision of the revolution, as well as a connection between new mobilizations for heritage and increased grass-roots political involvement in Putin's Russia. What follows gives an overview of the actors involved in preservation of the avant-garde until 2017, and of their motivations and practices.[53] On the one hand, this movement involves connoisseurs of this type of architecture from similar professional backgrounds: professors of art history or architecture, cultural specialists, architects, and restorers. These actors form a significant part of the new Russian *intelligentsia*. Condemning the incompetence and corruption of the government officials in charge of preserving heritage buildings, these experts affirm their mandate, as well as that of Russian society, to protect avant-garde architecture as a national treasure. The heirs of Soviet architects are also deeply involved: Natalia Dushkina, granddaughter of the architect Alexey Dushkin; Vladimir Shukhov, great-grandson of the engineer Vladimir Shukhov; and Alexei Ginzburg, grandson of the architect Moisei Ginzburg, to name a few. Their relation to Soviet architecture, and in particular to the works of their ancestors, is in many aspects a legacy issue. This hereditary filiation creates a desire to protect and enhance this heritage that is not only cultural and historical but also personal.

The "heritage emotions" aroused by the state's patent abandonment of the avant-garde as well as these actors' personal sensitivity to issues related to monument preservation explain their involvement.[54] The internationalization of this issue, previously evoked, has also greatly contributed to shedding light on this phenomenon and to raising awareness among professionals who had not previously been actively engaged in this movement. These experts are the ones who are actually documenting, identifying, and monitoring avant-garde buildings, and their work is vital.

In addition, the "Moscohipsters" or, now, "Yekathipsters" – "trendy" youth, mostly students in architecture, art, or design – form a stronghold for those committed to the avant-garde. The American photographer and activist Natalia Melikova has confirmed this by saying, with humour, "Avant-garde is a cool thing again."[55] Indeed, the Constructivist aesthetic, recognizable by its geometric patterns and evocative colours, seems to have recently become a new fashion phenomenon in Russia.[56] One cannot visit Russia, especially the capital, without noticing how these motifs have infinitely increased on postcards, notebooks, posters, badges, jewellery, clothes, soap, and other consumer products. While sometimes used by actors in the grass-roots movements to raise people's awareness – an effective tool – these products are also sometimes simply part of a marketing trend. Indeed, the "Melnikov House made an appearance in the form of coffee stands, its roundness an ideal shape for setting up a street cafe. Muscovites lined up to buy coffee, knowingly or not, from a replica of a building that, despite all of its architectural merits recognized internationally, has had to fight for its existence in Moscow."[57] More generally, books, conferences, exhibitions, cultural events, guided tours, new websites, and pages dedicated to the avant-garde have increased. In this sense, popular fashion has undeniably played a role in the new involvement of people, at least in contributing to a better awareness of this artistic style.

The presence of foreign actors is a very particular and characteristic element of these new mobilizations. Indeed, foreign journalists like Clementine Cecil, Moscow correspondent for *The Times* from 2001 to 2004, and Kevin O'Flynn, correspondent for the *Moscow Times* at the same time – as well as historians of architecture such as the world-renowned

Jean-Louis Cohen and artists like Natalia Melikova – have contributed significantly to the defence of the avant-garde. Born in Russia in 1984, but raised in the United States, Melikova rediscovered the Russian culture she had left behind thanks to the photographs of Alexander Rodchenko. Coming to Moscow to carry out her dissertation project, she fell in love with these buildings. From a "random" appreciation of the avant-garde, she has become one of its most emblematic defenders and considers herself to be an activist, publicly recognizing her political role.[58]

Although the circle of people involved is nevertheless quite small, this recent increase in interest in the avant-garde was brought on by the urgent need to improve the condition of heritage structures. Furthermore, the fact that citizen engagement has recently come back in style has contributed to this process.[59] Yet most of these actors consider their actions to be non-political ones.

At the same time, another track of analysis has been introduced by historian of architecture Anna Bronovitskaya, who developed the idea that the renewed interest in the avant-garde could also be explained by a better understanding nowadays of the modernity of these buildings.[60] This theory is also supported by Ajrat Bagaudinov, the young director of the successful business Moscow through the Eyes of an Engineer, which offers guided tours of Moscow's (not only Soviet) buildings.[61] To Bagaudinov, the literal and figurative revolutionary aspect of these buildings is better understood by young people today than it was when they were built. Despite this, it appears that young people are often more interested in the aesthetic form of the buildings than in their revolutionary content.

Yekaterinburg: Revolutionary Identity and Tourism

The case of Yekaterinburg exemplifies this heightened interest in avant-garde architecture. The city – the fourth largest in Russia – had seen its urban face radically changed during the 1920s and the 1930s: more than 550 avant-garde buildings were erected. After being rejected, forgotten, and mostly abandoned, these buildings have been, since the 2000s, strongly revalued as world heritage sites, so that the city is nowadays promoted as the capital of Constructivism in Russia, if not in the world. This radical change in the way of perceiving these buildings especially underlines the fact that interest in the avant-garde is not only a Moscow phenomenon but takes a different form in each city. The acquisition of the White (Water) Tower in 2012 by a group of young architects named Podelniki was one of these, and may be the most relevant example of this new dynamic (figure 3.3).

Figure 3.3. White (Water) Tower (Moisey Reischer, 1929–30). Photographed by the author, 2016

Although the tower ceased being used for its original function in the late 1960s, it has been reused and newly appropriated in the late 2010s after being totally abandoned. Podelniki's architects wanted not only to preserve or restore the tower but also to convert it into an open cultural space with tours, exhibitions, conferences, and performances.[62] The "White Tower Project" has been a great success. After years of work with experts and volunteers, since August 2016 the tower has been the "cultural place to be" in Yekaterinburg. Although the initiative started with young, educated, dynamic, cosmopolitan, virtually connected, and often politically engaged citizens, it today attracts more and more "ordinary" citizens from the town and beyond. All these initiatives participate in a broader positive revaluation of avant-garde heritage sites that have been transformed from lost and forgotten monuments to a source of pride; objects to protect, promote, and reuse.

In addition, since 2010 Yekaterinburg has hosted the Contemporary Art Biennale of the Industrial Ural, which is recognized worldwide for its academic and artistic quality.[63] In 2015, the main event of the Biennale, "Mobilization," curated by Alisa Prudnikova, took place in the Hotel Iset', a building with an astonishing aesthetic that was part of the so-called House of the Chekist (figure 3.4).[64] The "hotel" hosted exhibitions, installations, and performances. As one of the Biennale's organizers, Li Zhen-Hua, declared:

> This is a very rich context, with the constructivist ideas of the buildings and all over the city, with the communist ideas of an ideal society, with the ideas of the industrial revolution and, of course, with the people of this place. Art and this Biennale must serve the people who live here, creating on the site, and should be a new opening of this locality.[65]

The revolutionary aspect of the building and, more broadly, of the town, is thus recognized and highlighted. Moreover, it is promoted as a strong argument for present-day use of these buildings. If the Biennale is an international cultural tourist event, the way it uses the avant-garde allows for its revalorization and revitalization. Ilchenko examines this "cultural discourse" as the last phase in the symbolic transformation of the sotsgorod that participates in introducing the monuments into the present – what, to him, "heritage discourse" does not do – making it possible to address a broader audience. In my view, however, these cultural projects should be considered entirely as part of a new heritagization of these monuments. Once the heritage value has been (re)projected onto the buildings, they instantaneously become a part of the present while serving as a way of understanding and protecting the past. This new heritagization is inseparable from the new uses of heritage sites. Despite the fact that the Biennale of Contemporary Art gathers together large numbers of professional and future avant-garde lovers, it seems for the time being the Constructivist brand is not yet truly revalorized. Nevertheless, the increasing interest in Constructivism has resulted in new restorations: seven monuments were restored in 2012 and eleven in 2015. In addition, in 2014 the Palace of Culture that hosts the Yekaterinburg Academy of Contemporary Art was designated as a protected monument.[66]

Nevertheless, Yekaterinburg's case remains unique in Russia. The avant-garde is seen there as an opportunity to enhance the unique identity of this city of the Ural Mountains as compared to the capital.

Figure 3.4. Hotel Iset' during the 3rd Industrial Biennale, Yekaterinburg. Photograph by Anna Korkodinova, courtesy of Wikimedia. Used under a CC-BY-SA license

Constructivist heritage is now even considered as a new brand for this modern city that is trying to create new forms of urban development. However, the uniqueness of this movement lies in the fact that, for the first time, the avant-garde has a tourist value at the national and international level. The backing that this touristic turn received from the authorities seems to be, for the moment, specific to Yekaterinburg. The mayor at that time (2013), Evgeny Roizman, supported the movement, declaring that Constructivism was a tool to attract tourists, while the minister of culture, Vladimir Medinsky, also encouraged this new development.[67] Moreover, the proposal to inscribe two groups of buildings on the World Heritage list was made in order to internationally recognize the role of Yekaterinburg in the development of the modernist movement. The two groups were buildings constructed under the First Five-Year Plan and the monuments of Prospekt Lenin – Hotel Iset', Uralskii rabochii, and Dom sviazi.[68] The proposal has not (yet) been officially presented to UNESCO.

In comparison, in St Petersburg avant-garde architecture is not included at all in tourism at the official level. This is in contrast with the Soviet period, during which the sites of the revolutions of 1905 and 1917 became part of touristic programs.[69] However, despite its rich revolutionary identity, St Petersburg is promoted today as an open-air museum of the Russian empire rather than as a museum of the Great October Revolution. In any case, visits to the sites of avant-garde monuments would be disappointing for any visitors in search of well-preserved heritage buildings. And the fact that the local authorities are not developing any tourist venues dedicated to the avant-garde is a key to understanding the state of preservation (or lack of preservation) of these sites. As with any vicious circle, it can only be broken by taking action.

Revolutionary Actions for the Heritage of the Revolution?

This is precisely why the different groups of people mentioned above organized to defend avant-garde architecture, to involve both public and media in their fight, and to mobilize new resources to make this heritage attractive. These new actions are part of a nation-wide dynamic that includes events, flash mobs, and public and humorous performances.[70] These groups stage and organize cultural events related to heritage objects, with the goal of getting national and international media coverage. This repertoire of post-Soviet actions borrows from the vocabulary of Soviet demonstrations with two types of references: the means of action and the iconography associated with events. During a day of protest for the maintenance of the Shukhov Tower (which was officially scheduled to be destroyed) on 20 April 2014, a red hot-air balloon was seen floating in the sky – although securely attached to the ground.[71] This balloon recalled the spectacular dimension of Soviet public manifestations and the aspiration to go beyond the USSR (figure 3.5). In Yekaterinburg, it is the *"subbotnikis"* – citizen mobilization groups organized on Saturdays for the cleaning of a district, inherited from the Soviet period – which were regularly deployed for maintenance of the White Tower. Dozens of inhabitants of the city volunteered to clean it, with makeshift equipment, and this in a joyous and friendly atmosphere (figure 3.6). Straightforwardly reviving Soviet practices proved to be a success. The dominant iconography employed to announce events and to raise citizens' awareness – flamboyant colours, catchy slogans, and easily identifiable symbols – was characteristic of the years 1920 to 1930. This new iconography reflects how much the representations of these buildings, including the Shukhov and White Towers, have gradually replaced the architectural objects they promoted.

The marketization of the avant-garde is an effective way to mobilize the population at the local level, and in the case of the two towers mentioned above, it turned out to be an essential tool that contributed to their safeguarding. Ironically, however, these buildings are today branded in ways that were rejected by their architects: the reproduction of these buildings' images, a perfect embodiment of consumer processes, is indeed in total contradiction to the intellectual and political ideals held by the buildings' original architects (figures 3.7–3.10).

Figure 3.5. Hot-air balloon ascension in the Shabolovka district on Moscow on 20 April 2014. Photograph by Alexandra Selivanova

Figure 3.6. Subbotnik around the White Tower of Yekaterinburg. Source: Facebook page of the "White Tower Project"

Figures 3.7 and 3.8. Marketization of avant-garde buildings. Store of the association Moscow through the Eyes of an Engineer. Dom Narkomfin, Moscow. Photograph by the author, 2017

Figures 3.9 and 3.10. Marketization of the White Tower. Source: Facebook page of the "White Tower Project"

The objectives that underlie this conscious reminder of Soviet codes and practices deserve to be questioned: is it to "contextualize" the monuments in the Soviet period, a way of bringing attention to the problem by addressing people who might have lived during the Soviet period, or to attract a new public that enjoys these kinds of "kitsch" activities, or, finally, to attract the public with evocative images? The answer seems to lie in a combination of all these possibilities. This reference to the past signals knowledge of the nation's revolutionary heritage rather than nostalgia for it. However, these activities clearly pose a question about the uses of the past, especially the revolutionary past, in promoting the avant-garde. This theme emerged even more strongly in 2017, during the revolution's centenary.

Conclusion – 2017 and the "De-ideologization" of the Avant-Garde: From Rejection to Schizophrenia?

As expected by many observers, 2017 was not, in Russia, a year of grandiose celebration of the revolutions.[72] There were nevertheless some celebrations, especially in the cultural field. Interestingly, these celebrations consisted largely of references to the avant-garde artistic movement in exhibitions, film viewings, concerts, conferences, and excursions. Among these, I would like to draw attention to a particular event: "Avant-Garde: Revolution in 10 Days," because it reflects a certain way of dealing with avant-garde architecture.[73] Organized in Moscow in April 2017, this event celebrated ten different kinds of revolutions over three days: social, industrial, artistic, cultural, cinematographic, engineering, architectural, poetical, musical, and theatrical. Essentially, it celebrated everything but the political revolution – however, this could be understood because the October Revolution was implied in the title. Still, the political nature of the avant-garde was, in a way, totally set aside so that all those "revolutions" could be divorced from their political context. Avant-garde architecture was somehow *dehistoricized* or even *de-ideologized*. The paradox, though, is that the organizers, as researchers and experts, are perfectly aware of the history of these buildings. When they publish papers and books about architecture, they never try to hide its political history. However, during events that are represented as non-political, the political – and fundamental – aspect of the avant-garde is not directly invoked. This celebration of the avant-garde without reference to revolution may simply be an attempt to avoid a divisive topic. The evocation of the revolution might even repel some people by reminding them how hard the times were when these buildings were built, and that the life people led in them was sometimes not a joyful one. But while the political context is not developed, the "utopian life" embodied in these buildings is often enhanced. As a unique testimony to this period, these buildings can be seen as a way to better understand the past. For instance, while visiting Dom Narkomfin during one of the several tours organized by Moscow through the Eyes of an Engineer, visitors were invited to imagine, feel, and absorb the past in a visit to several restored apartments. In that context, these buildings are mostly presented in terms of their innovative aspects, their unique aesthetic, and their contribution to architecture at a global level. The difficulty in reconciling the political history of these buildings and the artistic genius of their architects remains a weakness at the heart of the grass-roots movement to preserve this national heritage.

At the same time, the official use of the avant-garde in public celebrations has gradually been increasing. In the same year of the 1917 revolutions' silent jubilee, Moscow loudly celebrated its 870th anniversary, and Constructivism was selected as the single style used to promote the event and decorate the city.[74] First, all the official posters, videos, and website designs were inspired by the famous textile ornaments created by the Russian artists Varvara Stepanova and Lyubov Popova in the early 1920s. Then, Moscow's streets were decorated with art works by Wassily Kandinsky and Kazimir Malevich – in three dimensions! – and Muscovites could also stroll past miniatures of avant-garde architecture's masterpieces, such as the Melnikov House (Melnikov, 1929), the Shukhov Tower (Shukhov, 1919–22), and the Bakhmetevsky Garage (Melnikov, 1926–9) (figure 3.11).

After analysing the current, sometimes worrying, condition of these buildings, their proud exhibition in the Moscow streets during an official event appears as a beautiful tension between reality and its political representation in public celebrations. As the head of the Department of Culture, and former head of the Department of Cultural Heritage, Alexander Kibovsky, declared in explanation of this choice: "We would like to show Moscow's contribution to international design, and therefore Constructivism was chosen as the most characteristic architectural and cultural style for our city."

Kibovsky added that the Russian avant-garde is recognized internationally as an original style and a significant innovation in the art world. And this seems to be just the beginning for this new phenomenon. As Natalia Melikova remarks, the website for the FIFA World Cup (2018) featured a special section introducing football visitors to "Constructivism. Legacy of the Soviet Era," and went as far as positioning Constructivism as "the country's brand identity along with

Figure 3.11.   Reproduction of the Bakhmetevsky Garage during Moscow's 870th anniversary celebrations. Photograph by Natalia Melikova

ballet, hockey and space exploration."[75] Further, in January 2018, the Russian tourist board unveiled a new visual identity inspired by suprematist art, with the slogan "the whole world within Russia" (figure 3.12).[76]

While the avant-garde was rejected for decades precisely because of its "non-Russian" appearance, the fact that this architectural style is now used as an advertisement for contemporary Russia should be understood both as a promotional victory and as instrumental politics. Indeed, this recent avant-garde promotion campaign addresses at the same time three segments of the public: first, Russian citizens who could be interested in this style – noticing the current fashion phenomenon; second, Russian citizens engaged in the preservation of the avant-garde, showing them that a step (effective or not) has been taken at the official level. The third group is the international public, who would understand at first glance that the image these buildings present and promote does not fit their current state of preservation. Enhancing not

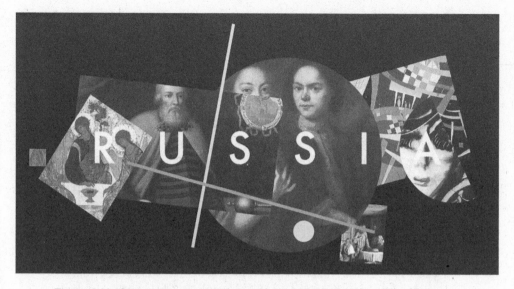

Figure 3.12. Suprematist visual identity for the Russia brand project. Source: Website of the project: http://russia-brand.com/en/

only the exceptionality of Constructivism but also the role of Russian art during the twentieth century perfectly fits the officially promoted state vision of history, which highlights the greatness and uniqueness of Russia. Finally, to promote the avant-garde in 2017 while not celebrating the 1917 revolution could also be considered as a discreet way to evoke 1917 not through its historical development and consequences but through artistic productions and architectural heritage. However paradoxical, this may be the most neutral and consensual solution to the problem of celebrating Russia's past.

NOTES

1 Exhibition held from 16 November to 3 December 2017, Rosfoto, Yard Building Exhibition Hall, 2nd floor. Website: http://rosphoto.org /events/heritage-revolution/. Exhibition visited on 18 November 2017. Part of the exhibition was presented again in Moscow during the festival "Arkhitekturnoe nasledie" (Architectural Heritage), Manezh, 2–5 July 2018.

2 The first program of construction was the well-known "plan of monumental propaganda," launched in April 1918 by Lenin, whose purpose was to erect an impressive number – although never achieved – of statues of revolutionary personalities. This plan had above all the aim to create a new and tangible political imagery and to build a new memory that had been hitherto non-existent. See Lodder, "Lenin's Plan for Monumental Propaganda."

3 http://rosphoto.org/events/heritage-revolution/.

4 The Krasnoe Znamia factory (Red Banner Textile Factory) was commissioned by the Leningrad Trust of Textile Manufacture in 1925 from the German architect E. Mendelson, that he designed together with S.O. Ovsyannikov, E.A. Tretyakov, and H. Pretreaus – the construction began in 1926. The Water Tower was constructed in 1930–1 by architect Y.G. Chernikhov. One of the first workers' districts in Leningrad was located in the Traktornaia ulitsa where residential buildings were built according to the designs of A.I. Gegello, A.S Nikotsky, and G.A. Simonov (1925–7). This observation on their conservation status dates back from a guided tour I participated in, on 18 November 2017, held by the historian of architecture Boris Kirikov. Kirikov is the co-author, among others, of Kirikov and Shtiglitz, *Arkhitektura leningradskogo avangarda. Putevoditel'* [Avant-Garde Architecture of St Petersburg. A Guide]. Since then, however, restoration, renovation, and reconstruction of these buildings have started.

5 Amacher, "Révolutions et révolutionnaires en Russie. Entre rejet et obsession."

6 For a global history of the revolutions, see, for instance: Holquist, *Making War*; Reynolds, *Shattering Empire*; Sandborn, *Imperial Collapse*; Werth, *Les Révolutions russes* [The Russian Revolutions]; and Rendle, "Making Sense of 1917." For an attempt to encapsulate the heritage transition in 1917, see Deschepper, "Between Future and Eternity."

7 For a more in-depth development of this topic see Gough, *The Artist as Producer*; K. Romberg, "Aleksei Gan's Constructivism, 1917–1928."

8 Anatoly Vasilyevich Lunacharsky (1875–1933) played a key role in the protection of cultural heritage. To grasp his role in the Commissariat of Education (Narkompros), see Fitzpatrick, *The Commissariat of Enlightenment*; A. Lunacharsky, *Ob iskusstve*, tom 2, 103.

9 Thouvenot, "Architecture constructiviste, quotidien et culture révolutionnaire": accessed 15 July 2016.

10 Cooke, *Russian Avant-Garde*, 118.

11 For illustrated examples of this architecture see Vassiliev and Ovsianikova, eds, *Arkhitektura Moskvy perioda NEPa i pervoi piatiletki, Putevoditel'* [Moscow Architecture from the NEP Period and First 5-Year Plan,

A Guidebook]; Elizarieva and Kubenskii, eds, *Yekaterinburg. Arkhitekturnii putevoditel', 1920–1940*.

12 See the map on the website of *The Constructivist Project*: http://theconstructivistproject.com/ru.

13 "Social condenser" is the expression of Ginzburg, quoted by Cooke, *Russian Avant-Garde*, 118.

14 Ilchenko, "Utopian Space," 33.

15 Vassiliev and Ovsianikova, *Arkhitektura Moskvy perioda NEPa i pervoi piatiletki, Putevoditel'*, 86–7.

16 See for instance: Werth, *Histoire de l'Union Soviétique de Lénine à Staline (1917–1953)*; Holquist, *Making War, Forging Revolution*.

17 Quoted by E.R. Krupnova in her conference paper "The Restoration of Monuments of the 1920s–1930s."

18 Zalivako, "2000–2006."

19 Decree "On the Restructuration of Literary and Artistic Organization of the 23 April 1932." [Text available in: Clark and Dobrenko, *Soviet Culture and Power*, 151–3]; Zalivako, "2000–2006," 64.

20 Cohen, "La conservation de l'architecture moderne entre savoirs et pouvoirs."

21 On the process of rehabilitation of the avant-garde in the 1960s, see: S.V. Bittner, "Remembering the Avant-Garde."

22 On the new interest in the past, see in particular: Kozlov, "The Historical Turn in Late Soviet Culture"; Kropotkine, "Les ambiguïtés du dégel"; Kelly, "From 'Counter-Revolutionary Monuments' to 'National Heritage.'"

23 Gosudarstvennyi arhiv Rossiiskoi Federatsii (GARF), f. A 639, op. 1.t.1, d. 6, l. 90.

24 List proposed by the Governmental Inspection. See Protocol 13 of the VOOPIK Architecture section meeting, 18 September 1967, GARF, f. A 639, op. 1.t.1, d. 126.

25 Ordinance of 4 December 1974, "Additions and partial modification of the RSFSR Ministers Council Ordinance of 30 August 1960, 'On the improvement of the activities linked to the protection of cultural monuments in the RSFSR.'" Available online at: http://www.libussr.ru/doc_ussr/usr_8454.htm. More broadly, on this topic, see Deschepper, "The Cycles of Avant-Garde."

26 RGALI, f. 674, op. 8, d. 1047, d. 1048, d. 1049.

27 RGALI, f. 674, op. 8, d. 1048, p. 96–105.

28 Decision No. 647 of the Moscow Executive Council, "On the registration under governmental protection of the architectural monument of the Soviet period," 23 March 1987.

29 Decision No. 1085 of the Moscow Executive Council, "On the events linked with the 100th anniversary of Konstantin Melnikov's birth," 23 June 1990.

30 To read more about this law, see Rakhmatullin, "Building Conservation Law – the Latest Developments."

31 Zalivako, "2000–2006"; Dushkina, "Reconstruction and Its Interpretation in Russia," 17; N. Vassilev: http://archi.ru/russia/69283/restavraciya-kluba-imeni-rusakova; Melikova, "Il construttivismo russo tra brand e realta"; Round table, "Past and Present of the Avant-Garde Architecture: Avant-Garde as a Disputed Heritage," with Alexandra Selivanova, Clementine Cecil, Natalia Melikova, and debate by Julie Deschepper, 9 December 2017, Inalco, Paris: http://www.labex-arts-h2h.fr/1917-2017-regards-croises-sur-les.html?lang=fr.

32 Stubbs, "Mobilizing Support for Conserving 20th Century Architecture."

33 To have a precise chronology of all the events and the evolution, see: Pronina, *Printsipy naslediia avangardskoi arkhitektury v sovetskoi i postsovetskoi epokhi.*

34 ICOMOS is the International Council of Monuments and Sites, created in 1965. Docomomo is the International Working Party for Documentation and Conservation of Buildings, Sites, and Neighbourhoods of the Modern Movement, created in 1968.

35 "Moscow Declaration on the Preservation of 20th Century Cultural Heritage," ICOMOS, Docomomo, UIA, 2006, Online: http://www.icomos.org/risk/2007/pdf/Soviet_Heritage_02_Moscow_Declaration.pdf. Accessed 20 November 2014.

36 "Repressed Architecture. Preservation of Architectural Avant-Garde in Russia and Germany." Curators: Anke Zalivako and Irina Chepkunova (17 April–17 May 2006).

37 Dushkina and Kudryavtsev, eds, *Heritage at Risk*; Haspel, Petzel, Zalivako, and Ziesemer, *The Soviet Heritage and European Modernism.*

38 Richard Pare's exhibition, *The Lost Vanguard: Soviet Modernist Architecture, 1922–32*, MOMA. Symposium 28 and 29 September 2007. Funded by the World Monuments Fund through its Modernism at Risk Program and funding from Knoll Inc. Program of the Symposium: http://v3.arkitera.com/e1660-vanguard-lost-and-found-symposium.html.

39 Cohen and Bergdoll, eds, Special Issue on the Preservation of Soviet Heritage, *Future Anterior: Journal of Historic Preservation, History, Theory, and Criticism.*

40 Haspel, *Arkhitekturnoe nasledie avangarda v Rossii i Germanii.*

41 Marja Makogonova, "Leningradskii konstruktivizm, nasledie pod ugrozoi," *Petersburg Arkhitekturnoe nasledie avangarda*, 151–3.

42 Resolution 17A 2011/24 – "Patrimoine de l'architecture russe d'avant-garde," 2011, XVIIᵉ Assemblée générale de l'ICOMOS, Paris, France, 27 novembre au 2 décembre: http://www.icomos.org/Paris2011/GA_2011_Resolutions_FR_finaldistr_20120109.pdf. Accessed 20 January 2017.

43 Raviot, "Moscou, les 'Moscobourgeois' et le patrimoine urbain."

44 Cultural Forum of St Petersburg, 16–18 November 2017.

45 Morisset, *Des régimes d'authenticité*, 24.

46 Casciato, "Modern Monuments and Heritage at Risk," 22–3.

47 See for instance the creation of the School of Heritage (*Shkola Naslediia*). Free and open to all, this non–degree-granting school offers a series of conferences and multidisciplinary round tables devoted to heritage. Although supported by the Moscow City Department of Culture, this initiative only works thanks to the volunteers' work: http://heritage -school.ru.

48 Source: http://tass.ru/obschestvo/3330968.

49 Forest and Johnson, "Unraveling the Threads of History."

50 Ibid., 532.

51 Amacher and Berelowitch, *Histoire et mémoire dans l'espace postsoviétique*.

52 Y. Luzhkov, "What Is the Capital's Architectural Style?," *Izvestia*, 19 May (No. 86), 2004.

53 This section is a short extract from the paper by Julie Deschepper, "Mémoires plurielles et patrimoines dissonants."

54 Fabre, *Émotions patrimoniales*.

55 Interview with Natalia Melikova, 24 April 2015.

56 Interviews with Jana Safronova, 1 June 2017, and with Tatiana Zaitseva, 19 June 2017, both involved in the preservation of avant-garde in Moscow.

57 Melikova, "Il construttivismo russo tra brand e realta."

58 Round table, "Past and Present of the Avant-Garde Architecture: Avant-Garde as a Disputed Heritage," with Alexandra Selivanova, Clementine Cecil, Natalia Melikova, and debate by Julie Deschepper, 9 December 2017, Inalco, Paris: http://www.labex-arts-h2h.fr/1917-2017-regards-croises-sur -les.html?lang=fr.

59 Le Huérou, "Les mouvements de protestation," 4.

60 Bronovitskaya, "Glimpses of Today in Visions of Russian Avant-Garde Architects."

61 https://engineer-history.ru. Interview with Ajrat Bagaudinov, 2 April 2016.

62 Interview with Evgeny Volkov, member of Podelniki, 17 April 2016.

63 See the following websites: http://first.uralbiennale.ru (2010); http:// second.uralbiennale.ru (2012); http://third.uralbiennale.ru (2015); http:// uralbiennale.ru (2017).

64 Hotel Iset' is part of the Chekists' Village (1929–36, I. Antonov, V. Sokolov, A. Tumbasov).

65 Quotation on the website of the event: http://third.uralbiennale.ru /гостиница-исеть/.

66 Ilchenko, "Utopian Space," 50.

67 The extract of Medinsky's comments may be read at http://tass.ru/ural
    -news/3202829.
68 See also http://tass.ru/ural-news/3202829.
69 Koenker, "The Russian Revolution as a Tourist Attraction."
70 See Merlin and Brenez, "Face au pouvoir russe, des mobilisations ténues
    mais vivaces," 13.
71 Deschepper, "Spectacularisation et patrimonialisation dans la Russie
    contemporaine."
72 Koustova, "Un malaise commémoratif"; Amacher "Révolutions et
    révolutionnaires en Russie."
73 http://avantgarde.center/avantgardedays.
74 On the silent jubilee, see the paper of Megan Swift in this volume.
75 Source: http://welcome2018.com/en/cities/moscow/constructivism
    -legacy-of-the-soviet-era/.
76 Source: https://www.dezeen.com/2018/01/17/russian-tourist-board
    -unveils-new-identity-inspired-suprematism-rebrand-graphics-design/.

REFERENCES

Amacher, Korine. "Révolutions et révolutionnaires en Russie. Entre rejet et
    obsession" [Revolutions and Revolutionaries in Russia. Between Rejection
    and Obsession]. *Revue d'études comparatives Est-Ouest* 45, 2 (2014): 129–73.
Amacher, Korine, and Wladimir Berelowitch. *Histoire et mémoire dans l'espace
    postsoviétique. Le passé qui encombre* [History and Memory in Post-Soviet
    Space. A Past That Encumbers]. Geneva: Université de Genève, 2014.
Bittner, Stephen V. "Remembering the Avant-Garde: Moscow Architects and
    the 'Rehabilitation' of Constructivism, 1961–64." *Kritika: Explorations in
    Russian and Eurasian History* 2, 3 (Summer 2001): 553–76.
Bronovitskaya, Anna. "Glimpses of Today in Visions of Russian Avant-Garde
    Architects." In lecture series *Modernism: Between Nostalgia and Criticism*,
    Architekturos leidiniu fondas, 2013: http://www.archfondas.lt/leidiniu
    /en/alf-02/eanna-bronovitskaya-glimpses-today-visions-russian-avant
    -garde-architects. Consulted 8 February 2015.
Bronovitskaya, Anna, and Natalia Bronovitskaya. *Arkhitektura Moskvy 1920–
    1960: Putivoditel'* [Moscow Architecture 1920–1960: Guidebook]. Moscow:
    Zhiraf, 2006.
Bronovitskaya, Anna, Clementine Cecil, and Edmund Harris, eds. *Moscow
    Heritage at a Crisis Point.* Moscow: MAPS, 2009.
Casciato, M. "Modern Monuments and Heritage at Risk." In *The Soviet Heritage
    and European Modernism,* edited by J. Haspel, M. Petzel, A. Zalivako, and
    J. Ziesemer, 22–3. Berlin: Heritage at Risk, 2006; ICOMOS, 2007.

Clark, Katerina, and Evgeny Dobrenko. *Soviet Culture and Power: A History in Documents, 1917–1953*. New Haven, CT: Yale University Press, 2007.

Cohen, Jean-Louis. "La conservation de l'architecture moderne entre savoirs et pouvoirs." *Patrimoine et architecture* 10–11 (June 2001): 82–5.

Cohen, J-L, and B. Bergdoll, eds. Special Issue on the Preservation of Soviet Heritage, *Future Anterior: Journal of Historic Preservation, History, Theory, and Criticism*, 5, 1 (2008). University of Minnesota Press, 2008.

Cooke, Catherine. *Russian Avant-Garde: Theories of Art, Architecture, and the City*. London: Academy ed., 1995.

Deschepper, Julie. "Mémoires plurielles et patrimoines dissonants: L'héritage architectural soviétique dans la Russie poutinienne" [Plural Memory and Dissonant Heritage: Soviet Architectural Heritage in Putin's Russia]. *Le Mouvement Social* 260 (July-September 2017): 35–52.

– "Spectacularisation et patrimonialisation dans la Russie contemporaine: Le cas sans précédent de la Tour Choukhov (Moscou)" [Spectacularization and Heritagization in Russia: The Unprecedented Case of the Shukhov Tower (Moscow)]. In *Le spectacle du patrimoine*, edited by Guillaume Ethier, 43–72. Quebec: Presses de l'Université du Québec, 2017.

– "Between Future and Eternity: A Soviet Conception of Heritage." *International Journal of Heritage Studies* 25, 5 (2019): 491–506. Special issue: "Heritage, Revolution and the Enduring Politics of the Past," edited by Pablo Alonso Gonzàlez, Margaret Comer, Tim Crowley, and Dacia Viejo-Rose. DOI: 10.1080/13527258.2018.1467949.

– "The Cycles of Avant-Garde. The Protection of Soviet Architecture or the Birth of Modern Heritage in the USSR (1960s-1980s)." In *"Old and New". Visual Culture and Cultural Heritage in Russia/USSR (1910–1940)*, edited by Federica Rossi and Gerhard Wolf. Florence and Moscow: KHI-Florenz and SIAF Moscow. Forthcoming.

Dushkina, Natalia. "Reconstruction and Its Interpretation in Russia." In 15th ICOMOS General Assembly and International Symposium, "Monuments and Sites in their Setting – Conserving Cultural Heritage in Changing Townscapes and Landscapes," 17–21 Oct 2005, Xi'an, China.

– "Survival or Fall? On the Fate of a 'New Heritage.'" In *20th Century Preservation of Cultural Heritage*, edited by Natalia Dushkina, 86–93. Moscow: Academy of Architectural Heritage, 2006.

Dushkina, N., and A. Kudryavtsev, eds. *Heritage at Risk: Preservation of Twentieth-Century Architecture and World Heritage*. Proceedings of the Scientific Conference, Moscow 17–20 April 2006. Moscow, 2006. https://www.icomos.org/risk/2007/pdf/Soviet_Heritage_01_Editorial.pdf.

Elizarieva, Anastasia, and Eduard Kubenskii, eds. *Yekaterinburg. Arkhitekturnii poutivoditel', 1920–1940* [Architectural Guide of Yekaterinburg, 1920–1940]. Yekaterinburg: Tatlin, 2015.

Fabre, Daniel. *Émotions patrimoniales*. Paris: Editions de la Maison des sciences de l'homme, 2013.

Fitzpatrick, Sheila. *The Commissariat of Enlightenment: Soviet Organization of Education and the Arts under Lunacharsky*. Cambridge: Cambridge University Press, 1970.

– *The Cultural Front: Power and Culture in Revolutionary Russia*. Ithaca, NY: Cornell University Press, 1992.

Forest, Benjamin, and Juliet Johnson. "Unraveling the Reads of History: Soviet-Era Monuments and Post-Soviet National Identity in Moscow." *Annals of the Association of American Geographers* 92, 3 (2002): 524–47.

Gough, Maria. *The Artist as Producer*. Berkeley, CA: University of California Press, 2005.

Hartog, François. *Régimes d'historicité: Présentisme et expérience du temps*. Paris: Editions du Seuil, 2003.

Haspel Jörg. *Arhitekturnoe nasledie avangarda v Rossii i Germanii: Vos'moe zasedanie Peterburgskogo Dialoga s 30 sentiabria po 3 oktiabria 2008 goda v Sankt-Peterburge*. Berlin: Bässler, 2010.

Haspel, Jörg, Michael Petzel, Anke Zalivako, and John Ziesemer, eds. *The Soviet Heritage and European Modernism*. Berlin: Heritage at Risk, 2006; ICOMOS, 2007.

Holquist, P. *Making War. Forging Revolution. Russia's Continuum of Crisis, 1914–1921*. Cambridge, MA: Harvard University Press, 2002.

Ilchenko, Mikhail. "Utopian Space: Symbolic Transformation of the 'Socialist Cities' under Post-Soviet Conditions." In *Re-Imagining the City: Municipality and Urbanity Today from a Sociological Perspective*, edited by Marta Smagacz-Poziemska, Krzysztof Frysztacki, and Andrzej Bukowski, 33–55. Krakow: Jagiellonian University Press, 2017.

Kelly, Catriona. "From 'Counter-Revolutionary Monuments' to 'National Heritage': The Preservation of Leningrad Churches, 1964–1982." *Cahiers du monde russe* 54, 1–2 (2013): 131–64. DOI: 10.4000 /monderusse.7928.

Kelly, Catriona, and David Shepherd, eds. *Constructing Russian Culture in the Age of Revolution 1881–1940*. Oxford: Oxford University Press, 1998.

Kirikov, Boris, and M. Shtiglitz. *Arkhitektura leningradskogo avangarda. Putivoditel'* [Avant-garde Architecture of St Petersburg. A Guidebook]. St Petersburg: Kolo, 2008.

Koenker, Diane P. "The Russian Revolution as a Tourist Attraction." *Slavic Review* 76, 3 (Fall 2017): 753–62.

Koustova, E. "Un malaise commémoratif: La Russie face au centenaire de sa revolution." In *Russie 2017: Regards de l'Observatoire franco-russe*, edited by A. Dubien, 497–505. Paris: Editions L'Inventaire, 2017.

Kozlov, Denis. "The Historical Turn in Late Soviet Culture: Retrospectivism, Factography, Doubt, 1953–91." *Kritika: Explorations in Russian and Eurasian History* 2, 3 (Summer 2001): 577–600.

Kropotkine, Anne. "Les ambiguïtés du dégel. Que faire du patrimoine culturel?" *Cahiers du Monde russe* 47, 1/2 (January–June 2006): 269–301.

Krupnova, E.R. "The Restoration of Monuments of the 1920s–1930s." Rossiiskii gosudarstvennyi arhiv literatury i isskustva (RGALI), f. 674, op. 8, d. 1047, l. 96–105.

Le Huérou, A. "Les mouvements de protestation: Une nouvelle génération dans la rue." In "À l'Est, du nouveau. Les élections 2011–2012 en Russie à l'heure du 'printemps russe,'" edited by A. de Tinguy. Les Dossiers du CERI; février 2012: http://www.ceri-sciences-po.org/ cerifr/kiosque.php.

Lodder, C. "Lenin's Plan for Monumental Propaganda." In *Art of the Soviets: New Perspectives on Post-Revolutionary Soviet Art*, edited by Matthew Bown, Brandon Taylor, and Matthew Cullerne Brown, 16–32. Manchester: Manchester University Press, 1993.

Lunacharsky, A. *Ob Iskustve [about Art], Tome 2 « Russkoe Sovetskoe Iskusstvo [Russian Soviet Art]*. Moscow: Iskusstvo, 1982.

Melikova, Natalia. "Il construttivismo russo tra brand e realta" [Russian Constructivism: Between Brand and Reality]. In *La città d'acciaio. Mosca costruttivista 1917–1937*, edited by Luca Lanini and Natalia Melikova, 84–94. Pisa: Pisa University Press, 2018.

Merlin, A., and L. Brenez. "Face au pouvoir russe, des mobilisations ténues mais vivaces." *Critique internationale* 2, 55 (2012).

Morenkova, Elena. *Les représentations du passé soviétique en Russie*. Paris: Broché, Etudes, 2017.

Morisset, Lucie. *Des régimes d'authenticité: Essai sur la mémoire patrimoniale*. Rennes: Presses Universitaires de Rennes, 2009.

Peresleguin, Nikolaj. *Istoriia stanovleniia i razvitiia organov arkhitekturnovo naslediia Moskvy v kontekste ikh vzaimodeistvia s obshchestvom v sovetskii period (1917–1991)* [A History of the Construction and Development of the Organs of Architectural Heritage in the Context of Their Cooperative Action with Society during the Soviet Period (1917–1991)]. PhD diss., Institute of Architecture, Moscow, 2015.

Poliakova, Marta. *Okhrana kulturnovo nasledia Rossii* [The Protection of Cultural Heritage in Russia]. Moscow: Drofa, 2005.

Pronina, Anna. "Prinsipy nasledia avangardskoj arhitektury v sovetskoj i postsovetskoj epohy." MA thesis, Moscow State University (MGU), Moscow, 2017, unpublished.

Rakhmatullin, R. "Building Conservation Law – the Latest Developments." In *Moscow Heritage at Crisis Point*, edited by Anna Bronovitskaya, Clementine

Cecil, and Edmund Harris, 186–94. Moscow: Vypusk 2/ Updated, expanded edition, MAPS, 2009.

Raviot, J-R. "Moscou, les 'Moscobourgeois' et le patrimoine urbain." In *Patrimoine et architecture dans les États post-soviétiques*, edited by Taline Ter Minassian, 245–58. Rennes: Presses Universitaires de Rennes, 2013.

Rendle, Matthew. "Making Sense of 1917: Towards a Global History of the Russian Revolution." *Slavic Review* 76, 3 (Fall 2017): 610–18.

Reynolds, M. *Shattering Empire: The Clash and Collapse of the Ottoman and Russian Empire, 1908–1918*. Princeton, NJ: Princeton University Press, 2011.

Romberg, K. "Aleksei Gan's Constructivism, 1917–1928." PhD diss., Columbia University, 2010.

Sandborn, J. *Imperial Collapse: The Great War and the Destruction of the Russian Empire*. Oxford: Oxford University Press, 2014.

Shorban, Yekaterina. "On Preserving 20th Century Architectural Monuments in Russia." In *20th Century Preservation of Cultural Heritage*, edited by Natalia Dushkina, 94–9. Moscow: Academy of Architectural Heritage, 2006.

Silina, M. "Obshhestvennoe dostojanie kak travma" [Social Heritage as a Trauma], *Colta* 2017: http://www.colta.ru/articles/art/13464.

Smith, Laurajane. *Uses of Heritage*. London: Routledge, 2006.

Starikov, A., V. Zvagelskaya, L. Tokmeninova, and E. Cherniak. *Ekaterinburg – Istorija goroda v arhitekture* [Yekaterinburg: History of the City through Architecture]. Yekaterinburg: "Sokrat" Publishing, 1998.

Stubbs, J. "Mobilizing Support for Conserving 20th Century Architecture." In *The Soviet Heritage and European Modernism*, edited by Jörg Haspel, Michael Petzel, Anke Zalivako, and John Ziesemer, 24–7. Berlin: Heritage at Risk, 2006; ICOMOS, 2007.

Ter Minassian, Taline, ed. *Patrimoine et architecture dans les États post-soviétiques*. Rennes: Presses Universitaires de Rennes, Collection Art et Société, 2013.

Thouvenot, Claire. "Architecture constructiviste, quotidien et culture révolutionnaire." *Revue Période*: http://revueperiode.net/architecture-constructiviste-quotidien-et-culture-revolutionnaire/.

Trigg, D. *The Aesthetics of Decay: Nothingness, Nostalgia, and the Absence of Reason*. New York: Peter Lang, 2006.

Tunbridge, John, and George Ashworth. *Dissonant Heritage: The Management of the Past as a Resource in Conflict*. Chichester and New York: J. Wiley, 1996.

Vanlaethem, France, and M-J Therrier. *La sauvegarde de l'architecture moderne* [Safeguarding Modern Architecture]. Quebec: Presses Universitaires du Québec, 2014.

Vassiliev, N., and E. Ovsianikova, eds. *Arkhitektura Moskvy perioda NEPa i pervoi piatiletki, Putevoditel'* [Moscow architecture from the NEP period and first 5-Year plan, A Guidebook]. Moscow: ABCdesign, 2014.

Werth, Nicolas. *Histoire de l'Union Soviétique de Lénine à Staline (1917–1953)*. Paris: Presses Universitaires de France, 2013.
– *Les Révolutions russes* [The Russian Revolutions]. Paris: Presses Universitaires de France, Que sais-je?, 2017.
Zalivako, Anke. "2000–2006: Monitoring Moscow's Avant-Garde Architecture." In *The Soviet Heritage and European Modernism*, edited by Jörg Haspel, Michael Petzel, Anke Zalivako, and John Ziesemer, 63–70. Berlin: Heritage at Risk, 2006, ICOMOS, 2007.

PART II

Social and Environmental Aftereffects

4 The Stalled Soviet Gender Revolution: Normalized Crisis in Contemporary Russia

JENNIFER UTRATA

[The family] will be sent to a museum of antiquities so that it can rest next to the spinning wheel and the bronze axe, by the horse drawn carriage, the steam engine, and the wired telephone.

S.Ia. Vol'fson, Soviet sociologist, 1929[1]

Women manage things better. Quite frequently when men no longer feel needed by society, they lose heart ... Two-thirds of the Russian population drink and they are drinking themselves to death ... But women are much less likely to do this. Women just have too many responsibilities at home to allow themselves to do this.

Igor, thirty-seven-year-old government official
and divorced father, Kaluga, 2005[2]

The key legacies of the Soviet revolution are contradictory, especially concerning issues of gender relations and families. While the early Bolsheviks discussed "liberating" women from unproductive housework and their related exploitation in families, they did so in order to bind women to the state rather than to private relationships in families. Instead of sending the family to the dustbin of history – or to a museum of antiquities, as Vol'fson puts it – we see from Igor's reflections in Putin-era Russia that women are frequently defined by the unpaid labour they perform in families. In spite of Russian women's very high labour market participation rates, Igor, like many ordinary Russians, accepts and naturalizes women's "many responsibilities at home."[3]

Yet although superficial differences exist, there are also surprising continuities over the past 100 years. The continuing devaluation of women's unpaid labour, as well as the lack of a gender revolution at home (notwithstanding Russian women's strong commitment to paid labour) are major legacies of the Russian Revolution. This chapter highlights Russia as the preeminent case of a stalled gender revolution.[4] From the early days of Soviet rule, when families and what Lenin characterized as the "barbarously unproductive, petty, nervewracking, and stultifying drudgery" of the home were seen as signs of backwardness that progressive policies and socialized labour could eventually overcome, to Igor's comments implying that women's unpaid labour at home is almost an inevitability, continuities between 1917 and today abound.[5] Whether in Soviet or Putin-era Russia, women's work in families has been devalued and dismissed and grass-roots feminism suppressed – all while the state, and men, have benefited directly from women's unpaid labour in families.

The 100-year anniversary of the Russian Revolution offers an opportunity to assess the most enduring, important legacies of the gender revolution. The revolution included a groundbreaking reconfiguration of gender relations that granted women formal equality with men. This state-imposed emancipation of women was a key cornerstone of the broader revolution. While the dramatic change in the gender regime was clearly revolutionary for its time, the radical changes occurred from the top down, a circumstance that limited the impact of these changes somewhat over the years. Furthermore, there were large gaps between what the Soviet state proclaimed it had achieved and what people experienced in everyday life. The reality of the gender revolution fell far short of its promise. But rather than focusing exclusively on why the Bolshevik gender revolution failed to sufficiently build upon its radical roots, this chapter highlights three important legacies emanating from Russia's gender revolution. These three gender legacies are critical for understanding contemporary Russia.

First, Russia is the preeminent case of a stalled gender revolution.[6] The concept of a stalled revolution has been influential for understanding the contradictions in Western women's lives, whereby most women work full-time for pay but, to varying degrees, also still bear primary responsibility for the unpaid work of the home (i.e., housework and childcare). This unpaid work is often experienced as a "second shift" in addition to the paid work done by women.[7] There is a vast literature on the "second shift" and its import for understanding why gender equality remains elusive in many Western countries in spite of women's significant educational and labour market gains. Yet Russia is an extreme case of these "second shift" inequalities in that it combines "historically and comparatively high female employment with a starkly unequal gender division of domestic labor."[8] Women's lives have changed dramatically in terms of the large number of women working for pay, but men's behaviours in sharing the work of the home as well as social-structural arrangements (i.e., both state and work-place policies) supporting the pronounced changes in women's lives have lagged behind. Though scholars of Russia have written about women's "double burden," they should do much more to frame Russian women's continuing commitment to full-time work and primary responsibility for the unpaid labour at home and with children as a longstanding problem for women's advancement, whether in Soviet or contemporary Putin-era Russia. Even though Russia had a ground-breaking gender revolution in 1917, to varying degrees over the years there has been a long period, with varied twists and turns, of a significant stall in that revolution. With the revolution's promise long unfulfilled, it will require a dramatic jumpstart in the contemporary period.

Second, though closely related to this first legacy, everyday discourse in Russian society suggests not only a stalled gender revolution with a long trajectory but also what I call a normalized gender crisis. Even health indicators such as men's premature mortality rates relative to women's justify this use of crisis language. In this normalized gender crisis, women are expected to be strong, or must work to become stronger, in what they see as a world with few "real men"; and many men, often considered weak, remain detached from or uninterested in family life. This is not a minor issue. As a result of this crisis of cultural imagination, other ways of doing gender seem unthinkable. Yet rather than taking these gender legacies of a stalled revolution and normalized gender crisis for granted, we should instead remain intensely curious about how these legacies may evolve and change in the contemporary period. Indeed, alternative femininities, represented by the growth and acceptance of single motherhood, might in time change the status quo of gender relations, putting pressure on masculinities.[9]

Third, although gender has long been used as a tool of state power and legitimation in Russia, contemporary Russia has amplified this practice. Putin-era Russia builds upon this tradition of using gender in the service of the state to remedy the perceived demasculinization and humiliation of the Yeltsin-era 1990s. Putin's hypermasculinity, or at least his clear efforts to remasculinize Russia, attempts to restore collective male dignity while also strategically using gender and including some prominent women as tokens. Russia is thus remasculinized without changing existing gender hierarchies in the broader society.[10]

Beyond these three major legacies – a stalled gender revolution, a normalized gender crisis, and the widespread use of gender as a tool of state power – this chapter will explore an overarching leitmotif of the past 100 years: the paired themes of men without women and women without men. Specifically, there is a trend toward the remasculinization of the political sphere, just as there was during the early years of the revolution.[11] Official Russian politics and culture, both 100 years ago and today, are very masculine, with issues such as childcare, education, healthcare, and social services feminized and clearly subservient to masculinized politics, industry, and the military. In contemporary Russia, Putin's remasculinization strategies are meant to shore up demoralized men, while also bringing women instrumentally in to the remasculinization of the Russian state, society, and culture.[12] Gender relations have always been significant in Russia, both for Soviet power and for the authoritarian power wielded by Putin, his United Russia party, and his strategies to legitimize his political power. But in stark contrast to official Russian politics and society, Russian everyday life is increasingly one of women without men. While this pattern likely solidified mostly after the Second World War, single motherhood and absent or marginalized fatherhood are also prominent features of the post-Soviet gender order. These tendencies are not brand new, given that Russia had the second-highest divorce rate in the world in the late 1970s, but these trends have intensified and have become infused with new meaning during the transition to authoritarian-style market capitalism in the Putin era. Understanding the contours of these legacies requires further theorizing and research.

Although many studies of gender in the field of Russian and Eurasian studies conceptualize gender as a tool used by the state, more work also remains to be done in terms of theorizing gender as a source of power and inequality in everyday life, particularly in families.[13] Scholars of the region have noted that "studies of public policies often focus on administrative regulations and treat norms and practices of everyday family life as secondary in importance."[14] Instead, a robust understanding of gender relations in Russian society requires that we engage gender at multiple levels of analysis, from the macro-structural level of Russian state power and politics to the micro-structures of everyday life. Before delving deeper into the three major Soviet legacies outlined here, I describe highlights of the radical progress promised, and partially achieved, in those heady early years after the Bolshevik Revolution, sketching major continuities and changes in gender relations through the late Soviet period. Then I highlight the three legacies of the Russian Revolution through examining contemporary, Putin-era Russia.

Soviet Russia: Radical Roots, Unfulfilled Promise (1917–1991)

Gender is a primary way of signifying power, and it works to legitimate power relations.[15] Furthermore, gender was critical to the Soviet state from the very beginning, given that women were needed for a successful revolution and for a productive, stable Soviet society. In spite of gender's importance for understanding Soviet society and the formation of the working class, it has often not been treated with the same importance as have other political and economic developments in Russia. But gender is central to any thorough understanding of the legacies of the Russian Revolution and should be used "not simply to fill a descriptive gap or to add a missing piece to a largely completed puzzle but rather to rearrange the puzzle itself."[16]

The Bolshevik Revolution: Radical Roots (1917–1927)

Before 1917, women had few rights: women owed husbands complete obedience according to state law, marriage was a sacrament controlled by the Russian Orthodox Church, divorce was nearly impossible, and fathers had the ultimate power and control over their children, with illegitimate children having no rights. The Bolsheviks sought to modernize Russia in this regard, by introducing new legislation on marriage and family.[17] Many of these laws sought to bring the state into private life more fully.

In October 1918, just one year after the revolution, the Central Executive Committee of the Soviet Union established a new Code on Marriage, the Family, and Guardianship. Provisions on the registration of civil marriage, which tended to bring Russia in line with changes in European countries, were important in taking control of marriages away from the church.[18] Yet "its provisions on illegitimacy, gender equality, marital obligations, and divorce surpassed the legislation of any other country," representing significant advances for its time relative to European countries, Canada, and the United States.[19] The 1918 code attempted to equalize the rights of women and men in marriage, making it easier to marry and to divorce. Besides simplifying the registration of marriage with civil authorities, the code eliminated men's rights in families to exercise power over wives and children, abolishing the system that gave the Orthodox Church authority over family issues. Specifically, the code established a network of local statistical bureaus (ZAGS) for registering marriage, birth, death, and divorce; and divorce could be requested by either spouse. The idea of "illegitimacy" was abolished, and all children became entitled to parental support. Adoption was forbidden in favour of state guardianship for fear that peasants might exploit children as unpaid labour. Through the code, women came to have full control of earnings after marriage, and neither spouse had claims on the other's property.

Although the 1918 code was seen as a first step towards the eventual withering away of the family in favour of "free unions" based on love rather than coercion, establishing "a multifaceted vision of women's liberation rooted in a long revolutionary tradition," the revolutionary moment was temporary.[20] As the 1919 program of the Communist Party proclaimed, "Not confining itself to formal equality of women, the party strives to liberate them from the material burdens of obsolete household work by replacing it with communal houses, public eating places, central laundries, nurseries, etc."[21] In the early days of revolution, women were a sign of everything backward in Russian society, and the Bolsheviks hoped to "bring them up" to the level of male workers. Wood shows that although male workers and peasants were also considered backward by the Bolsheviks, their masculinity was not implicated in the way that being a "baba" rather than a "comrade" marked women as not only backward, but backward *women*, a marked category that prevented women from becoming full comrades.[22] Women were seldom the ideal-typical Soviet workers; instead, they were a marked category at best, defined as worker-mothers.

From a literary perspective, Borenstein has explored the theme of *Men without Women*, where the absence or marginalization of women reflected masculine values associated with the post-revolutionary era: not only heavy industry and struggle, but production instead of reproduction, and labour force participation instead of the "drudgery" of the home. Borenstein argues that

> When the cult of (masculine) productive labour is combined with the degradation of (feminine) domestic and reproductive pursuits, one sees that post-revolutionary Soviet society was characterized by a reverence for traditionally masculine values at the expense of conventional femininity. Domesticity, femininity, nature, and the family were objects of scorn for the Bolsheviks, while the social sphere, science, productive labor, and implicitly, masculinity were established as ideals.[23]

So while the first family code was revolutionary for its time in terms of formal laws and official equality, culturally women were still seen as backward.

Although women constituted 46 per cent of the industrial workforce in 1920, women were generally the first fired and last hired, and discrimination against women workers proceeded relatively unchecked.[24] In addition to their vulnerability to loss of employment and to being pushed into prostitution (often to support their children), women were concentrated in the most poorly paid, unskilled jobs, a circumstance that only reinforced their economic dependence on men. Women, after all, earned only about two-thirds of what men earned.[25] The Zhenotdel, the Women's Department of the Communist Party, was established in 1919 in order to help forge "a new political community," in working to transform popular attitudes and practices on a massive scale. While its mission was often met with controversy, including the hostility of local Party committees, it worked during the 1920s to increase female literacy and host delegate meetings, and began to mobilize for communal cooking and childcare facilities. Zhenotdel leaders were often in the challenging position of having to advance women's causes while differentiating themselves from Western feminism thought to be the "antithesis of the proletarian revolution."[26] Ultimately the Zhenotdel sought to bring women's domestic lives under state control.[27] Because the Zhenotdel had set the precedent for the state's regulation of private lives, by the time Stalin shut down the organization in 1930 he was able to reverse many of its gender advances. At the same time, Stalin built upon the paradigm of the state as a surrogate husband and father.

In addition to this cultural lag and intrusion of the state into the regulation of private lives, the Family Code of 1926, which replaced the 1918 code, represented a retreat of sorts. Certainly the 1926 code represented a retreat in terms of the commitment to socialized childrearing, which the state recognized could not be realized because of the millions of *besprizorniki* (homeless waifs) sleeping in the streets and blamed for rampant crime and delinquency. Goldman notes that "The family was resurrected as a solution to *besprizornost'* because it was the one institution that could feed, clothe, and socialize a child at almost no cost to the state."[28] While the 1926 code simplified divorce procedures even further relative to the 1918 code, recognized cohabitation as the equal of registered civil marriages, and established joint property between spouses after divorce, women were still far from economically independent from men in practice. Already the revolution was stalled.

The revolution granted women equal rights from above, but there was no accompanying revolution at home. This missing revolution seriously impeded overall progress. Goldman argues that even though laws viewed women as men's equals, "women's role in the home undercut their independence."[29] Resisting the false dichotomy of whether the Soviet state "liberated" women or merely exploited them further, scholars such as Ashwin and Wood argue that the state was always ambivalent about the place of women. Ashwin has argued that "the Bolshevik state was never directed at the liberation of women from men, it was directed at breaking the subordination of women to the patriarchal family in order to 'free' both men and women to serve the communist cause."[30] In a similar vein, in spite of achievements such as suffrage, paid leave and family allowances, childcare, legal abortion, the simplification of divorce, civil registration of marriage, and the abolition of the concept of illegitimate children, Wood argues that "Bolshevik attention to the woman question was not primarily focused on women themselves but rather on competition with other groups in society for the allegiances (and in these early years, the votes) of a new group in society."[31] Indeed, Wood explains that the real issues that Russian women had to deal with every day – such as sexual harassment, job discrimination, overcrowded housing, and insufficient child care – were met, mostly, with silence.

Of course, countries elsewhere also grapple with issues related to women and work, but the Soviet state was unique in that it had boldly proclaimed, at least by 1930, to have solved the "Woman Question."[32] Rather than holding a monolithic view of gender relations, Wood argues, the Soviet state was distinguished by "an ambiguous policy that constantly shifted to bring ideological demands in line with the everyday needs of the state."[33]

From Stalin's Ascent to Power to the End of the Second World War (1927–1945)

While the Stalin years cover more than a quarter-century, from the early period of Stalinism to the victory of the Great Patriotic War (as the Second World War is known in Russia) and the death of Stalin in 1953, it has frequently been characterized as a period of retrenchment from the promise of the first Soviet decade. The 1930s and 1940s brought a "stifling of discussion" in many spheres of life, including discussions of women's liberation under socialism, and by 1930 the Zhenotdel was dissolved, the "woman question" proclaimed to have been solved.[34]

Yet in terms of gender relations, this period merely reconstructed families more fully according to a Soviet vision. Given that the Soviet state never really sought to "liberate" women but instead sought to disrupt the authority of patriarchal families by binding men and women to the Soviet state, "one can identify significant continuities between early Soviet and Stalinist gender politics."[35] As Ashwin argues,

> This means that the supposed "resurrection" of the family in the Stalin era should not be viewed as a conservative retreat which curtailed the revolutionary potential of the 1920s. Rather, what occurred was an attempt to recreate the family as a specifically *Soviet* family, which, instead of serving

as a "conservative stronghold of the old regime," would become a functio-
nal unit in the new polity.[36]

In the 1930s, the regime accepted families and the family unit as the cell
of Soviet society, but only as long as people realized that their primary
duty was to the state. In Putin-era Russia, families are less politicized,
but there is still great concern that families should fulfil the function
of reproduction in order to replenish a declining population. This is so
even though other benefits for families and for women have declined
with the onset of market capitalism and neoliberal policies.

Although the Stalin era included restrictions on divorce and abortion
in 1935 and 1936 in order to fight the declining birthrate, these restrictions were presented "not as limiting women's choices but as the result
of improved material and cultural life under socialism."[37] Other policies promoted ideals of a large family by giving incentives to mothers
to have many children, and a new law expanded working women's
access to childcare facilities. Women began to be ranked according to
their reproductive contributions to the state.[38]

In spite of the hypermasculinization of the Stalin era, the state relied
heavily on women's labour during this period. Goldman argues that
women were used as "a key reserve of labor."[39] She notes that "The
family served as a unit to support the unwaged at the expense of
the waged – to raise children and care for the sick, the disabled, and the
elderly."[40] In 1945, women made up half of the Soviet Union's labour
force. Yet in the years after the war ended, the state was mostly concerned with encouraging women to once again bear more children. The
tensions between women's paid work and unpaid reproductive labour
at home were never resolved.

Postwar Russia to the End of the Soviet Union (1945–1991)

After the Second World War, Russia was literally a society where many
women were without men. The Soviet Union lost approximately 27 million soldiers and civilians during the war, about half of all the Second
World War casualties, and women's responsibility for children and family life became further institutionalized during this period, as did men's
marginalization in families. In order to achieve its pronatalist goals, the
1944 Family Law collapsed the distinction between war widows and
unwed mothers – even though unwed mothers had previously been
stigmatized and at best tolerated. It encouraged all men to marry, form
families, and raise children, but at the same time encouraged men to
sire more children than they could afford to support. Because the state

would assume some responsibility for raising out-of-wedlock children, both men and women were encouraged to have relationships outside of marriage that would lead to procreation. According to Mie Nakachi, the law resurrected a double standard of sexual morality that had been abolished after the revolution, since a single mother's sexual partner now had no legal responsibility for any resulting children, and fatherhood became a mere legal obligation related to official marriages.[41] In the absence of men, or more accurately in the absence of fathers, the state would support children. The effects of these postwar gender relations reverberate in today's Russia.

However, shortly after the fiftieth anniversary of the revolution (1967), some significant tactical shifts ensued. The 1968 Family Code, in particular, ushered in a new era of reproductive politics. Even though "the main family ideals remained unchanged"[42] after 1968, the legislation shifted tactics in balancing "the interest of the state in family stability and the need for greater freedom and equality in personal relationships."[43] Although women were still honoured symbolically as mothers and encouraged to bear children, the 1968 laws attempted to reduce the private costs of rearing children by investing further in maternity leave and childcare facilities. Distinctions between legitimate and illegitimate children were dissolved and, unlike in the immediate postwar years, women could make claims on their children's fathers for support. Moreover, although the state still upheld the two-parent-family ideal, it did more to encourage men "to assert their manhood by acting as responsible and protective husbands and fathers."[44] While the government remained a patriarchal authority, men were expected "to perform their masculinity by serving as more explicit heads and masters of their families."[45] After 1968, divorce became more frequent and single motherhood more common, although women who rejected marriage and childbearing were still stigmatized and traditional gender ideologies remained dominant. There was no revolution at home, even though there was renewed awareness of women's double and triple burdens, as shown by the controversial publication of Natalia Baranskaia's *A Week Like Any Other* (1969). In this novella, a Soviet-era heroine and scientist is constantly running everywhere between work and home, presenting a clear picture of Soviet women's stressful and unequal circumstances in juggling paid and unpaid work nearly singlehandedly (even when married). Women were still mostly encouraged to look to the state and their work for support in juggling the demands of paid and unpaid labour. Inequality on the home front, even if acknowledged as such, was still considered a "women's" problem.

Post-Soviet Russia (1991–Present): The Stalled Gender Revolution

Hochschild, in her classic book *The Second Shift*, argues that US women's lives have suffered from a stall in the gender revolution. Although the lives of women changed dramatically as they flooded into the paid labour market in the 1970s, men's involvement in the unpaid labour of childcare and housework, as well as social structural arrangements supporting women's advances in the workplace, lagged behind.[46] Russia should be understood as a case – and perhaps even the global exemplar – of what has been referred to in the United States as a stalled gender revolution. The Soviet Union long had a critical mass of women in the workplace, more so than in the West, yet lacked a grassroots feminism to address gendered patterns of unpaid work in the home. Russian women have long faced an intensified "second shift," the unpaid work of shopping, cooking, cleaning, and caring for family members after returning home from paid work. Inequalities at work and at home for Russian women are especially stark.

Recent research, my own and the most recent research of other gender scholars, suggests that the gender revolution in the Putin era is more stalled than ever. After the collapse of the Soviet Union, social supports for mothers were cut (in real value), childcare services were slashed, and families were extolled, thus privatizing motherhood. The notable exception to this trend has been the introduction of maternity capital in 2007 to halt the demographic decline. Now, in spite of a resurgence of neotraditionalism, Russian women are not only in the workplace but are extremely committed to the idea of paid work as critical for women, without which many feel diminished as women. Russia's gender gap in employment has long been one of the world's smallest, "with less than 4 percentage points' difference in labour force participation between men and women between the ages of 30 and 55."[47] This low gap in employment is a Soviet legacy, but one that exists alongside one of the largest gender gaps in pay among high-income countries, at just above 30 per cent. There is high occupational segregation, many restrictions on women's employment, and rampant discrimination against women in the workplace.[48]

During the Soviet era, women's emancipation was proclaimed from above even though the state never did enough to support women as worker-mothers; they paid lip service to women's equality but never fully committed to supporting women's equality to men. Although women were encouraged to rely on the state for support rather than relying on individual men in families, women's role in serving as worker-mothers made them responsible for cultural mores and standards. In terms of state support, while there was more than there is in contemporary Russia, in practice it was frequently lacking, whether in terms of childcare slots or quality of care. Women played this secondary role as worker-mothers, with access to childcare and job protections, even as men were encouraged to take on leadership positions in Soviet enterprises, or in military service, and were discouraged from sharing the work of the home or becoming involved fathers.

Ultimately, the Soviet state marginalized men as fathers and normalized women's "double shift" of paid work and responsibility for nearly the entire second shift of work at home. Women could complain to the Party about men who were especially burdensome (due to inebriation, serial philandering, etc.), and they could access divorce as a last resort, but the responsibility for managing the home and children was theirs – doing shopping, cooking, and cleaning in shortage conditions and without many modern conveniences. It was exhausting to be a Soviet woman, at least for mothers, and the theme of having no time for self or adequate sleep continues with post-Soviet women, especially for single mothers. In fact, my research suggests that bearing almost singlehandedly the work of managing the home also resonated with many married mothers, whose husbands were not necessarily engaged in sharing the work of the home. Given the matrifocality of Russian family life, where women often depend on other women and heterosexual bonds are quite frail, grandmothers often shape women's experiences with second shift work. Grandmothers are often pressured culturally to do unpaid work on behalf of their adult children and grandchildren.[49] Furthermore, in many cases there are blurred boundaries rather than strong divisions between the discourses of married and single mothers in Russia, depending on the level of support in their lives. The "second shift" has long been considered women's responsibility in Russia, and men's contributions to domestic labour and childcare are low by international standards.[50] This is all the more notable considering women's high labour participation rates.

Many Russian women feel overburdened and that they must become stronger to make it in the "man's world" of today's Russia. But while the Soviet state at least supported women's double burden rhetorically, and provided some material supports for juggling paid work and motherhood, objectively many of those state supports for women's double burden have declined sharply.[51] Institutional supports for women as worker-mothers have been cut back as a result of economic reform, making things more difficult for women than before, and during a period when pressures at work, both in getting a job and keeping it, have expanded. The 2007 policy of "maternity capital" is also relevant here, in extending into the post-Soviet era themes of pronatalism, a general commitment to women's employment, and the idea that women should turn to the state for support rather than to individual men, as well as continued marginalization of fatherhood relative to motherhood.[52]

Some scholars debate whether Russian women want more equality, and surveys indicate that more traditional divisions of labour are still popular. But I found that women long for more "help" and "support" from partners, although it is still rather unthinkable to many that they might reasonably receive this help. Women do not want to expend energy longing for something they cannot have, or that it seems unlikely they can achieve. In fact, women are fatalistic about the chances that men or the state will do much to help them and their families.[53]

Therefore, while policies supporting gender equality ebbed and flowed depending on the Soviet leadership and decade, on balance the idea of the Soviet superwoman was normalized and became a taken-for-granted part of Russian culture and society. She could work for pay all day, and then go on to do the "second shift" for her kids and family – to shop for food and household items in conditions of "deficit" and scarcity, prepare food for her family with few conveniences, clean – and on and on. Men were encouraged to focus their efforts at work, while perhaps occasionally "helping" at home but not taking primary responsibility for domestic work or childcare. In fact, many have argued that men's main link to the home and family, in spite of Soviet women's paid work, was the paycheque they brought home, and at various points in time the Soviet state actively discouraged men from doing much carework at home.[54]

Although the Soviet-style and now Putin-era Russian superwoman is normalized, it also takes a great deal of cultural work, and oftentimes assistance from the older generation of women, to sustain this image. Participation in the paid labour force is a major part of Russian women's identity, as well as a strong force helping to restrain some neotraditional tendencies afoot in Russia, including Putin's policies of suppressing dissent (and feminism) and the ultra-conservative policies of the Russian Orthodox Church. Considering the state's reduced supports for women and families, the reduction of penalties for domestic violence since February 2018, and related efforts of the Russian Orthodox Church to mobilize against abortion, Putin's Russia is becoming an increasingly conservative country hostile to women's rights.[55]

Most single mothers I interviewed in the early part of the Putin period (2003–4) were disillusioned about the chance that men or the state would come to their aid, but they felt they had more control over improving their own material circumstances. They constantly spoke of "relying upon myself alone," embracing a neoliberal discourse of "going it alone" without many other alternatives, turning to self-help discourses and adhering to the cultural code of what I call "practical realism" in how they presented themselves to others.[56] In lieu of the stereotype of Russian women as somehow naturally strong superwomen, I argue that they are conforming to a dominant cultural code, a kind of neoliberal ideology of self-reliance, and that they engage in cultural work to transform the self, to become strong. In other words, in the case of single mothers, they work to create the socially necessary selves required to get by in what most see as a man's world of market capitalism.

The stalled gender revolution has also intensified in Russia in more subtle ways. It used to be acceptable for women to lament their burdens, including the double shift of paid and unpaid work, but the women I interviewed argued that it is no longer acceptable to talk about your problems.[57] If you are having a hard time in today's Russia, several women explained, then you have no one to blame but yourself. In fact, I had to probe in order for women to talk about material burdens they faced as single mothers (often reflecting on a difficult period when they were married). Mothers were not eager to talk about problems, and they frequently diminished some problems as "only material difficulties," claiming that their lives are simpler in some ways as single mothers. For instance, as one of my respondents, Nastya, a twenty-nine-year-old widowed mother, exclaimed,

> For some reason everyone thinks, "Oh, she's raising a child alone, how hard things must be for her!" But really for me it's much simpler raising my son on my own! Because fathers don't take on any responsibilities and you end up running around and looking after your husband, too, so your child gets much less time with you than when you are raising a child alone. When you're married with one child, it's often more like having two. As we say, "I have two children, one is five years old and the other is thirty!"

Women's paid work alongside an unequal gender division of labour is not the only reason Nastya feels that being a single mother is in some ways simpler. Yet in this case her late husband was a heavy drinker, often burdensome on the home front, who died in a drinking-related car accident. The unequal gender division of labour at home is part of the story of a stalled gender revolution.

Throughout much of the Soviet period and at least since after the Second World War, in Russia matrifocal families predominate even though two-parent, nuclear-family cultural ideals remain stronger than ever, often encouraged by the state. In matrifocal families, the mother-child unit is more central culturally than the father-child unit or the mother-father conjugal relationship. Matrifocality does not imply domestic maternal dominance (given that Russia is solidly a patriarchal society), but rather suggests that the role of mothers in family life is more elaborated, and conjugal relationships are relatively weak.[58] In fact extended mothering has long been the norm in Russia in spite of the state's efforts to propagate a "traditional family" kind of ideal based on a male primary breadwinner and a female household manager-nurturer-secondary breadwinner.

This legacy of matrifocal families (in spite of two-parent-family ideals) is also related to the stalled gender revolution. Even though many women long for a "good man," often arguing, relatedly, that there are no "real men" in Russia ready to take responsibility for family life and live a relatively sober life, in practice many Russian mothers are significantly more reliant on capable grandmothers who serve as co-parents, or at least as a strong source of practical support, whether for housework, cooking, or childcare. In fact, most Russian women see very little conflict between work and family, as long as there is a grandmother nearby to provide on-call backup support, especially with childcare. The cultural (and gendered) expectation that Russian women serve as a caregiver to grandchildren as they age leads to a "third shift" that is performed by many Russian women in the period when Russian men are retired. While this intergenerational involvement helps to ease the child-rearing burdens on many Russian mothers, it likely contributes to the generalized "stall" in the gender revolution – or at least does little to jumpstart it. There is less of a need to turn to men and the state for support if grandmothers will continue to take on significant responsibility for raising the next generation.

Russia is a society with high levels of gender distrust. Even though Soviet women were expected to be "supermoms" by working for pay in shortage conditions with few amenities, they could at least complain about their burdens and join with other women. Today they are expected to be supermoms "relying on themselves alone," and because of the constraints and new rules of neoliberal capitalism in Russia, they are not supposed to admit to feeling overburdened. Instead, women encourage one another to work on the self, and on changing their own attitudes to deal more effectively with a new system. In the new system, you have only yourself to blame if you cannot "do it all" at work and at home. Meanwhile, if more women are expected to do it all, many men are demoralized and marginalized as fathers and seldom serve as the successful breadwinners they are increasingly expected to be.

Of course, Putin-era Russia has changed dramatically since the early 2000s. While the early Putin years reflected his focus on restoring order and solidifying state power – and economic growth from 2000 to 2008 led to rising living standards for a time – the last decade has been marked by greater conservatism and nationalism. Since 2011 the situation has changed, and mostly worsened from a gender perspective. Russia's recovery from the 2008 global crash was sluggish, and Putin's return to the presidency in 2012 was met with unprecedented protests. Putin intensified his use of gender politics and his regime, in alliance with the Orthodox Church, began using gender traditionalism as a signifier of Russianness. Both Putin and church leaders have presented demographic decline as a threat to national security, restricting women's abortion rights in 2011 as part of a pronatalist agenda focused on women's maternal "duty." The "punk prayer" of the feminist opposition group Pussy Riot provided a focus for this neotraditional backlash, which continued with new laws banning gay "propaganda" in 2013.[59] The backlash continued further in February 2017 with a law decriminalizing domestic violence, eliciting international outcry given Russia's serious domestic violence problem. Contemporary Russia is experiencing one of the most repressive periods of the post-Soviet era, alongside the resurgent power of the Russian Orthodox Church, rising traditionalism, regressive domestic violence policies, and anti-LGBTQ legislation.

Normalized Gender Crisis

Perhaps one of the most critical legacies has to do with a pervasive, entrenched cultural discourse of Russia as a place where the women are strong and adaptable and the men are frequently considered weak and dispirited. In my research many men also agreed in general terms with this negative discourse about men, where women are positioned as "naturally" more responsible, flexible, and accustomed to managing things and men are spoken of in terms of more easily feeling demoralized and turning to drink, often accompanied by the camaraderie of other men. Many Russian men and women lament the state of the gender status quo, arguing that men *should* be strong, and women *should* be able to work less and rely on a man's "strong shoulders"; but, at least among women, there is considerable fatalism about this gender status quo, reflecting profound disillusionment with men and the state. While this is hardly true for all women, single motherhood is an increasingly common life stage in a Russian woman's life course. Given that Russia has long had high divorce rates (now considerably higher than the US rate, by most recent indicators), and that the post-Soviet period has seen a growth in non-marital births in addition to men's premature mortality rates, it is hardly surprising that single motherhood has become so common that it is normalized as the way things are in Russia, even if it is also a departure from the normative two-parent-family ideal.

The normalized gender crisis is exemplified by the cultural discourse of strong women/weak men, but typically scholars have written about men in crisis in Russia in the post-Soviet years because of men's heavier drinking and premature mortality rates. Russia has one of the largest gender gaps in mortality in the world (second only to Syria), and drinking heavily is routine masculine behaviour in Russia. While heavy drinking was also a prominent feature of men's lives in the Soviet Union, men in post-Soviet Russia are drinking more than they did before.[60] Furthermore, the consequences for men's heavy drinking, and the stakes involved in managing men's drinking successfully (or attempting to do so) are much different under market capitalism than they were previously under state socialism. Importantly, men's behaviours require the invisible management labour of women, especially as wives and mothers, even as women attempt to shape those same behaviours in order to maximize their families' well-being.[61]

There is a paradox implicit, if not explicit, in studies of gender relations in Russia, especially those foregrounding masculinities. Much of the recent literature on Russian men's health crisis, mostly quantitative, documents how much more negatively affected men have been by the transition to capitalism relative to women, especially in terms of men's decreased longevity, poor health, likelihood of accidents, and more. Scholars generally concur that men's premature death rates are caused in large part by men's greater likelihood of drinking heavily, especially of engaging in the binge drinking of vodka. With vodka accounting for about 75 per cent of the alcohol consumed in Russia, this preference for distilled spirits, the normality of episodic binge drinking, and a high tolerance for heavy drinking and related behaviours tends to make the Russian case distinctive.[62] According to survey data, approximately one-third of Russian men acknowledge binge drinking spirits (whether vodka or substitutes) at least once a month.[63]

Yet at the same time that men are undeniably "in crisis" and dying earlier than ever, in recent decades post-Soviet Russia has also been experiencing a period of intensified patriarchy and a resurgence in neo-traditionalism. In a special issue of *Signs*, Holmgren argues that "To a great extent, the transition years have bared, glorified, and globalized the patriarchal state that lay just beneath the socialist veneer of the Soviet Union."[64] So in spite of men's health crisis, in a more openly patriarchal system with fewer state guarantees, men hold most positions of influence in business and government. Women, in contrast, face increased employment discrimination (typically as mothers or potential mothers) and multiple disadvantages in new capitalist labour markets.[65] So while men suffer from a range of disadvantages, and indeed men suffer much more globally from lifestyle-related health problems relative to women, men also reap patriarchal dividends from intensified masculine dominance of business, government, and the public spheres of life.[66] This paradox, of men in crisis and requiring help while dominating positions of power in key areas of social life, is perhaps nowhere more vivid than in the case of contemporary Russia.

Remasculinization as a Legitimizing Political Strategy

Gender has long been used in the service of state power, but Putin's regime has taken this to an extreme. Some scholars even argue that masculinity is wielded as a kind of ideology, given the ideological vacuum of postsocialism.[67] Putin's hypermasculinity, or at least his clear attempts to remasculinize Russia, attempts to restore collective male dignity while also strategically using gender and including women while leaving existing gender hierarchies intact.[68] Sperling has also highlighted how Putin has relied on masculine dominance to enhance his power.[69]

In a recent *Washington Post* op-ed and related publications, Johnson argues that Russia has increased the numbers of women in politics somewhat, with the recent elections in Russia bringing in the most women since the collapse of the Soviet Union, but that "like the Soviet regime before ... It has learned how to subvert the connection between the increase of women in politics and gender equality."[70] Putin's remasculinization strategy attempts to assuage demoralized men who cannot serve as primary breadwinners while bringing in overburdened women looking for a sober, reliable leader as well. While much scholarship highlights how Putin's strategy is successful among men looking for Russia to be a leader in the world once more, the idea of a leader as a strong, sober, reliable breadwinner – the embodiment of the ideal man among the 130 or so women I interviewed in the early Putin era – was quite strong. Many looked to Putin to get the country back on track after the chaotic 1990s. As Putin defends the nation, he is focused on creating a particular kind of nation, one where feminists, LGBTQ individuals, and others are deviants with no place. Many scholars consider the Russian government's reaction to Pussy Riot in February 2012 an overreaction, given clear signs of support for neotraditionals trying to reshape society. Ashwin and Isupova argue that gender traditionalism is being used as a sign of Russianness, even though polls indicate greater support for egalitarian ideals among a younger generation of Russians.[71] While Putin provides some rhetorical support for working mothers, and the "worker-mother" gender contract in which women are secondary breadwinners continues in Russia, recent steps backward, especially with the recent law decriminalizing domestic violence unless it involves repeat offences, as well as the decline in state supports overall in Russia, make Putin's commitment to improving the lives of working women in Russia seem rather tepid.

Recent Developments: Heightened Gender Inequality, Continued Mixed Messages

In Russia, gender inequality has increased since the fall of the Soviet Union.[72] The façade of liberation common in the late-Soviet period has had several twists and turns over the past few decades and is constructed somewhat differently under market capitalism. Generally, however, women's position in society has deteriorated, as rights and guarantees assisting women in managing their paid work and unpaid home responsibilities have weakened, and neotraditional ideologies have gained traction in the past several years. Gender inequality occurs at multiple levels. In spite of overall economic growth, for instance, a recent study suggests that there are exacerbated family inequalities on the basis of gender in Russia. The relative "winners" of the postsocialist transition, such as affluent households and younger couples, have the highest levels of intrahousehold gender inequality, with more male-dominated patterns of managing family finances predominating in most contexts.[73]

Recent years have been marked by the continued remasculinization of Russia, in spite of some superficial changes that could be misread as advances in gender relations. Instead, these superficial changes are at best distractions and at worst cynical moves by the Putin regime to give the appearance of allowing for real opposition. In terms of gender strategy, little has changed. Putin remains the most popular and trusted politician in the country, with other parties trailing behind, in large part because of the association between the incumbent president and positive changes in the country, including overall stability after the tumultuous Yeltsin years. New arrivals to the political scene, such as presidential candidate Ksenia Sobchak, a well-known journalist, actress, activist, and wealthy socialite who positioned herself as critical of the Putin government, do not change the major strategy of Putin's regime. Massive public protests in March and June 2017 notwithstanding, Putin's regime attempted to marginalize the more serious opposition while allowing the candidacy of Sobchak. Her candidacy gave the appearance of Russia's openness to a pro-Western, anti-Putin opposition and suggested that the opposition had representation in the elections, all without seriously threatening the regime's power. Some have argued that the Kremlin wants to include opposition candidates who differ from the usual Communist Party opposition leaders, making Sobchak's candidacy especially enticing. Alexei Navalny, the opposition candidate who mobilized the masses successfully in 2017 and still commands a large audience on his YouTube channel at the time of this writing,[74] had been marginalized in the media and imprisoned several times because of what Navalny calls politically motivated charges.

The legacies I have outlined here – the stalled gender revolution, a normalized gender crisis in Russia's matrifocal families, and the continued use of gender as a tool of state power and legitimation – are individually important, and interrelated. When we think overall about Russia, it seems critical to note that even with women's high rates of employment and commitment to paid work, gender equality will be elusive unless there are policies and movements to support changes that motivate men to more fully share the work of the home, whether with children as fathers, or with domestic work – or, ideally, both. Few societies have gender convergence between men and women, but women want and need additional supports for the work of home and family if they are to engage fully in the paid labour force. And increasing gender convergence is the prevailing tendency in more egalitarian countries worldwide.

There are few feminist voices that are not heavily censored and stigmatized in Russia, and in this respect the post-Soviet gender order is not markedly different from the Soviet regime.[75] Women still engage in paid work and do the lion's share of domestic labour and childcare, with the help of their own mothers if at all possible, but women's expectations are also higher than they were previously.[76] Neoliberal ideas positing that anyone can make it and that you control your own destiny appear to be on the rise, and more, too, is expected of male breadwinners, even though it is objectively more difficult to earn enough income for a family than it was in the Soviet era. There is less state support tying men to families, since even child support enforcement has weakened in the post-Soviet era, in addition to other institutional supports.

With high gender distrust, essentialized gender ideas, and neotraditionalism on the rise – especially from the Orthodox Church – plus high rates of marital dissolution, stigmatized feminism, and more, the outlook for jumpstarting Russia's stalled gender revolution is perhaps not especially promising. New laws such as the February 2017 law decriminalizing domestic violence in Russia have justly elicited international outcry. In addition, given that Russia has one of the largest gender gaps in drinking in the world, and one of the highest rates of male drinking worldwide, coping mechanisms in Russia, too, seem especially gendered. In spite of inequalities at home and at work, Russian women have some independence through relying on paid work and, quite often, practical support from their own mothers. But a normalized gender crisis continues in Putin-era Russia, with many overburdened women who are disillusioned with men and the state, and many demoralized men who turn to the bottle, or even violence, rather than family life, for solace. Certainly, there are exceptions to these patterns, but the idea of overburdened "strong" women and demoralized "weak" men is reinforced at several levels of society, including everyday cultural discourse. This normalized gender crisis is likely to continue without a grass-roots feminist movement, even as Putin's masculinist legitimization strategies continue. While there are pockets of advocacy work on behalf of women's issues in Russia, without a strong feminist movement – and a genuinely bottom-up one, from below – change will likely be slow and gradual, instead of jumpstarting the stalled gender revolution.

The gender achievements stemming from the 1917 revolution– including women's access to paid work and divorce, but also, often, matrifocal family networks with extensive babushka support – remain achievements in today's Russia. But given the stalled gender revolution, Russia teaches us that the gender-progressive advances and legislation inspired by the Russian Revolution failed in their mission to truly transform the gender order, especially given the missing domestic revolution at home and the top-down suppression of feminism. If there is a shortage of men able to offer sober breadwinning or equality, the status quo in Russia will likely continue, in spite of women's gains.[77] Women will attempt to manage everything on their own, with many disillusioned with men and the state, but this will not necessarily change the contours of the stalled gender revolution. Certainly, increased egalitarianism in domestic labour would benefit most Russian women, but it would also benefit many men, especially in terms of parenting involvement. Given the stark inequalities in the gender division of labour in Russia, we can too easily lose sight of the fact that some men desire closer relationships with their children and families. Breadwinning alone as a main link to families is a precarious, burdensome position for many men.[78] Both women and men would benefit from a radical jumpstart in Russia's stalled gender revolution.

NOTES

1 S.Ia. Vol'fson, *Sotsiologiia braka i sem'i* (Minsk, 1929), 450, as cited in Goldman, *Women, the State and Revolution*, 1.
2 Interview excerpts are from the author's fieldwork, conducted in 2003 and 2004. All names used in reference to this research are pseudonyms.
3 Atencio and Posadas, "Gender Gap in Pay in the Russian Federation," 2.
4 Hochschild, *The Second Shift*, 12; Ashwin and Isupova, "Anatomy of a Stalled Revolution," 441–3, 463–5.
5 Lenin 1934, as cited in Goldman, *Women, the State and Revolution*, 5.
6 Ashwin and Isupova, "Anatomy of a Stalled Revolution," 441–3.
7 Hochschild, *Second Shift*, 11–14.
8 See Utrata, *Women without Men*, 23. See also Ashwin and Isupova, "Anatomy of a Stalled Revolution."
9 Utrata, "Invisible Labor and Women's Double Binds."
10 Johnson, "Fast-Tracked or Boxed In?," 643–7. See also Riabov and Riabova, "The Remasculinization of Russia," 23–6.
11 Borenstein, *Men without Women*.
12 Riabov and Riabova, "Remasculinization of Russia," 23–7.
13 Utrata, "Youth Privilege," 616–20.
14 Carlbäck, Gradskova, and Kravchenko, *And They Lived Happily Ever After*, 6.
15 Scott, "Gender: A Useful Category," 1069.
16 Goldman, *Women at the Gates*, 3.
17 Goldman, *Women, the State and Revolution*, 26–7.
18 Ibid, 56.
19 Ibid, 56–7.
20 Ibid, 58.
21 Ibid, 58.
22 Wood, *The Baba and the Comrade*, 15–18.
23 Borenstein, *Men without Women*, 17.
24 Ibid, 110–12.
25 Lapidus, *Women in Soviet Society*, xxi.
26 Mouton, "The Boundaries of Women's Work," 168–9.
27 Ashwin, ed., *Gender, State and Society in Soviet and Post-Soviet Russia*, 8–9.
28 Goldman, *Women, the State and Revolution*, 100.

29 Ibid., 131.
30 Ashwin, ed., *Gender, State and Society*, 5.
31 Wood, *The Baba and the Comrade*, 38.
32 Silverman and Yanowitch, *New Rich, New Poor, New Russia*.
33 Mouton, "Boundaries of Women's Work," 168.
34 Buckley, *Women and Ideology in the Soviet Union*, 108.
35 Petrone, "Soviet Women's Voices in the Stalin Era," 199.
36 Ashwin, ed., *Gender, State and Society*, 9.
37 Nakachi, "N.S. Khrushchev and the 1944 Soviet Family Law," 43.
38 Ibid., 44.
39 Goldman, *Women at the Gates*, 279.
40 Ibid.
41 Nakachi, "N.S. Khrushchev and the 1944 Soviet Family Law," 65–6.
42 Rotkirch, *The Man Question*, 20.
43 Lapidus, *Women in Soviet Society*, 239.
44 Randall, "'Abortion Will Deprive You of Happiness!'"
45 Ibid., 30.
46 Hochschild, *Second Shift*, 12.
47 Atencio and Posadas, "Gender Gap in Pay," 2. In contrast to increasing
    rates of later childbearing in Europe and North America, Russian women
    typically have an earlier entry into motherhood (e.g., early twenties
    instead of late twenties/early thirties), with low overall numbers of
    children. The gender gap in labour force participation might be higher if it
    included women under the age of thirty.
48 Gerber and Mayorova, "Dynamic Gender Differences in a Post-Socialist
    Labor Market," 2064–6.
49 Utrata, "Youth Privilege," 620–2.
50 Lapidus, *Women in Soviet Society*; Fuwa. "Macro-level Gender Inequality
    and Division of Household Labor in 22 Countries," 756–7, 763.
51 Teplova, "Welfare State Transformation," 290–9, 315–16.
52 Rivkin-Fish, "Pronatalism, Gender Politics, and the Renewal of Family
    Support in Russia," 701 and 712–16.
53 Utrata, *Women without Men*, 94–7.
54 Ashwin and Lytkina, "Men in Crisis in Russia," 192–6.
55 Ferris-Rotman, "Putin's War on Women."
56 Utrata, *Women without Men*, 100–18.
57 Ries, *Russian Talk*, 18–27.
58 Utrata, *Women without Men*, 5–6.
59 Johnson, "Pussy Riot as a Feminist Project."
60 Pridemore, "Heavy Drinking and Suicide in Russia."
61 Utrata, "Invisible Labor and Women's Double Binds," 7.
62 Pridemore, "Heavy Drinking and Suicide in Russia," 415.

63 Bobak, McKee, Rose, and Marmot, "Alcohol Consumption in a National Sample of the Russian Population," 859–60.
64 Holmgren, "Toward an Understanding of Gendered Agency in Contemporary Russia," 537.
65 Gerber and Mayorova, "Dynamic Gender Differences," 2047.
66 Connell, *Masculinities*, 82.
67 Wood, "Hypermasculinity as a Scenario of Power," 329–36.
68 Riabov and Riabova, "Remasculinization of Russia," 23–35.
69 Sperling, *Sex, Politics, and Putin*, 29–43.
70 Johnson, "Putin's Russia Promotes both Women and Misogyny in Politics."
71 Ashwin and Isupova, "Anatomy of a Stalled Revolution," 451–4.
72 Gerber and Mayorova, "Dynamic Gender Differences," 2047; Ibragimova and Guseva, "Who Is in Charge of Family Finances in the Russian Two-Earner Households," 2426–7.
73 Ibragimova and Guseva, "Who Is in Charge of Family Finances in the Russian Two-Earner Households," 2444–5.
74 *The Economist*: https://www.economist.com/europe/2021/09/18/vladimir-putin-is-still-rattled-by-alexei-navalny.
75 Sperling, *Sex, Politics, and Putin*, 245–70.
76 Utrata, *Women without Men*, 221–2.
77 Ashwin and Isupova, "Anatomy of a Stalled Revolution," 463–5.
78 Utrata, "Keeping the Bar Low," 1308–9.

REFERENCES

Ashwin, Sarah. "'A Woman Is Everything': The Reproduction of Soviet Ideals of Womanhood in Post-Communist Russia." In *Work, Employment, and Transition: Restructuring Livelihoods in Post-Communism*, edited by A. Rainnie, A. Smith, and A. Swain, 117–33. London: Routledge, 2002.
Ashwin, Sarah, ed. *Gender, State and Society in Soviet and Post-Soviet Russia*. London: Routledge, 2000.
Ashwin, Sarah, and Olga Isupova. "Anatomy of a Stalled Revolution: Processes of Reproduction and Change in Russian Women's Gender Ideologies." *Gender & Society* 32, 4 (2018): 441–68.
Ashwin, Sarah, and Tatyana Lytkina. "Men in Crisis in Russia: The Role of Domestic Marginalization." *Gender & Society* 18 (2004): 189–206.
Atencio, Andrea, and Josefina Posadas. "Gender Gap in Pay in the Russian Federation: Twenty Years Later, Still a Concern." World Bank Policy Research Working Paper No. 7407, 2015.
Baranskaia, Natalia. *Nedelia kak Nedelia. [A Week Like Any Other]*. Copenhagen: Rosenkilde and Bagger, 1969.

Bobak, Martin, Martin McKee, Richard Rose, and Michael Marmot. "Alcohol Consumption in a National Sample of the Russian Population." *Addiction* 94, 6 (1999): 857–66.

Borenstein, Eliot. *Men without Women: Masculinity and Revolution in Russian Fiction, 1917–1929*. Durham, NC: Duke University Press, 2001.

Buckley, Mary. *Women and Ideology in the Soviet Union*. Ann Arbor: University of Michigan Press, 1989.

Carlbäck, Helene. "Lone Motherhood in Soviet Russia in the Mid-20th Century – in a European Context." In *And They Lived Happily Ever After: Norms and Everyday Practices of Family and Parenthood in Russia and Eastern Europe*, edited by Helene Carlbäck, Yulia Gradskova, and Zhanna Kravchenko, 25–46. Budapest: Central European University Press, 2012.

Carlbäck, Helene, Yulia Gradskova, and Zhanna Kravchenko. *And They Lived Happily Ever After: Norms and Everyday Practices of Family and Parenthood in Russia and Eastern Europe*. Budapest: Central European University Press, 2012.

Connell, Raewyn. *Masculinities*. Cambridge: Polity Press; Sydney: Allen & Unwin; Berkeley: University of California Press, 1995.

Ferris-Rotman, Amie. "Putin's War on Women." *Foreign Policy*, 9 April 2018: https://foreignpolicy.com/2018/04/09/putins-war-on-women/.

Fuwa, Makiko. "Macro-Level Gender Inequality and the Division of Household Labor in 22 Countries." *American Sociological Review* 69 (2004): 751–67.

Gerber, Theodore P., and Olga Mayorova. "Dynamic Gender Differences in a Post-Socialist Labor Market: Russia, 1991–1997." *Social Forces* 84, 4 (2006): 2047–75.

Goldman, Wendy Z. *Women, the State and Revolution: Soviet Family Policy and Social Life, 1917–1936*. Cambridge: Cambridge University Press, 1993.

– *Women at the Gates: Gender and Industry in Stalin's Russia*. Cambridge: Cambridge University Press, 2002.

Hochschild, Arlie Russell, with Anne Machung. 1989. *The Second Shift*. New York: Avon.

Holmgren, Beth. "Toward an Understanding of Gendered Agency in Contemporary Russia." *Signs: Journal of Women in Culture and Society* 38, 3 (2013): 535–42.

Ibragimova, Dilyara, and Alya Guseva. "Who Is in Charge of Family Finances in the Russian Two-Earner Households?" *Journal of Family Issues* 38, 17 (2017): 2425–48.

Issoupova, Olga. "From Duty to Pleasure? Motherhood in Soviet and Post-Soviet Russia." In *Gender, State, and Society in Soviet and Post-Soviet Russia*, edited by S. Ashwin, 55–70. London: Routledge, 2000.

Johnson, Janet Elise. "Pussy Riot as a Feminist Project: Russia's Gendered Informal Politics." *Nationalities Papers* 42, 4 (2014): 583–90.

– "Fast-Tracked or Boxed In? Informal Politics, Gender, and Women's Representation in Putin's Russia." *Perspectives on Politics* 14, 3 (2016): 643–59.
– "Putin's Russia Promotes both Women and Misogyny in Politics. Wait, What?" *Washington Post*, 6 November 2016.
– "Gender Equality Policy: Criminalizing and Decriminalizing Domestic Violence." *Russian Analytical Digest* 200 (28 March 2017): 2–5. http://www.css.ethz.ch/content/dam/ethz/special-interest/gess/cis/center-for-securities-studies/pdfs/RAD200.pdf.
Kukhterin, Sergei. "Fathers and Patriarchs in Communist and Post-Communist Russia." In *Gender, State and Society in Soviet and Post-Soviet Russia*, edited by S. Ashwin, 71–89. London: Routledge, 2000.
Lapidus, Gail Warshofsky. *Women in Soviet Society: Equality, Development, and Social Change*. Berkeley: University of California Press, 1978.
Mouton, Michelle. "The Boundaries of Women's Work: Political Battles and Individual Freedoms." *Journal of Women's History* 11, 4 (2000): 166–75.
Nakachi, Mie. "N.S. Khrushchev and the 1944 Soviet Family Law: Politics, Reproduction, and Language." *East European Politics and Societies* 20, 1 (2006): 40–68.
Petrone, Karen. "Soviet Women's Voices in the Stalin Era." *Journal of Women's History* 16, 2 (2004): 197–208.
Pridemore, William Alex. "Heavy Drinking and Suicide in Russia." *Social Forces* 85, 1 (2006): 413–30.
Randall, Amy E. "'Abortion Will Deprive You of Happiness!' Soviet Reproductive Politics in the Post-Stalin Era." *Journal of Women's History* 23, 3 (2011): 13–38.
Riabov, Oleg, and Tatiana Riabova. "The Remasculinization of Russia? Gender, Nationalism, and the Legitimation of Power under Vladimir Putin." *Problems of Post-Communism* 61, 2 (2014): 23–35.
Ries, Nancy. *Russian Talk: Culture and Conversation during Perestroika*. Ithaca, NY: Cornell University Press, 1997.
Rivkin-Fish, Michele. "Pronatalism, Gender Politics, and the Renewal of Family Support in Russia: Toward a Feminist Anthropology of 'Maternity Capital.'" *Slavic Review* 69, 3 (2010): 701–24.
Rotkirch, Anna. *The Man Question: Loves and Lives in Late 20th Century Russia*. Helsinki: University of Helsinki, 2000.
Rotkirch, Anna, A. Temkina, and E. Zdravomyslova. "Who Helps the Degraded Housewife? Comments on Vladimir Putin's Demographic Speech." *European Journal of Women's Studies* 14, 4 (2007): 349–57.
Scott, Joan W. "Gender: A Useful Category of Historical Analysis." *The American Historical Review* 91, 5 (1986): 1053–75.
Silverman, Bertram, and Murray Yanowitch. *New Rich, New Poor, New Russia: Winners and Losers on the Russian Road to Capitalism*. New York: Routledge, 1997.

Sperling, Valerie. *Sex, Politics, and Putin: Political Legitimacy in Russia*. New York: Oxford University Press, 2015.

Teplova, Tatyana. "Welfare State Transformation, Childcare, and Women's Work in Russia." *Social Politics* 14 (2007): 284–322.

Utrata, Jennifer. "Keeping the Bar Low: Why Russia's Nonresident Fathers Accept Narrow Fatherhood Ideals." *Journal of Marriage and Family* 70, 5 (2008): 1297–310.

– "Youth Privilege: Doing Age and Gender in Russia's Single-Mother Families." *Gender & Society* 25 (2011): 616–41.

– *Women without Men: Single Mothers and Family Change in the New Russia*. Ithaca, NY: Cornell University Press, 2015.

– "Invisible Labor and Women's Double Binds: Collusive Femininity and Masculine Drinking in Russia." *Gender & Society* 33 (2019): 911–34.

Wood, Elizabeth A. *The Baba and the Comrade: Gender and Politics in Revolutionary Russia*. Bloomington: Indiana University Press, 1997.

– "Hypermasculinity as a Scenario of Power: Vladimir Putin's Iconic Rule, 1999–2008." *International Feminist Journal of Politics* 18, 3 (2016): 329–50.

5 *"Etnos*-Thinking" in 1917 and Today

DAVID G. ANDERSON

Introduction

Just before the 2012 presidential elections, Vladimir Putin published an article devoted to the "national question."[1] There the term *etnos* appeared as a category for understanding how post-Soviet migrants from Central Asia and the Caucasus were guided by the leading vision of the Russian people. The Russian president noted that "[t]he self-determination of the Russian people [hinges] on a poly-ethnic civilization strengthened with Russian culture as its foundation."[2] In this article he coined the phrase a "single cultural code" (*edinyi kulturn'yi kod*), which elaborates a sort of centralized version of multiculturalism wherein Russia is seen as a multinational society acting as a single people (*narod*). Originally, his ideas seem to have been aimed at creating a law that would protect the identity of this single people by reviving Soviet-era nationality registers, which tracked the *etnos* identity held by each individual. Most recently, Putin argued that his ethnocultural definition of the *Rossiiskii narod* should be militarized. At his speech at the 9 May celebrations in 2017, he spoke of the need to deploy military strength to protect the "very existence of the Russian people (*Rossiiskii narod*) as an *etnos*."[3] Here we witness a slippage from the use of *etnos* to denote non-Russian migrants to the use of *etnos* to diagnose a possible life threat to the biological vibrancy of a state-protected people. This led to a further controversy in October 2017 when Putin expressed worry about foreign scholars' collecting genetic samples from "various *etnoses*" across Russia. Spokespersons from the Kremlin further speculated that by holding this "genetic code," foreign interests might be able to build a biological weapon.[4]

For most readers the term *etnos* will be unfamiliar. Incorrectly glossed as "ethnicity," the term refers to a somewhat transhistorical collective identity held by people speaking a common language, sharing a common set of traditions, and often said to hold a "common psychology" and share certain key physiognomic attributes. At first glance, the term is a biologically anchored definition of collective identity. It is distinctive since it diverts itself from the standard, postwar North Atlantic definition of ethnicity, which stresses that an individual has a choice over which social, linguistic, or confessional groups he or she might belong to.[5] It however falls completely in line with early Bolshevik thinking, including Stalin's infamous 1913 pamphlet "Marxism and the National Question."[6] Peter Skalník, an expert observer of the history of Soviet ethnography, distinguishes *etnos* as "a reified substance" distinct from the "relational" understandings of ethnicity that developed in North America and Europe.[7] In other words, if modern European and North American analysts see ethnicity as a bundle of qualities – any one of which an individual might cite to describe his or her identity – Russian or Kazakh ethnographers experience an *etnos* as a coherent and enduring set of traits that only knowledgeable experts can see. Circulating around this single term are a number of strong assumptions about the durability of identities over time, the role of the expert eye in assigning identity, and the importance of physical bodies to stabilize and reproduce identities. The role of experts in identifying *etnoses* accentuates the concept's arcane quality. At times, the concept seems anchored like an internal family squabble among a relatively small group of ethnographers and geographers. At other times, the enduring *sameness* of a particular *etnos* is spoken of as so natural and self-evident that both politicians and scientists do not waste more than a few lines justifying how they associate people with a particular group. This naturalized, unreflective, and often hegemonic grouping together of a certain collection of people as an *obchshnost'* (a set of stable commonalities) links both early Bolshevik thinking on nations and nationalities and early twenty-first-century arguments about the biosocial careers of nations within the Russian Federation.

1917 and *Etnos*

The October Revolution was an epoch-changing event wherein scientists and politicians worked together to craft a new technology of rule. As historian Francine Hirsch argues, this "revolutionary alliance" was built upon a set of significantly overlapping vocabularies of nationality that were not quite the same.[8] Recent archival work suggests that academicians were already seeking to embed themselves within imperial state structures before the 1917 revolution, and that the revolution offered them a new window of opportunity. Therefore, this politically evocative alliance was also rooted in deeply embedded ideas of co-cultural "sameness," expressed at a collective level and recognized by qualified experts. This bundle of ideas – *etnos*-thinking – was deployed practically and politically in the early Soviet period. It was somewhat unreflectively built into Soviet modernization itself – and came to haunt the Russian Federation after the fall of the Soviet Union.

Discussions about national identity and co-cultural "sameness" were erected upon a long tradition of empirical fieldwork through-out the Russian empire, and especially in eastern Siberia. Historians of anthropology often link the development of Russian ethnography to the founding of the Ethnological Division of the Imperial Russian Geographic Society in 1845.[9] The history of that division is one of a con-stant alternation between the study of Slavic cultural forms and those of the non-Russian *inorodtsy* (pagan-foreigners), which the empire sought to incorporate but could never quite assimilate. Hirsch grounds her "revolutionary alliance" between imperial-era experts and Bolshe-vik organizers in the personal acquaintance and perhaps friendship of Vladimir Ulianov (Lenin) and Sergei Ol'denburg – the secretary of the Academy of Sciences. It is an interesting detail that this prominent Orientalist and ethnographer was brought up in Zabaikal'e – a fron-tier region on the eastern side of Lake Baikal bordering upon China. In Hirsch's account, their long acquaintance, and important reacquain-tance in 1917, may have cemented the collaboration between the acad-emy's scientists and the new Bolshevik government.[10] An important part of their collaboration was the redeployment of at least two imperial-era scientific commissions to produce ethnographic studies on how to improve the lives of non-Russian nationalities. It is not commonly known that Ol'denburg's homeland – Zabaikal'e – was one of several major ethnographic, geographic, and linguistic laboratories where these commissions experimented with their ideas. In particular, both the Commission for Establishing Ethnographic Maps and the Russian Committee of the International Association for the Study of Central Asia and the Far East sponsored several field projects in the area.[11] Both organizations were founded by Ol'denburg. These intersecting sets of field studies launched between 1903 and 1919 among Buriats and Tun-guses (Evenkis) in Zabaikal'e, as well as in Turkestan, Sakhalin, and Mongolia, generated a wealth of data but more importantly opened a debate on the links between biological form and national identity. Soviet and post-Soviet *etnos*-thinking bears the unmistakable signs of this early revolution-era debate.

Vocabularies of Identity in the Early Soviet Period

Standard accounts of nationality policy in the early Soviet Union revolve around Joseph Stalin's 1913 pamphlet "Marxism and the National Question," which would become a theoretical foundation of Bolshevik nationalities policy. After 1917, the recommended lexica for discussing identity and difference were the hierarchy of terms approved by Stalin, who held the post of People's Commissar of Nationalities from 1917 to 1923: *natsiia* (nation), *narodnost'* (nationality), *plemiia* (tribe).[12] Against the position of Austrian social democrats that "cultural national autonomy" could be held by minorities "personally" as an "association of peoples" not necessarily living together in a defined space, Stalin, at the behest of the Russian Bolshevik faction, argued for a much more holistic and territorially anchored definition of a nation, wherein a nation inhabited a defined region (*oblast'*),[13] In that text he also introduced what came to be a standard shorthand for the gradual evolution of national consciousness from the stage of being tribal (*plemia*), to consolidating into that of a nationality (*narodnost'*), until finally achieving the status of a nation (*natsiia*). Each type of national consolidation was seen as justifying different types of territorial autonomy – the end result of which was reflected in the complex nested system of national autonomous districts and republics that characterized the Soviet Union. Hirsch was one of the first scholars to draw attention to the special conditions under which Stalin's text was written.[14] She argued, convincingly, that the "sacred" status of this text needs to be contextualized within the polemics of the time. She draws attention to the fact that different groups of politicians and scholars held varying "vocabularies of nationality," which sometimes harmonized with each other and sometimes generated dissonance, creating the ensemble that came to be recognized as a single Soviet policy on nationality.[15] While noting that there was a "significant overlap" in the terms used by Bolshevik party organizers and the ethnographers, geographers, and anthropologists working within the Imperial Academy of Sciences, she pointed out that they nevertheless only "seemed to speak the same language."[16] Her classic work is devoted to demonstrating how maps, censuses, and museums in the early Soviet period were the venues where specialists expressed these differing vocabularies, eventually creating a distinctive cultural technology of power.

I would like to argue that this early revolutionary discussion is part of a long-standing discussion on the nature of biosocial identities across Eurasia. Like Francine Hirsch, I recognize the important role of competing vocabularies of nationality held by scholars and political actors at the time of the 1917 revolution. Her account implies that this process led to a unique "revolutionary alliance" between imperial scholars and Bolshevik organizers. I would like to contextualize this process further. Much of this debate hit upon very old ideas on how identities have been anchored in evocative landscapes, not to mention older "alliances" between ethnographers and the imperial state. To frame this argument, I would like to draw attention to a different aspect of Stalin's classic text – a little-noticed but significant turn of phrase in which he describes the role of "stable commonalities" *(obshchnost')* (literally "the quality of being the same") in forming national identities.[17] In this section, he links these commonalities to his now standard formula of connecting a nation to collectively held qualities such as language, a common territory, and economic "life," as well as a particular psychological outlook. Although it is indisputable that the language of "tribes," "nationalities," and "nations" captures the formal political architecture of early Soviet thought, the conviction that people have a recognizable and enduring "sameness" falls into line with a distinctive narrative of power that has re-emerged in Putin-era ethnic governance, as well as in the nationalist discourse of strategist Aleksandr Dugin, where the use of *etnos* is associated with powerful collectivities who have a moral right to control social behaviour.[18] In the following section I will argue that, while the surprising reappearance of *etnos* and what I have termed *etnos*-thinking in Russia today is anchored in revolutionary policymaking, like many revolutionary legacies, the concept is not as straightforward as it appears.

The Soviet Resurgence of *Etnos*-Thinking

Soviet nationalities policy continued to be driven by Stalin's formulaic expressions of nationality, nations, and sameness, but it is perhaps significant that these terms barely survived Stalin's death. After 1953, ethnographers began to question state-sanctioned rhetoric, but in 1964 *etnos* was reinstituted in a prominent opening address at the 1964 Congress of the International Union of Anthropologic and Ethnographic Sciences in Moscow to a largely indifferent audience of European and American anthropologists.[19] In 1966, upon the nomination of the historian Iulian Bromlei as the new director of the Institute of Ethnography of the Soviet Academy of Sciences, *etnos* became the keystone in a new architecture of ethnic governance.

This resurgence around the fiftieth anniversary of 1917 harked back to the revolutionary year itself. Although strands of *etnos*-thinking can be traced as far back as the seventeenth century, the first scholar to employ the term as a stand-alone, compact concept was Nikolai N. Mogilianskii (1871–1933) – a curator at the Russian Ethnographic Museum in St Petersburg.[20] In 1917 he published his definition of the term, which reads as follows:

> The ἔθνος (*etnos*) concept – is a complex idea. It is a group of individuals united together as a single whole (*odno tseloe*) by several general characteristics. [These are:] common physical (anthropological) characteristics; a common historical fate, and finally a common language. These are the foundations upon which, in turn, [an *etnos*] can build a common worldview [and] folk-psychology – in short, an entire spiritual culture.[21]

His off-the-cuff definition was published in the context of a wide-ranging debate on the institutionalization of ethnography within Russian universities between 1914 and 1917 – a debate which overlaps entirely with Bolshevik polemics on the question of the collective qualities that go into the building of a nation.

Although Bromlei's late-Soviet foray into *etnos* did not ignore the work of Mogilianskii, nor of course the work of Stalin, he did give the strong impression that his theory of *etnos* was self-invented. Yet his writing owed a great and unacknowledged debt to the émigré ethnographer Sergei M. Shirokogoroff, whose work, though not banned, was difficult to access. Peter Skalník even accused Bromlei of covertly plagiarizing Shirokogoroff's work using his privileged access to the special collections of the Lenin library.[22] The writings of this colourful and controversial figure, published primarliy in English outside the Soviet Union, ironically serve as a central link between the *etnos*-thinking during the period of the Russian Revolution and civil war and the ethnographic imaginations of the Russian public in the contemporary period.

The Shirokogoroffs' Field Research in Zabaikal'e

Sergei Shirokogoroff was appointed head of the Department of [Physical] Anthropology at the Museum of Anthropology in 1917 – a post he held until 1923 – despite the fact that by that time he was living in self-imposed exile in China.[23] Shirokogoroff is well known in the English language anthropological literature for his ethnographic work on Evenkis, whom he referred to alternately as Orochens and Tunguses. He is also renowned as an expert on Tungus shamanism.[24] Shirokogoroff's interest in how bodily forms reflected aspects of national identity overlapped with many strands of developing social science, some of which was of interest to Bolshevik politicians. Sergei and his wife, Elizaveta Shirokogoroff, would conduct three long-term field studies, first in Zabaikal'e among a mixed group of Orochens, nomadic Tunguses, and Buriats (1912; 1913), and then with Orochens and Manchus in Russian-controlled Manchuria (1915; 1916–17). Revolutionary events led to a situation where the couple had to make a choice whether or not to remain in Bolshevik-controlled Petrograd or to live in emigration. They chose to relocate first to Vladivostok, and then to a series of cities across China.[25] The bulk of their research was written up in English, although they continued to correspond intensively both with colleagues in the Soviet Union and with Russian colleagues living overseas. They each died in Beiping during the Japanese occupation of Manchukuo. The fieldwork that the couple first did would be analysed and published only in 1923 in a wide-ranging volume entitled *The Anthropology of Northern China*, comparing a number of peoples across eastern Eurasia.[26]

This publication shortly followed the Russian-language debut of Shirokogoroff's *etnos* theory, first in pamphlet form and then in book form in 1922.[27] Although physically situated within a vibrant community of émigré scholars outside the Soviet Union, Shirokogoroff's thinking on "guiding" nationalities and territorially compact ethnic groups would remain influential for Soviet ethnographers, who cited his work, discreetly, in specialist publications.[28] However, like many of the slippery moments in this play of "vocabularies," the way in which his thinking was implemented by Bromlei in the 1960s was far from what he had intended.

Etnos theory in the late Soviet period came to be seamlessly integrated into the way the state allocated resources, and as a result, became a guiding theme in the way in which professional Soviet ethnographers defined themselves. It was widely assumed that with the collapse of central state control over regional development, the term would disappear from public life and ethnography would move to querying local understandings of how individuals saw themselves. Instead, the term gained increasing influence both within some sectors of the academy and increasingly within public life.

In the 1980s, as the mass movements began to question the hegemony of the Soviet state, prominent Russian intellectuals distanced themselves from the term and tried to introduce liberal and individualist notions of ethnic choice. The most evocative attack came from former director of the Institute of Ethnography Valerii Tishkov, in his *Requiem for Etnos*.[29] Yet this resilient term did not vanish; rather, in the post-socialist period, it became more popular in the press, in Dugin's ideology, in provincial academies, and most conspicuously in the speeches of President Putin himself.

Etnos Theory in Putin's Russia

The biosocial identities forged at the beginning of the Soviet period are arguably indispensable to ordering the world in the contemporary Russian Federation. One way to explain this persistence is through the long-term survival of variants of *etnos*-thinking within the "revolutionary alliance" that structured the Soviet state, as well as the resilient way in which this biosocial lineage propagated itself within a set of circumlocutory expressions. The explosion of *etnos*-talk in the Putin era is most tangible among regional elites. Since the fall of the Soviet Union there has been an upsurge in publications on the ethnogenetic histories of various national groups. There is a strong quality to these works on cultural resilience and survival that one might identify as a type of Indigenous-rights discourse. Indeed, this quality is arguably closer to the way in which scholars like Shirokogoroff conceived of the term. The *etnos* term itself appears directly in the title of a number of regional collections as a way to emphasize their sense of pride and their expectation of respect for their nationality. Volumes such as *The Reality of the Etnos* or *The Etnoses of Siberia* place their emphasis on the longevity, energy, and persistence of cultural minorities.[30] They have manifesto-like qualities in that they insist on the vibrancy of cultural difference. This process, which I once called "nationality inflation," can be seen in a number of examples such as in the "somatic nationalism" analysed by Serguei Oushakine in the Altai republic.[31] Even Valerii Tishkov in the 2016 retrospective review of his *Requiem* was forced to acknowledge that "etno-identities" are characteristic of Russia now, and likely "forever" (*navsegda*).[32] The passion with which regional elites have been attracted to *etnos* theory was a major theme in the analysis of Mark Bassin.[33] Ranging from nostalgia for Stalinist essentialism to the Eurasian geopolitics of the twenty-first century, he sees this "biopolitical" term as able to stand in for concerns about modernization and environmentalism, cultural survival, and the strengthening of the newly independent Turkic states.

Conclusion

Etnos theory in contemporary Russia can trace its roots to a "revolutionary alliance" between scholars and politicians in the early revolutionary period, and arguably beyond. The theory differs subtly but distinctively from North American writing on ethnicity in its concern for collective identities, which cannot be curated by a single individual and which are crafted inter-generationally. Many adherents of the theory in the imperial period, the Soviet period, and the post-Soviet period further mark a certain somatic or physical anthropological consistency to an *etnos* – a type of discourse that is read uneasily by Euro-American scholars. It was the surprise of the century that, with the fall of the Soviet Union, this collectivist and biosocial theory did not wither away but instead became even more prolific. It left the safe haven of the academy and continued to expand in the public sphere, appropriated alike by right-wing nationalists such as Dugin and the Russian president. *Etnos*-talk is one of the more substantial artefacts of the Russian Revolution in the post-socialist present and, at the same time, a testament to the *longue durée* persistence of certain concepts in Russian ethnic governance.

ACKNOWLEDGMENTS

The research for this chapter was supported by a grant from the Economic and Social Research Council "ES/K006428/1 Etnos: A Life History of the *Etnos* Concept among the Peoples of the North." I am grateful as always to my colleagues Dmitry Arzyutov and Sergei Alymov, who gave advice on the Soviet implementation of *etnos* theory.

NOTES

1 Putin, "Rossiia: natsional'nyi vopros."
2 Ibid. All translations from Russian are mine.
3 "'Putin predlozhil tost v chest' Dnia Pobedy."
4 Zyrianova, "'Utechka biodannykh.'"
5 Lachenicht, "Ethnicity."
6 Stalin, "Marksizm i natsional'nyi vopros."
7 Skalník, "Gellner vs Marxism," 116.
8 Hirsch, *Empire of Nations*, 35–45.
9 Knight, "Constructing the Science of Nationality"; Tokarev, *Istoriia russkoi Etnografii*.
10 Hirsch, *Empire of Nations*, 23.
11 Histories of this committee can be found in Alymov and Podrezova, "Mapping Etnos"; Ol'denburg, "Russkii komitet dlia izucheniia Srednei i Vostochnoi Azii"; and Kisliakov, "Russkii Komitet dlia izucheniia Srednei i Vostochnoi Azii (RKSVA)."
12 Stalin, "Marksizm i natsional'nyi vopros."
13 Bottomore and Goode, *Austro-Marxism*; Bauer, *The Question of Nationalities and Social Democracy*, 281.

14 Hirsch, *Empire of Nations*, 28.
15 Ibid., 35–45.
16 Ibid., 35–6.
17 Stalin, "Marksizm i natsional'nyi vopros," 291–302.
18 Dugin, "Evoliutsiia Natsional'noi idei Rusi (Rossii) na raznykh istoricheskikh Etapakh."
19 The indifferent reception of the term is described in Anderson and Arzyutov, "The Etnos Archipelago."
20 For the early eighteenth- and nineteenth-century roots of *etnos* discourse see Vermeulen, *Before Boas*; and Alymov, "Ukrainian Roots of the Theory of Etnos."
21 Mogilianskii, "Predmet i zadachi etnografii," 11.
22 Skalník, "Towards an Understanding of Soviet Etnos Theory."
23 Anderson and Arzyutov, "The Etnos Archipelago," Section 2.
24 Shirokogoroff's key works on Tungus ethnography and shamanism are in Shirokogoroff, *Social Organization of the Northern Tungus*; and *Psychomental Complex of the Tungus.*
25 Anderson and Arzyutov, "The Etnos Archipelago."
26 Shirokogoroff, *Anthropology of Northern China.*
27 Shirokogorov, *Etnos – issledovanie osnovnykh printsipov izmeneniia etnicheskikh i etnograficheskikh iavlenii*; and *Mesto etnografii sredi nauk i klassifikatsiia etnosov.*
28 A full list of Soviet-era citations to Shirokogoroff's work can be found in Anderson and Arzyutov, "The Etnos Archipelago."
29 The *Requiem* was published in Russian as Tishkov, *Rekviem po etnosu.* Tishkov also published an English-language version of his arguments in a prominent American anthropology journal: Tishkov, "The Crisis in Soviet Ethnography."
30 Goncharov, Gashilova, and Baliasnikova, eds, *Real'nost' etnosa*; Makarov, ed. *Etnosy Sibiri.*
31 Nationality inflation was discussed in Anderson, *Identity and Ecology in Arctic Siberia.* Oushakine discussed somatic nationalism in Oushakine, "Somatic Nationalism."
32 Tishkov, "Ot etnosa k etnichnosti i posle."
33 Bassin, *The Gumilev Mystique.*

ARCHIVAL REFERENCES

St Petersburg Filial of the Archive of Russian Academy of Sciences.
SPF ARAN 4–4-672. Delo kantseliarii pravleniia Imperatorskoi Akademii Nauk ob opredelenii S. M. Shirokogorova na gosudarstvennuiu sluzhbu

na dolzhnost' mladshego antropologa Muzeia Antropologii i Etnografii Ak. Nauk 1917.

SPF ARAN 849–6-806: 239, 242, 244–56. Shirokogorov, Sergei M. [vmeste s E.N. Shirokogorovoi?]. Untitled typescript [Kochevye tungusy Zabaikal'skoi oblasti Chitinskogo uezda. Antropologicheskii ocherk, 1912–1913].

REFERENCES

Alymov, Sergei Sergeevich. "Ukrainian Roots of the Theory of Etnos: Saint-Petersburg Anthropology and Ukrainian National Movement in the Late 19th–Early 20th Century." In *Etnos-thinking in Eurasia: Life Histories of a Controversial Concept*, edited by David G. Anderson, Dmitry V. Arzyutov, and Sergei Sergeevich Alymov, 77–144. Cambridge: Open Book Publishers, 2019.

Alymov, Sergei Sergeevich, and Svetlana Podrezova. "Mapping Etnos: The Geographic Imagination of Feodor Volkov and His Students." In *Life Histories of Etnos Theory in Russia and Beyond*, edited by David G. Anderson, Dmitry V. Arzyutov, and Sergei Sergeevich Alymov, 145–202. Cambridge: Open Book Publishers, 2019.

Anderson, David George. *Identity and Ecology in Arctic Siberia: The Number One Reindeer Brigade*. Oxford: Oxford University Press, 2000.

Anderson, David George, and Dmitry Arzyutov. "The Etnos Archipelago: Sergei M. Shirokogoroff and the Life History of a Controversial Anthropological Concept." *Current Anthropology* 60, 4 (2019): 741–73.

Anderson, David George, Sergei Sergeevich Alymov, and Dmitry Arzyutov. "Introduction." In *Life Histories of Etnos Theory in Russia and Beyond*, edited by David G. Anderson, Dmitry V. Arzyutov, and Sergei Sergeevich Alymov, 1–20. Cambridge: Open Book Publishers, 2019.

Arutiunov, S.A. "Etnichnost' – ob'ektivnaia real'nost' (otklik na stat'iu S.V. Cheshko)." *Etnicheskoe obozrenie* 5 (1995): 7–10.

Arzyutov, Dmitry. "Order Out of Chaos: Political Intrigue and the Anthropological Theories of Sergei M. Shirokogoroff (1920–1930)." In *Life Histories of Etnos Theory in Russia and Beyond*, edited by David G. Anderson and Dmitry Arzyutov, 249–92. Cambridge: Open Book Publishers, 2019.

Bassin, Mark. *The Gumilev Mystique: Biopolitics, Eurasianism, and the Construction of Community in Modern Russia*. Culture and Society after Socialism. Ithaca, NY: Cornell University Press, 2016.

Bauer, Otto. *The Question of Nationalities and Social Democracy*. Minneapolis: University of Minnesota Press, 2000 [1907].

Bertrand, Frédéric. *L'anthropologie soviétique des années 20–30: Configuration d'une rupture*. Pessac: Presse de Université de Bordeaux, 2002.

Bottomore, T.B., and P. Goode. *Austro-Marxism*. Oxford: Clarendon Press, 1978.

Briusov, A.Ia. "Arkheologicheskie kul'tury i etnicheskie obshchnosti." *Sovetskaia arkheologiia* (1956): 5–27.

Bromlei, Iu.V. "Etnos i endogamiia." *Sovetskaia etnografiia* 6 (1969): 84–91.

– *Ocherki teorii etnosa*. Moscow: Nauka, 1983.

– *Theoretical Ethnography*. Moscow: Nauka, 1984.

– "Teoriia etnosa." In *Svod etnograficheskikh poniatii i terminov. Vyp.2: Etnografiia i smezhnye distsipliny*, edited by Iu.V. Bromlei, 41–53. Moscow: Nauka, 1988.

Bromlei, Iu.V., and G.E. Markova., eds. *Etnografiia: Uchebnik*. Moscow: Vyshaia shkola, 1982.

Bromley, Julian V., ed. *Soviet Ethnology and Anthropology Today*. Studies in Anthropology, vol. 1. The Hague, Paris: Walter de Gruyter, 1974.

– *Soviet Ethnography: Main Trends*. Moscow: Progress, 1977.

Castren, Matthias Alexander. *Grundzüge einen Tungusichen Sprachlehre nebst kurzem worterverzeichnis*. St Petersburg: Kaiserlichen Akademie der Wissenschaften, 1856.

Cheshko, C.V. "Davnie idei v novom prochtenii." *Etnograficheskoe obozrenie* 3 (1994): 111–13.

Cvetkovski, Roland, and Alexis Hofmeister, eds. *An Empire of Others: Making Ethnographic Knowledge in Imperial Russia and the USSR*. Budapest: CEU Press, 2014.

Davydov, Vladimir Nikolaevich. "People on the Move: Development Projects and the Use of Space by Northern Baikal Reindeer Herders, Hunters and Fishermen." PhD diss., University of Aberdeen, 2011.

d'Encausse, Hélène Carrère. *L'Empire éclaté: La révolte des nations en URSS*. Paris: Flammarion, 1978.

Dugin, A.G. *Osnovy geopolitiki (geopoliticheskoe budushchee Rossii)*. Moscow: Arttogeia, 1997.

– "Evoliutsiia Natsional'noi idei Rusi (Rossii) na raznykh istoricheskikh etapakh." In *Teoriia etnogeneza i istoricheskie sud'by Evrazii: Materialy konf.: Posviashch. 90-letiiu so dnia rozhd. vydaiushch. evraziitsa XX v. – L.N. Gumileva*, edited by L.R. Pavlinskaia, 9–36. St Petersburg: Evropeiskii Dom, 2002.

– "Strukturnaia sotsiologiia." TSentr konservativnykh issledovanii sotsiologicheskogo fakul'teta MGU (16.11.2009): http://konservatizm.org /161109164821.xhtml.

– "Sergei Mikhailovich Shirokogorov: Vozvrashchenie zabytogo klassika." In *Etnos. Issledovanie osnovnykh printsipov izmeneniia etnicheskikh i etnograficheskikh iavlenii*, edited by N.V. Melenteva, 5–8. Moscow: Librokom, 2010.

– *Etnosotsiologiia*. Moscow: Akademicheskii Proekt, 2011.

Dunn, Stephen Porter. "New Departures in Soviet Theory and Practice of Ethnicity." *Dialectical Anthropology* 1, 1 (1975): 61–70.

Dzhunusov, M.S. "Sblizhenie sotsial'no-klassovoi struktury natsii i narodnostei." Moskva Inst. Sotsiologicheskih issledovanii, 1977.

Gellner, Ernest. "Modern Ethnicity." In *State and Society in Soviet Thought*, edited by Ernest Gellner, 115–36. Oxford: Basil Blackwell, 1988.

Goncharov, S.A., L.B. Gashilova, and L.A. Baliasnikova, eds. *Real'nost' etnosa: obrazovanie i etnosotsializatsiia molodezhi v sovremennoi Rossii*. St Petersburg: RGPU im. Gertsena, 2012.

Hart, Bradley W. *George Pitt-Rivers and the Nazis*. London: Bloomsbury Publishing, 2015.

Hirsch, Francine. *Empire of Nations: Ethnographic Knowledge and the Making of the Soviet Union*. Ithaca, NY: Cornell University Press, 2005.

Kisliakov, V.N. "Russkii Komitet dlia izucheniia Srednei i Vostochnoi Azii (RKSVA) i kollektsii po Vostochnoi Azii MAE RAN." In *Kiunerovskii sbornik: Materialy vostochnoaziatskikh i IUgo-vostochnoaziatskikh issledovanii: Etnografiia, fol'klor, iskusstvo, istoriia, arkheologiia, muzeevedenie, 2011–2012*, edited by Iu.K. Chistov and M.A. Rubtsova, 114–31. St Petersburg: MAE RAN, 2013.

Knight, Nathaniel. "Constructing the Science of Nationality: Ethnography in Mid-Nineteenth Century Russia." PhD diss., Columbia University, 1995.

Kozlov, B.I. "Etnos i ekonomika. Etnicheskaia i ekonomicheskaia obshchnosti." *Sovetskaia Etnografiia* 6 (1970): 47–60.

Kozlov, V.I. *Etnicheskie i etno-sotsial'nye kategorii: Svod etnograficheskikh poniatii i terminov*. Moscow: Institut etnologii i antropologii RAN, 1995.

Kuznetsov, A.M., and A.M. Reshetov, eds. *Etnograficheskie issledovaniia v 2-x kn., Izbrannye raboty i materialy S.M. Shirokogorova*. Vladivostok: Izd DV univ, 2001–2.

Lachenicht, Susanne. "Ethnicity." In *Oxford Bibliographies Online*, 10.1093/OBO/9780199730414–0022. Oxford: Oxford University Press, 2011.

Laruelle, Marlene. "Aleksandr Dugin: A Russian Version of the European Radical Right." In *Kennan Institute Occasional Papers*. Washington, DC: Woodrow Wilson International Centre for Scholars, 2006.

Makarov, Nikolai Polikarpovich, ed. *Etnosy Sibiri. Proshloe. Nastoiashchee. Budushchee*. Krasnoiarsk: Krasnoiarskii kraevoi kraevedcheskii muzei, 2004.

Martin, T.D. *The Affirmative Action Empire: Nations and Nationalism in the Soviet Union, 1923–1939*. Ithaca, NY: Cornell University Press, 2001.

Miller, Aleksei I. "Istoriia poniatiia natsiia v Rossii." *Otechestvennye zapiski* 1 (2012): http://magazines.russ.ru/oz/2012/1/m22-pr.html.

Miller, Alexei I. "The Romanov Empire and the Russian Nation." In *Nationalizing Empires*, edited by A.I. Miller and Stefan Berger, 309–68. Budapest: Central European University Press, 2015.

Miller, Alexey. "Natsiia, narod, narodnost' in Russia in the 19th Century: Some Introductory Remarks to the History of Concepts." *Jahrbücher für Geschichte Osteuropas* 56, 3 (2008): 379–90.

Mogilianskii, Nikolai M. "Predmet i zadachi etnografii." *Zhivaĩa starina* 25 (1916): 1–22.

Mühlfried, Florian, and Sergey Sokolovskiy. *Exploring the Edge of Empire: Soviet Era Anthropology in the Caucasus and Central Asia.* Halle Studies in the Anthropology of Eurasia. Berlin: Lit, 2011.

Mühlmann, Wilhelm. "Nachruf auf S.M. Sirokogorov (nebst brie ichen Erinnerungen)." *Archiv für Anthropologie, Völkerforschung und kolonialen Kulturwandel* NFB 26 (1940): 55–64.

Okladnikov, Aleksei Pavlovich. "K izucheniiu nachal'nykh etapov formirovaniia narodov Sibiri." *Sovetskaia Etnografiia* 2 (1950): 26–52.

Ol'denburg, S.F. "Russkii komitet dlia izucheniia Srednei i Vostochnoi Azii." *Zhurnal Ministerstva narodnogo prosveshcheniia* (1903): 44–7.

Oushakine, Serguei A. "Somatic Nationalism: Theorizing Post-Soviet Ethnicity in Russia." In *In Marx's Shadow: Knowledge, Power, and Intellectuals in Eastern Europe and Russia,* edited by C. Brădăţan and S. Oushakine, 155–74. Plymouth: Lexington Books, 2010.

Pimenov, V.V. *Moia professiia – etnograf.* Moscow, St Petersburg: Avrora, 2015.

Putin, Vladimir. "Rossiia: Natsional'nyi vopros." *Nezavisimaia gazeta,* 23 January 2012.

"Putin predlozhil tost v chest' Dnia Pobedy: 'Za pobeditelei, za mir na nashei zemle, za velikuiu Rossiiu!'" *Pravda,* 9 May 2017.

Riasanovsky, Nicholas V. *Nicholas I and Official Nationality in Russia, 1825–1855.* Vol. 3. Berkeley: University of California Press, 1959.

Semenov, Iu.I. "Etnos, natsiia, diaspora." *Etnograficheskoe obozrenie* 2 (2000): 64–74.

Shanin, Teodor. "Soviet Theories of Ethnicity: The Case of a Missing Term." *New Left Review* 158 (1986): 113–22.

Sharp, John S. "The Roots and Development of *Volkekunde* in South Africa." *Journal of Southern African Studies* 8, 1 (1981): 16–36.

Shirokogoroff, Sergei Mikhailovich. *Anthropology of Northern China.* Northern China Branch of the Royal Asiatic Society Extended Volume. Vol. 2. Shanghai: Commercial Press, 1923.

– "Ethnological Investigations in Siberia, Mongolia, and Northern China Part 1." *The China Journal of Science and Arts (Shanghai)* 1, 5 (1923): 513–22.

– *Ethnical Unit and Milieu: A Summary of the Ethnos.* Shanghai: E. Evans and Sons, 1924.

– *Social Organization of the Northern Tungus.* Shanghai: Commercial Press, 1929.

– "Ethnological and Linguistic Aspects of the Ural-Altaic Hypothesis." *Qīnghuá xuébào* 6, 3 (1930): 199–396.

– *Psychomental Complex of the Tungus*. London: Kegan Paul, Trench, Trubner & Co. Ltd, 1935.

– *A Tungus Dictionary: Tungus-Russian and Russian Tungus Photogravured from the Manuscripts*. Tokyo: Nippon Minzokugaru Kyokai, 1944.

Shirokogoroff, Sergei Mikhailovich, and Koichi Inoue. "Tungus Literary Language." *Asian Folklore Studies* 50 (1991 [1939]): 35–66.

Shirokogorov, Sergei Mikhailovich. "O metodakh razrabotki antropologicheskikh materialov." *Uchenye zapiski istoriko-filogicheskogo fakul'teta v Vladivostoke* 1, chast' 2 (1919): 3–20.

– *Mesto etnografii sredi nauk i klassifikatsiia etnosov*. Vladivostok: izd "Svobodnaia Rossiia," 1922.

– *Etnos – issledovanie osnovnykh printsipov izmeneniia etnicheskikh i etnograficheskikh iavlenii*. Shanghai: Sibpress, 1923.

Shirokogorov, Sergei Mikhailovich, and Elizaveta N. Shirokogorova. "Otchet o poezdkakh k tungusam i orochonam Zabaikal'skoi oblasti v 1912 i 1913 gg." *Izvestiia Russkogo komiteta dlia izucheniia Srednei i Vostochnoi Azii* 3 (1914): 129–46.

Shlapentokh, Dmitry. "Alexander Dugin's Views of Russian History: Collapse and Revival." *Journal of Contemporary Central and Eastern Europe* 25, 3 (2017): 331–43.

Sirina, Anna Anatol'evna, Vladimir Nikolaevich Davydov, Olga Alekseevna Povoroznyuk, and Veronika Vital'evna Simonova. "S.M. Shirokogoroff's Book *Social Organization of the Northern Tungus* and Its Russian Translation: History, Structure, and Interpretations." *Asian Ethnicity* (2015): 1–17.

Skalník, Peter. "Towards an Understanding of Soviet Etnos Theory." *South African Journal of Ethnology* 9, 4 (1986): 157–66.

– "Gellner vs Marxism: A Major Concern or a Fleeting Affair." In *Ernest Gellner and Contemporary Social Thought*, edited by S. Malešević and M. Haugaard, 103–21. Cambridge: Cambridge University Press, 2007.

Smele, Jonathan D. *The "Russian" Civil Wars, 1916–1926: Ten Years That Shook the World*. Oxford: Oxford University Press, 2015.

Solovei, T.D. "'Korennoi perelom' v otechestvennoi etnografii (diskussiia o predmete etnologich. nauki k. 1920-kh – n. 1930-kh gg.)." *Etnograficheskoe obozrenie* 3 (2001): 101–20.

Stagl, Justin. "Rationalism and Irrationalism in Early German Ethnology. The Controversy between Schlözer and Herder, 1772/73." *Anthropos* 93, 4/6 (1998): 521–36.

Stalin, I.V. "Marksizm i natsional'nyi vopros." In *Sochineniia, t. 2 (1907–1913)*, edited by Institut Marksa – Engel'sa – Lenina pri TSK VKP(b), 290–367. Moscow: Gosudarstvennoe izdatel'stvo politicheskoi literatury, 1946 [1913].

Terletskii, P.E. "Natsional'noe raionirovane Krainego Severa." *Sovetskii Sever* 7–8 (1930): 5–29.

Tishkov, Valerii Aleksandrovich. "The Crisis in Soviet Ethnography." *Current Anthropology* 33, 4 (1992): 371–94.

– *Rekviem po etnosu.* Moscow: Nauka, 2003.

– "Ot etnosa k etnichnosti i posle." *Etnograficheskoe obozrenie* 5 (2016): 5–22.

Tokarev, S.A. "Problema tipov etnicheskoi obshchnosti (k metodologicheskim problemam etnografii)." *Voprosy filosofii* 11 (1964): 43–53.

– *Istoriia russkoi etnografii (Dooktiabr'skii period).* Moscow: Nauka, 1966.

Tokarev, S.A., and N.N. Cheboksarov. "Metodologiia etnogeneticheskikh issledovanii na materiale etnografii v svete rabot I.V. Stalina po voprosam iazykoznaniia." *Sovetskaia etnografiia* 4 (1951): 7–26.

Umland, Andreas. "Formirovanie pravoradikal'nogo 'neoevraziiskogo' intellektual'nogo dvizheniia v Rossii (1989–2001 gg.)." *Forum noveishei vostochnoevropeiskoi istorii i kul'tury* 1 (2009): 93–104.

– "Alexander Dugin and Moscow's New Right Radical Intellectual Circles at the Start of Putin's Third Presidential Term 2012–2013: The Anti-Orange Committee, the Izborsk Club and the Florian Geyer Club in Their Political Context." *Europolity – Continuity and Change in European Governance, New Series* 10, 2 (2016): 7–31.

Vasilevich, Grafira Makarevna, and A.V. Smoliak. "Evenki." In *Narody Sibiri*, edited by M.G. Levin and L.P. Potapov, 701–41. Moscow: AN SSSR, 1956.

Vermeulen, Han Frederik. *Before Boas: The Genesis of Ethnography and Ethnology in the German Enlightenment.* Lincoln: University of Nebraska Press, 2015.

Wang, Mingming. "The Intermediate Circle." *Chinese Sociology & Anthropology* 42, 4 (2010): 62–77.

Zorin, Andrei. "Kormia dvuglavogo orla." *Literatura i gosudarstvennaia ideologiia v Rossii v poslednei treti XVIII – pervoi treti XIX veka.* Moscow: NLO, 2004.

Zyrianova, Anastasiia. "'Utechka biodannykh': Kto i zachem sobiraet biomaterialy rossiian." *Russkaia sluzhba Bi-Bi-Si* (9 November 2017).

6 Building the National Park System after 1917: Environmental and Political Empowerment in Territorial Constructs

MICHAEL W. TRIPP

2017 was named the "Year of Ecology and Protected Areas" by Russian President Vladimir Putin in honour of the revolution's centenary and of the declaration of Russia's first protected area (*zapovednik*) in 1917.[1] But the question of the way in which 1917 shaped national parks in Russia is not a straightforward one. First there is a conceptual complexity: in foregrounding modernization and industrialization, the goals of the revolution are typically assumed to be antithetical to the goals of nature protection. Nonetheless, after the 1917 revolution, the Soviet state systematically created and supported a system of protected areas, the components of which fulfilled many national park functions. The revolution empowered the reformation of the country's social system and attendant reconfiguration of land-based ownership, enlarging the scope and territorial extent of protection to fulfil Marxist utilitarian objectives. Despite this early network of protected areas, Soviet Russia did not establish a true national park system. Preservation was an immediate result of 1917, while national park designation became a longer-term legacy. When a national park system did arise, after the fiftieth anniversary of the revolution, the issue of parks' geographical placement underlined the reality that political exigencies played a role alongside environmental ones. Soviet Russian national parks were set in a way that favoured the more-populated west, south, and centre, only gradually diffusing into the more biodiverse east. These processes and developmental patterns can be understood as consistent with recurring ideological shifts, changing hierarchies of place loyalties between macro-scale centralized governmental constructs and localized allegiances, and, eventually, the re-emergence of environmental consciousness as a socio-political force. Furthermore, the establishment of a Soviet national park system in fact contributed to the political devolution of the Soviet Union itself. Finally, all of these complexities and legacies are very much at work in the national park system of the Putin era, where park designation has become realigned with a non-divisive post-Soviet definition of "national": uniting Russia and defending its borders. Since 2000, vast swaths of land have been designated national parks, especially in Russia's Arctic. Their existence bears a dual mandate, one stated and one implied, the first ecological, the second territorial. Thus, the establishment of a national park system is a difficult, long-term, understudied legacy of 1917, an aftereffect shaped by conflicting objectives that continues to influence state protected-areas policymaking in Russia today.

1917: A New Era for Parks

While the conservationist movement in Russia began in the second half of the nineteenth century, it was not until the February Revolution of 1917 that Russia's first piece of ecological legislation was introduced.[2] Kerensky's Provisional Government prepared a resolution titled "On the Types of Sites Where It Is Necessary to Establish *Zapovedniki* on the Model of the American National Parks" for legislative passage. Conceived by Veniamin Semenov-Tian-Shanskii in conjunction with the first meeting of the Moscow Society for Conservation, the bill included a list of specific sites for nomination.[3] But this mid-November 1917 gathering had the misfortune of being scheduled concurrently with the Bolshevik putsch and was cancelled by the turbulence of the times. Given the advantage of historical hindsight, the dispatch in that same year of personnel to the Crimean Imperial Hunting Preserve, "to supervise its conversion to a national park," does appear as yet another mote in a maelstrom.[4] Yet, contrary to expectations, the legislative interruptions and political indeterminacies of 1917 were not viewed by Russian conservationists as necessarily negative. There were even some justifications for exhilaration. The tsar, the aristocracy, and now the ultimate purveyor of the status quo, the all-pervasive bureaucracy, seemingly had been eliminated. Depredations of capitalism and class privilege could be superseded by societal will and scientific reason. Lenin himself shared the common Russian love for "*pokhody*" – long, no-frills wilderness treks – and showed interest in natural resource conservation. On 16 September 1921, he signed into law the decree "On Protection of Monuments of Nature, Gardens and Parks." This act provided mechanisms for "declaring parcels of nature and individual components thereof having special scientific or cultural-historical value to be inviolable monuments of nature, *zapovedniki* or national parks."[5] Theoretically, such sites could now be open to the public rather than for the exclusive use of elites and valued for their intrinsic, non-exploitive qualities. In practice, over time new elites did emerge, establishing as Soviet norms much the same pre-revolutionary constraints and perspectives and with it their own set of antipathies to the constraints of the protected areas concept.

Previous attempts to create protected areas, especially *zapovedniki*, did proceed to fulfilment, at least in part to wrest control from the anarchic upheavals raging in the countryside. For instance, in 1919 the Astrakhanskii Zapovednik was established to defend the Volga delta from depredation. In 1920, Lenin created another equivalent site by special decree, the Central Urals Zapovednik of Ilmenskii. Other *zapovedniki*, however, such as the Komi region's Pechoro-Ilychski Zapovednik, were "founded precisely as national parks and because of this, their organizational structure was planned using elements more characteristic of national parks than of [nature] reserves."[6] Here, taking full advantage of the enabling legislation's definitional breadth, unlike the exclusionary strict *zapovedniki*, the Komi site protected cultural as well as natural elements, with visitation and habitation allowed. This dichotomy was not unique to the Russian context but reflective of ongoing tensions embedded in the constructs of protected areas since their beginnings – between nature users and nature protectors.

The establishment in 1924 of the All-Russian Society for Conservation (VOOP) provided institutional legitimization of nature protection as well as an avenue for continuing dialogue with individuals and organizations abroad. Botanist Ivan Borodin continued the collaboration with his German counterpart Hugo Conwentz, and Grigorii Kozhevnikov's work with the Swiss botanist and founder of Europe's first national park, Paul Sarasin, proceeded unabated. Contacts were made with the national park services of both the United States and Canada. VOOP initiated publication of its widely read journal, *Okhrana Prirody* [*Nature Conservation*], which included articles on national parks.[7] In 1929, the First All-Russian Conference on the Protection of Nature formally proposed the founding of a network of national parks, each internally zoned to fulfil three objectives: organized educational tourism, the provision of worker relaxation through recreational activities, and nature preservation.[8] These guiding principles were embedded in site planning documents when Russian national parks did begin to be established. However, as international influence increased, prioritization shifted from recreation to nature preservation, with "organizational educational tourism" reformatted as a means both of controlling visitation and as a source of foreign tourism funds.

Expanding its constituency, advocacy for national parks drew some of its strongest support from emerging *"landschaft"* (landscape) societies, which envisioned preserving the fullness of regional identities – both in their human and natural elements – within the new protected area construct.[9] The largest of these organizations, the Central Bureau for the Study of Local Lore, grew by the end of the 1920s to include 2,270 branches with 60,000 members.

The momentum of these events, however, was largely illusory. What could be interpreted as continuing progression towards the establishment of a national parks system within a developing protected areas framework, in hindsight represented vestiges of pre-revolutionary visions first buffeted by the disillusionment of war and then overwhelmed by perceptual reorganizations of Soviet society that disparaged and eventually condemned the ideals of the structures represented. Given the loss of adherents, the realization of Russian national parks was to be held in abeyance for another five decades, after 1917 had already celebrated its fiftieth anniversary.

Hiatus for the National Park Concept

Late-Soviet-era sources tend to gloss over or, even more frequently, simply bypass the reasons for this half-century hiatus. The only transition, for instance, between Reimer and Shtil'mark's discussion of calls for national parks in 1929 and their statement that "only in the second half of the 1960s [was the country] once again reminded of their necessity" is the end of one paragraph and the beginning of the next.[10] Post-Soviet protected areas literature, from within the country and internationally, followed this format, casting intervening history aside as fraught with other overriding circumstances or relegating it to generic "Green Red Horror Stories" about communism's environmental damage. The founding of Barguzinski Zapovednik in 1918 followed by seven decades of Soviet history marked by hardship, war, industrialization, and the arms race with America is illustrative of the first variant.[11] Funding proposals for protected areas often exemplify the second approach, repeatedly substituting the brevity of current legitimizing paradigms for the complexities of past perspectives.[12] Western post-Soviet works on the subject such as Feshbach and Friendly's 1992 *Ecocide in the USSR: Health and Nature under Siege* and Pryde's 1995 *Environmental Resources and Constraints in the Former Soviet Union* illustrate the latter well-tested reportorial exposé.[13] Set within what was viewed as the passing of the cold war, only the tense needed to be changed – from what communism was doing to what it had done, from its profligacy to its legacy.[14]

Upon closer scrutiny, however, the fate of Russia's first flirtation with the national park concept can be readily understood as the consequence of a series of devaluations of nature and its adherents that impeded the ability of initiating groups to institutionalize their efforts. Movements for the protection of natural landscapes have invariably been started by segments of a nation's elite. In North America this was composed of a loose affiliation of individuals from various walks of life, sponsored and supported to differing degrees and for varying purposes by a few powerful industrialists and government leaders.[15] In the case of Russia, the original momentum for the establishment of protected areas came from within an equivalent academic "intelligentsia" and progressive gentry. In both instances, these constituencies split into two major factions – proponents of *in situ* wilderness preservation and adherents of "wise use" conservation, the economically productive, sustainable use of natural resources. The philosophies of John Muir and Gifford Pinchot epitomize this dichotomy in the United States, unbroken from the establishment of the country's first protected areas to the present. Muir and Pinchot were both of that inner circle of Americans who first recognized the need for controlling the plundering of nature; yet for all their shared "love of the woods, Pinchot's ultimate loyalty was to civilization and forestry; Muir's to wilderness and preservation."[16]

Weiner's apt categorization of Russian equivalencies subsumes within preservationists the cultural-aesthetic-moral (neo-Romantic) proponents of nature and divides conservationists between the scientific community of biologists/ecologists and the "pure" utilitarians. Here the Russian experience diverged from the perceptual pathways of its American equivalents. To put it succinctly, in Russia, the revolution intervened. With the consolidation of the Soviet regime, perspectives of nature other than those adhering to the most utilitarian conservation agendas were increasingly suppressed, or simply ceased to exist – and with them died the impetus for the establishment of national parks.

The vicissitudes (and survival) of the country's *zapovedniki* provide an explanatory text readily applicable for comprehending the demise of the momentum for establishing national parks. *Zapovedniki* are defined as untouched or at least relatively pristine parcels of land large enough to prevent external environmental impacts – in other words, self-sustaining exemplars of ecosystems. These "healthy nature" sites would in turn serve as laboratories for envisioning enlightened use of like landscapes. *Zapovedniki* were scientific in their methodologies and utilitarian in their objectives – qualities that enhanced the momentum for their establishment. Yet even during the initial phase of their formation, *zapovedniki* were being attacked as elitist enclaves antithetical to the necessary levelling of society. Academicians associated with the sites were stigmatized as remnants of the ruling class and their conservation efforts branded as reactionary.[17] Field-based ecological research came under increasing disparagement for not reflecting the ethos of or contributing sufficiently to socialist construction, which, reflecting Marxist ideology, viewed nature not as an entity unto itself, much less an object for deification, but primarily as raw material for the production of economic goods.[18] In this "brave new world," Maxim Gorky could proclaim that "Man, in changing nature, changes himself."[19] Put simply, academic science believed extensive research into nature's complexity to be an essential prerequisite for successful "sustainable development," while the ministries, straining to fulfil production goals, saw the resources of the reserves as not contributing their fair share to the task at hand. Increasingly corrupted by necessary compliance with socio-political objectives, these divergent perspectives coalesced around the doctrinal inanities of Lysenko's Lamarckian biology and, in consequence, its emphasis on vast, "nature improving" acclimatization and hybridization schemes.[20]

Confronted with these circumstances, by the late 1920s *zapovedniki* were jettisoning overtly preservationist objectives to concentrate first on the dialectically sound search for nature's mechanistic underpinnings and, when that proved politically unsupportable, descending to the role of game farms and bio-inventory tabulators.[21] Even these subterfuges probably would have failed to save the *zapovednik* system, its territory slashed by 85 per cent in 1951 and further contracted in 1960–3, if contingent events, principally the death of Stalin in 1953 and the ousting of Khrushchev in 1964, had not intervened.[22] Given the travails of *zapovedniki*, even with their legitimizing utilitarian "scientism," it is not surprising that the concept of national parks, based on the veneration and protection of nature and on the ideology of "national" identity, did not succeed in the depths of the Soviet Union.

When national parks finally did begin to appear in the Soviet Union's last two decades, followed by their proliferation in post-Soviet Russia, the emergence signalled a relegitimization of nature as an entity and its role as a mechanism in the reformation of societal organization and political empowerment.[23] With devolution and the weakening of the country's centralized administrative structures, the national park designation became a means to support regional claims to territorial autonomy under the auspices of environmental protection. Site selection was motivated by attachments to the specifics of place and attendant proclamations of self-identity rather than to normative ecological or recreational national park criteria. As a consequence, first Soviet then Russian national parks embraced complex matrices of historical, cultural, and natural landscape characteristics reflective of their specific socio-political constituencies. Whether it knowingly exploited the Soviet legislation's lack of clarity in distinguishing between ecological and cultural preservation, this ambiguity did provide a legitimizing mechanism in such park formation processes. Appearing first in the outlying republics, the national park formation process diffused inwards to the Russian heartland and eastwards into Siberia. This sequential development mirrored the devolution of Soviet sovereignty and the deconstruction of its empire.

Delayed Legacy: A Soviet National Park System

Estonia's Council of Ministers declared the first Soviet national park on 1 June 1971. This proclamation in itself did not constitute a breach of political etiquette, for such resolutions within the Soviet Union normally did originate at the republic level. What was unusual was that the action carried with it an understanding that the designation was a *fait accompli*. The area chosen did not appear in academic publications or on ministerial lists of potential Soviet sites, nor did its matrix of natural and cultural elements readily conform to such national park formulae as were then being discussed and developed. In fact, Lakhemaa National Park most closely resembled the rural countryside of Britain's national parks, categorized by the IUCN not as national parks but as "protected landscapes." As with the British sites, the primary motivation behind Lakhemaa's founding was a need to embrace and protect essential elements of a people's heritage. The eclectic mixture of forests, seashores, glacial boulder fields, bogs, burial mounds, agricultural lands, villages, and manor houses did not detract from the appropriateness of the selection, for it was the quintessential representativeness of the territory that had been sought. To paraphrase a basic contention of the geographer Donald Meinig's *Interpretation of Ordinary Landscapes*, it is the heterogeneity of such places that makes them valued symbols of continuity and identity and thus a vital part of the iconography of nationhood.[24]

Estonia's lead was followed in 1973 by the other Baltic republics. Latvia established Gauya National Park, and Lithuania founded a national park in its own name. Both sites enclosed landscapes with high degrees of historic cultural modification unique to their respective republics. Lithuania National Park's proximity to a massive Chernobyl-type nuclear reactor also presented an early example of the "national park designation being used as a weapon in the arsenal of territorial defense."[25] That the Baltic states shared the shortest tenure as Soviet republics, as a result of a forced union after the Second World War, undoubtedly contributed to their initiation of this process of self-nominated national heritage selections.

In the decade that followed the Baltic designations, five more national parks were established in the Soviet Union, each in one of the peripheral republics – Tbilisi in Georgia (1973), Ala-Archa in Kirghizia (1976), Sevan in Armenia (1978), Uzbekskoi in Uzbekistan (1978), and Karpatski (1980) in Ukraine. The sites included a wide variety of landscapes. Tbilisi, located near its Georgian namesake capital, encompassed rural countryside. Created in 1973, the park was not officially recognized by Soviet central ministries until 1984, giving further credence to the proposition that the emergence of the country's national park system was the direct result of local initiatives rather than the product of central planning. Sevan in Armenia constituted by far the largest of the first group of Soviet national parks. Its borders encompassed the entire watershed of the lake for which it is named – a lake suffering the calamitous effects of Soviet water diversion projects. Here, once again, an environmental objective – the preservation and restoration of Lake Sevan – melded with nascent politics of self-determination. Such formative and structural stratagems were to be repeated when the momentum for the establishment of national parks shifted from the peripheral republics into Russia (see table 6.1).

In 1975, the Moscow Planning Research Institute proposed a "natural park" to encompass Losiny Ostrov, a remnant woodland and marsh on the city's northern periphery protected in various forms since 1406. The recommendation was adopted in 1979, and the site was then upgraded by fiat to a national park in 1981 because "the only way to truly preserve it was to give it the status of a national park."[26] Republic and federal governments approved this action only reluctantly and retroactively.[27] As with the first phase of Soviet Republic national parks, localized environmental concerns prompted action – in this case incremental losses to development prompted into action by construction of a major ring road that bisected the site.

In the same year, far to the south along the Black Sea coast and extending into the foothills of the Caucasus Mountains, a second Russian national park was founded. Sochinski National Park showed many of Losiny Ostrov's characteristics. The site bordered the city of Sochi, a major Soviet city and prime vacation destination. Its natural landscape of shoreline and forests, extending into the foothills of the

Table 6.1. Soviet Era National Parks – 1971–1991

National Park	Republic	Established
Lakhemaa	Estonia	1971
Gauya	Latvia	1973
Lithuania	Lithuania	1973
Tbilisi	Georgia	1974
Ala-Archa	Kyrgyzia	1976
Sevan	Armenia	1976
Uzbekskoi	Uzbekistan	1978
Karpatski	Ukraine	1980
Shatski	Ukraine	1983
Losiny Ostrov	Russia	1983
Sochinski	Russia	1983
Samarskaya Luka	Russia	1984
Mariya Chodra	Russia	1985
Bayanaul'ski	Kazakhstan	1985
Baskiria	Russia	1986
Pribaikalski	Russia	1986
Zabaikalski	Russia	1986
Prielbrusski	Russia	1986
Kurshkaya Kosa	Russia	1987
Pereyaslavski	Russia	1988
Shorski	Russia	1989
Valdaiski	Russia	1990
Kenozerski	Russia	1991
Nizhnyaya Kama	Russia	1991
Taganai	Russia	1991
Tunkinski	Russia	1991
Vodlozerski	Russia	1991

Caucasus Mountains, had been fragmented by industrial enterprises, forestry operations, and resort complexes. Intense development pressures threatened to continue the trend, further degrading the region's once famed environment.

The movement to establish Samarskaya Luka, Russia's third national park, followed much the same progression of events. Preservation impetus was provided by the "desecration" of Mogutova Mountain. Despite numerous purported closures, quarrying at the site had continued unabated since its wartime emergency opening in 1942. Residents of nearby Zhigulevsk protested both the destruction of the mountain itself and the high incidences of health disorders attributed to perpetual atmospheric dust and blasting. Once again local constituencies, supported by Moscow-based summer vacationers and recreationists, used the national park designation to attain social-political and environmental objectives.

Administrative affinities contributed substantially to site selection processes in the establishment of Russia's first three national parks. Attuned to the increasing politicization of the environment and to means for promoting its protection, Moscow elites, both at home and from the perspective of two favoured vacation destinations, provided empathetic conceptualization and process linkages to champion each of the site protection movements.[28] Such personal connections, always an important facet of accomplishing any task in the Soviet Union, gained increasing ascendancy in the 1980s as alternative avenues of information flow and empowerment. Local environmentalists, at times closely aligned with ministry personnel, used these lobbying channels, coupled with the rapid development and maturation of NGOs, to confront the same environmentally destructive practices of ministry branch organs that plagued the peripheral republics.[29]

Communism's Collapse, Parks' Expansion

From these beginnings through to the dissolution of the Soviet Union in December 1991, fourteen national parks were established, all but one located in the Russian Republic (see table 6.1). Thereafter, from 1992 through to the end of the Yeltsin era in 1999, with momentum undiminished by the collapse of the country, another nineteen sites were established. These post-Soviet national parks continued to replicate essential context and content characteristics of the sites that had preceded them (see table 6.2).[30] Reflecting the motivations of the peripheral republics and in reaction to their emerging hubris, the Russian Federation sited its national parks based on criteria for the preservation of landscapes of historical, religious, and occasionally mythological significance set within forest, meadow, and water. This choice of elements was and continues to be widespread

Table 6.2. Establishment of Russian National Parks – Yeltsin Era 1992 through 1999

National Park	Administrative Region	Established
Meshchyor	Vladimir	1992
Meschyorsky	Ryazan	1992
Paanajarvi	Karelia	1992
Russky Sever	Vologda	1992
Smolenskoye Poozerye	Smolensk	1992
Chavash Varmanie Bor	Chuvashia	1993
Pripyshminskiye Bory	Sverdlovsk	1993
Zyuratkal	Chelyabinsk	1993
Khvalynsky	Saratov	1994
Orlovskoye	Oryol	1994
Yugd Va	Komi	1994
Smolny	Mordovia	1995
Sochi	Krasnodar	1995
Sebezhsky	Pskov	1996
Ugra	Kaluga	1997
Pleshcheyevo Ozera	Yaroslav	1997
Alaniya	North Ossetia	1998
Alkhanay	Zabaikalski	1999
Anyusky	Khabarovsksi	1999

and ingrained. Its image appears repeatedly in park literature, often as a source of bodily and/or spiritual rejuvenation – at heart more conservative than conservationist.

Passage of the 1991 Law on Specially Protected Areas was nullified by the collapse of the Soviet Union. A second attempt in the fall of 1993 to pass legislation failed with the dissolving of parliament. In December 1994, *zapovednik* and national park directors petitioned President Yeltsin to:

create within the Ministry of Environmental Protection and Natural Resources a Department for Nature Reserves, and create within the Federal Forest Service, a Division of National Parks, giving these units all management functions over the *Zapovedniki* and National Parks, including planning, financing, construction, labour and wages, preparation and placement of staff.[31]

On 14 March 1995, a protected areas act was signed into law, affirming federal administration of national park and *zapovednik* territories, but leaving jurisdictional structures intact. Further reorganization followed Yeltsin's re-election in August 1996. Where previously the Federal Forest Service had included national parks within their budget as specific line items, now lump sum payments were forwarded to the regions, allowing them to choose where their monies should be spent – hardly a message portending the advent of a national parks system.

As to the supposition that establishment of Russian national parks has been strongly influenced by biological diversity preservation considerations, the distribution of sites provides a graphically cogent argument against such a surmise (figure 6.1). Well over half of all national parks (or 19 out of 36) are found within the single Kola-Karelian/ Eastern European Forest bioregion. Seven more are located in three ecologically similar mountainous zones (three in the Urals; two in Baikal; and two in the Caucasus). Virtually all protect the same aforementioned matrix of meadow, woodlands, and water, while the vast Arctic tundra and the truly magnificent biodiversity of the Russian Far East until the Putin era continued to be largely unrepresented. The "Greenwall" project of Russia's southern plain offers a case in point. What remains of this region's forests is mostly confined to fragments of once vast woodlands that served for centuries as barriers against Tatar and other nomadic invaders. An expanding chain of *zapovedniki* and national parks now traces this "abatis line" through much of Russia's southern heartland, most noticeably from Bryanski Les (Bryanski Woods) bordering Ukraine eastwards to the Meshchera forests in the east.[32] Though ostensibly components in an "ambitious program to provide … a single network of forests throughout the territory [and thus] … a key link in protecting the biodiversity of central and southern European Russia," the project's underlying motivation lies in the desire to restore an inherent element of Russian culture – its history-laden forests. Site observations tend to confirm this hierarchy of objectives, with rehabilitation of cultural/natural landscape elements far outweighing scientific inquiry.[33]

The Second Hiatus

Political recentralization of governmental authority in the Putin era that followed brought with it a significant diminishment of momentum in the establishment of national parks, beginning with a complete hiatus in their formation from 2000 to 2006.

Figure 6.1. Distribution of Soviet/post-Soviet national parks

The gap can be attributed to the rapid reascendance of Soviet-era environmental utilitarianism promoted by newly appointed like-minded administrators – a shock therapy heralded within months of Putin's investiture by the 17 May 2000 decree 867 abolishing both federal agencies directly involved with national parks: Goscompriroda (The State Committee for the Protection of Nature), tasked with nature protection, and the production-oriented Russian Forest Service, within whose jurisdiction the parks resided. The friction between these two entities, the former a Gorbachev-era newcomer and the latter a venerated institution harking back to the time of Peter the Great, replicated many of the same characteristic preservation/resource use antagonisms that have reverberated in perpetuity between equivalent North American governmental structures.[34] Both functions were transferred to the Natural Resources Ministry. National parks and *zapovednik* departments were eliminated, with responsibilities for their management redirected to ministry subdivisions. Reaction by defenders of nature from within the government and from the public was swift and effective, culminating in the establishment of a Department of Environmental Protection and Environmental Security (Minprirody) headed by Vsevolod Stepanitsky, a champion of protected areas and manager of Russian *zapovedniki* since 1991.[35] As one expert put it at the time, "Despite the seeming absurdity of the original 'reforms,' for the first time in history a united agency arose to manage both *zapovedniki* and national parks."[36] In a replay of the 1920s, however, this triumph of nature protection was illusory, most likely a misstep engendered by the new regime's being caught off guard by the strength of its opponents both individually and en masse. Soon thereafter, in summer 2001, a new minister of natural resources was shuffled in from a troubled tenure in transportation, bringing with him a reputation as "a tool of the oligarchs furthering privatization."[37] By the end of 2001, Stepanitsky had resigned, transferring his efforts to parallelling NGO activities.[38] In the ensuing years, many such organizations and their constituencies, especially those with international affiliations, were to be increasingly anathematized and eventually legislatively suppressed, with the government's retrenchment of pre-1991 attitudes towards the roles, if any, of civil society in decision-making processes.[39] In November 2003, the third All-Russian Congress of Nature Conservation held in Moscow was disrupted by denunciations of the assembly's rote acceptance of government plaudits to its protected areas efforts.[40] The following month brought a bizarre series of retaliations, retractions, and restructurings, whereby "suites of five" centrally appointed administrators were to be assigned to each protected area.[41] With his re-election in 2004, Putin appointed yet another minister of natural resources, this one previously associated with oil extraction companies in the Perm region. The Department of Specially Protected Nature Areas, a remnant of Stepanitsky's brief success, was abolished and its functions highly fragmented. Thus, protected areas and their adherents moved from crisis to crisis as Putin consolidated his vision of the Russian state. Given this political climate, the hiatus in the establishment of new protected areas should not be surprising.

Resurgence with a New Agenda

What is surprising, however, is that in 2007 four national parks were established, followed by an additional twelve through to the present (2018), with further sites proposed (see table 6.3).

This resurgence can be attributed to the same factors, hierarchically and perceptually reconstructed, that propelled the original bursts of activity. Local constituencies and with them the spontaneity of change are no longer prime motivators. Sites are now formulated rather than declared. Bureaucratic structures, weakened in the 1990s, have added

Table 6.3. Establishment of Russian National Parks in the Putin era, 2000 through 2018

National Park	Administrative Region	Established
		Seven-year hiatus 2000–2006
Buzulusky Bor	Samara/Orenburg	2007
Kalevalsky	Karelia	2007
Zov Tigra	Primorski	2007
Udegeyskaya Legenda	Primorsk	2007
Russian Arctic	Arkhangelsk	2009/2116
Saylyugemsky	Altai	2010
"Land of the Leopard"	Primorski	2012
Berengia	Chukotka	2013
Shantar Islands	Khabarorvsk	2013
Onezhskoye Pomorye	Arkhangelsk	2013
Chikoy	Zabaikalski	2014
Bikin	Primorski	2015
Sengilei Mountains	Ulyanovsk	2017
Lensliye Stolby	Sakha	2018
Khibiny	Murmansk	2018
Ladoga Kerries	Karelia	2018

their plodding pace to the process. According to Maleshin, "Many proposals for the creation of new protected areas had been with the Ministry for years and no one knew what to do with them."[42] A set of ten national parks identified for establishment during Putin's first term languished until he personally spurred them onwards.[43] More sites were identified by government resolution in 2011 for founding by 2020.[44] Continuing the pattern of the 1990s, the sites diffuse eastwards and to peripheries, though fulfilling objectives of national inclusion rather than regional ambitions of autonomy. Areas of economically significant natural resources were studiously avoided.[45] Where potential resource use conflicts existed, park boundaries were drawn to exclude them.[46]

Patterns of distribution and size, viewed again where they are, rather than where they are not, offer insights into government motivations for their establishment. The farther the sites stray from population centres, the more a *zapovednik* designation seems appropriate, yet the term "national park" continues to be the ultimate empowering seal of distinction. Four Arctic sites offer one variant, epitomized by the vast (1,426,000 hectare) Russkaia Arktika National Park, established in 2009 in the Arkhangelsk Oblast. Putin, when visiting, had proclaimed the landscape a rubbish heap in dire need of reclamation. After being granted the status of national park, it was consequently greatly enlarged, encompassing both land and maritime territories.

"Yet why do we need national parks in the Arctic? A mere eighteen people are asserting Russian presence in the archipelago. This territory is essentially open to foreign vessels. The aim of creating the park is not only and not so much to preserve nature as to ensure national security. If the territory were uninhabited it might come under international control. This is why all countries assign the status of national park to uninhabited territories. This is what happens in Alaska, Greenland, and the Canadian Arctic islands. Nobody may claim territory with this status."[47]

Here again, national parks are being used to proclaim territorial hegemony, but at a national rather than regional or local scale. Yet it is in Putin-era national parks, especially in Arctic sites, comparatively unconstrained by human habitation, that government to government (e.g., fisheries departments) and supra-governmental (UNESCO, WWF [World Wildlife Fund]) affiliations continue to find viability drawn by mutual environmental research interests, legitimizing both geopolitical and nature preservation objectives.[48]

The establishment of Shantar Islands National Park offers a different variant in terms of scale and purpose. With its unique flora and fauna, especially its bird and marine mammal populations, this isolated archipelago had long been envisioned as a *zapovednik*. Established as such in 1999 in the Sea of Okhotsk, the designation excluded potential visitors. In 2013 its status was changed to national park, thereby allowing "ecological tourism." Zov Tigra and Land of the Leopard National Parks cluster nearby within Primorsky Krai's Ussuri Mountains, the latter enfolding at its core Kedrovaya Pad *zapovednik*. Merging of the two protected areas is viewed by some as a profanation of *zapovednik* principles. The configuration, however, neatly replicates accepted international zoning principles that dominate national park planning models.[49] The question still to be resolved is whether such amalgamations represent a trend and, if a trend, to what purpose. If *zapovedniki* are being relegated to the status of a protected zone within national parks, depriving them of administrative and staffing autonomy, the outcome will be to diminish nature protection to the advantage of utilitarian use objectives, including tourism. The wisdom of the zoning model, however, is in its attractiveness to a wide range of regimes – including Putin's Russia – as a means of legitimizing a nation's environmental credentials. The zoning model, at least on the surface, provides something for everyone, including nature.

Most other post-hiatus national parks also "guard the borders," including two in Karelia and one in the Altai Mountains intersecting with Kazakhstan, Mongolia, and China. So peripheral as to be extraterritorial, two national parks excluded from table 6.3, Ritinsky (2007) in the breakaway region of Georgian Abkhazia, and Tarkhantul (2014) on the western shore of the Crimea, provide a further permutation on the theme of using the protected area construct, here to proclaim dubious extensions of national sovereignty.

Yet whatever the motivations and despite recent vicissitudes, the resurgence in establishment of Russian national parks is a reality. More significantly, that all of Russia's national parks still exist, even those declared in the midst of the turmoil of the 1990s, gives credence to the continued strength and resilience of their originators and their purposes – as signifiers of the resurrected environmental, aesthetic, and cultural/historical values with which they are imbued. Buryatia's national parks epitomize the intertwining of the rights of nature and of people first championed by VOOP and the landschaft societies in the 1920s then reforged during the breakup of the Soviet Union and in its Russian reconstruction. The region's immense Tunkinski National Park has not been diminished, nor has a projected oil pipeline been allowed to encroach on its territory.[50] With the addition of the Alkhanay and Chikoy sites, Buryatia continues to pursue its original "Republic as national park" objective. Representing the first in a significant subset of ethnic-based national parks, Mariya Chodra, founded in 1985, also survives, as does the first national park, municipally proclaimed Losiny Ostrov.[51] Even post-hiatus sites have adopted as legitimizers the protection of Indigenous peoples and their natural/cultural landscapes.[52] Throughout Russia, the annual March for Parks and similar events begun in the 1990s and rapidly replicated throughout the country have brought together a wide array of supporters, raising awareness of the importance of protected areas for preserving nature and its environment.[53] The World Wildlife Fund – Russia's website promoting the causes of numerous species and their habitats – boasts nearly 400,000 followers.

This volume deals with the legacies of the revolution, of its goals, policies, and priorities, and their outcomes. Whether Russia's nascent protected areas movement, and more specifically the establishment of national parks, would have flourished and along what pathways had not the revolution intervened can only be conjectured. What can be stated is that precisely because the process was interrupted and left unfinished, these sites are a legacy, to varying degrees unforeseen and unintended, of the revolution. In 1917 few beyond a narrow, privileged stratum of individuals acknowledged such a foreign concept as national parks, much less a need for their presence. The Soviet-era policies that followed, while effectively suppressing nature veneration, continued to support its utilitarian uses within designated areas, offering varying degrees of limited protection. Familiarity with their purposes and with the sites themselves formed the basis for the gestation of Russia's late and post-Soviet protected area systems, including the reintroduction of the national park concept. Today there is a wide acceptance of their existence and a shared understanding of their cultural and environmental goals – to the point that Russian national parks have become effectively national in their recognition while remaining legitimate signifiers of their local and regional beginnings. The principal legacy of 1917 with regard to national parks and their place in Russia is the fact that the environmental is ever contingent on the political. While a national park system might have come to pass without the Bolsheviks and their early decrees, the *particular* national park system that emerged in Russia, with regard both to the timeline of its creation and to the spatial distribution of parks within the national territory, remains an inheritance of 1917, bearing witness to the power of ideology in shaping landscapes and land use.

NOTES

1 The term *zapovednik* (strict nature reserve) derives etymologically from *zapoved/zapovednost*, commandment/inviolability, denoting a protected territory "for preserving and studying representative and unique landscapes as well as the genetic inheritance of their flora and fauna; refining principles for the protection of nature; and creating conditions that will secure and maintain the natural flow of nature processes" (Supreme Soviet, 25 July 1991). Placed in a familiar biogeographic context *zapovedniki* are representative natural areas withdrawn by legislation from anthropogenic impacts for baseline data collection and research into ecosystem interactions. These functions have, since the origin of the system, carried a corollary responsibility for extrapolating findings to restore and enrich nature, leaving the sites more or less vulnerable to interpretation of these latter objectives by prevailing political ideologies. On "The Year of Ecology and Protected Areas" see Conant, "Look Inside Russia's Wildest Nature Reserves Now Turning 100."

2 The early Russian conservationist movement emerged in response to growing industrialization and was led by a small but significant group including botanists Ivan Borodin and Valerii Taliev, physical geographer Alexander Voikov, and entomologist Grigorii Kozhevnikov. Landmarks included the establishment of the Permanent Conservation Commission of the Imperial Russian Geographical Society in 1911 and Russia's first Conservation Fair in 1913.

3 Chairman of the Russian Geographical Society's Biogeographical Commission, president of the Russian Entomological Society, and a noted aestheticist/humanist.

4 Weiner, *Models of Nature*, 22.

5 Though validating both designations within the framework of the legislation, the act lacked clarification in distinguishing one from the other – a bedevilling omission that would not be remedied until the early 1990s. See Statute on National Nature Parks of the Russian Federation, Resolution of the Council of the Russian Federation Government No.769, 10 August 1993, and Federal Statute on Specially Protected Natural Territories, section III, National Parks.

6 Reimers and Shtil'mark, *Osobo okhranniaemye prirodnye territorii* [Specially Protected Natural Territories], 52.

7 This journal, published bimonthly from 1928 to 1930, included an article on Yellowstone National Park with translated excerpts from Teddy Roosevelt's autobiographical reminiscences on the early exploration of that region. See Weiner, *Models of Nature*, 49.

8 Weiner, *Models of Nature*, 51.

9 Though never a dominant Soviet conservation paradigm, the *"landschaft"* model formed the basis for the United Kingdom's national park system, specifically that of Great Britain and Wales, stimulated by post-Second World War populism and given the composition of the highly modified countryside to be preserved. This national park paradigm has diffused worldwide as socio-political factors of necessity incorporated resident populations and their activities within proposed national park boundaries.

10 Reimers and Shtil'mark, *Osobo okhranniaemye prirodnye territorii*, 51.

11 See Conant. "Look Inside Russia's Wildest Nature Reserves."

12 World Wildlife Fund's 1994 regional synopsis, for instance, begins with the erroneous but self-justifying statement that "Russia's specially protected natural territories form a unified system whose primary purpose is biodiversity conservation and research of natural processes and phenomena." Krever, Dinerstein, Olson, and Williams, eds, *Conserving Russia's Biological Diversity*.

13 Feshbach and Friendly, *Ecocide in the USSR;* and Pryde, *Environmental Resources and Constraints in the Former Soviet Republics.*

14 A conspicuous exception to this genre continues to be the historian Douglas Weiner's treatise on *zapovedniki*, *Models of Nature*, though its chronological narrative unfortunately expires along with Stalin. Seminal works on the origins and development of North American national parks (e.g., Nash, *Wilderness and the American Mind*; Fox, *The American Conservation Movement*) tend to corroborate the tautology that historians are best at writing history.

15 See, for instance, Runte, *National Parks*; Albright, *The Birth of the National Park Service*; and Fox, *The American Conservation Movement*.

16 Nash, *Wilderness and the American Mind*, 135. Muir went on to found the Sierra Club, while Pinchot became the first director of the federal Forest Service.

17 An anecdote illustrates the prevalence of this attitude even in the early years of the Soviet Union. Mikhail Prishvin, one of Russia's great nature writers, in his book *Nature's Diary*, recalls during an expedition in the mid-1920s coming upon a group of young "proletariat" students shooting birds for biological study. Upon being asked why they perpetrated such carnage when specimens aplenty were available in the universities and science academies, their answer was that they wanted to begin afresh, untainted by bourgeois perspectives. Though comparatively benign in 1925, such biases rapidly hardened under Stalin into formulae for judging the legitimacy of thoughts, actions, and ultimately one's existence within Soviet society.

18 Marx, *Capital*, 199. Marx's perspective, though uncompromisingly utilitarian, was also influenced by the empiricist Francis Bacon's claim that "Nature can be conquered only by obeying her" (Bacon, quoted in Chappell, "The Ecological Dimension," 161). To obey, one must understand – thus the need for *zapovedniki*. It was Stalin's impatience with the pace of this formula, not Marx's original man-land theories, that brought about the full devaluation of Soviet nature.

19 Excerpted from Maxim Gorky's *Belomor*, a paean to the (forced labour) construction of the White Sea Canal connecting Leningrad on the Gulf of Finland northwards through lakes Lagoda and Onega to the White Sea and the Arctic Ocean.

20 It should be noted that this perspective, especially interest in the scientific manipulation of species and ecosystems, continues to find resonance amongst segments of Russian parks and protected areas personnel as well as within the general public.

21 The arch-villain in Weiner's work, I.I. Prezent (Stalin's appointed vice-regent of proletarian science), attacked ecological views that argued the existence of limits to the transformation of the earth's "vegetative and faunal cover," demoting nature to biomass in the process of asking the

rhetorical question, "Why study a concept that does not exist?" (see Weiner, *Models of Nature*, 221). In the post-Soviet era, the propensity for collecting observational rather than analytical data continued to be enshrined in the annual *Letopis Priroda* [Chronicle of Nature] reports, accounts of each *zapovednik*'s natural inventory forwarded upward through the ministry's decision-making process. An antiquated exercise even before the collapse of the Soviet system, it came to be viewed even by *zapovednik* personnel as a useless tool, "often no more scientific than the gossip one would collect at the market place" (Barguzinski Zapovednik, personal communication, July 1993). Whether cause or effect, the fact that "scientific workers" comprised only 9 per cent of total *zapovednik* personnel gave further credence to such observations (Ryzhikov, "Regional Differences in Expenditures on Maintenance of Nature Reserves," 381). Nevertheless, in their guise as a "vast biodiversity data base" (W.M. Eichbaum, World Wildlife Fund, personal communication, April 1995), these repositories gained a dubious respectability amongst international agencies enamoured of information management: for example, "Aid earmarked for improved information management will allow published and unpublished data on biodiversity within *zapovedniki* – painstakingly recorded over the decades in field notebooks – to be transferred into relational databases and geographic information systems" (Dinerstein, "An Emergency Strategy," 935; also see Grigoriew and Lopoukhine, "Russian Protected Areas Assistance Project," 4). For an example of the product's eclecticism, see Volkov, *Strict Nature Reserves (Zapovedniki) of Russia: Collection of "Chronicle of Nature" Data for 1991–1992.*
22 August 1951 Decree No. 3191, "On *Zapovedniki*," abolished 88 of the country's 128 *zapovedniki*.
23 Intertwining with the rise in the value of nature as a spiritual entity was a concurrent resurgence of religion as a core tenet of societal well-being.
24 Meinig, "The Interpretation of Ordinary Landscapes," 109.
25 Weiner, *Models of Nature*, 269.
26 Nikolai Maxakovsky, Ministry of Culture, personal communication, May 1993.
27 Guseva and Tseveliov, "Management of Protected Landscapes in Russia."
28 In Sochinsky's case, a jurisdictional anomaly may have contributed to the process. A portion of the territory that became the park was a Moscow-controlled (rather than regionally controlled) *leskhoz* (forest service) unit.
29 The *Directory of Environmental Groups in the Newly Independent States and Baltic Nations* published in 1992 includes 282 Russian NGOs. Over 60 per cent of these organizations espouse region-specific objectives, while at least another 10 per cent viewed their roles as that of coordinating "umbrella" associations. Of those that noted a founding date, none had existed before the mid-1980s.

30 The question does arise as to why the peripheral republics suddenly ceased proclaiming national parks. Most likely, with the rapid accrual of political autonomy followed by independence, establishment of national parks lost much of its symbolic significance, and attention shifted to the resolution of more immediate internal agendas.

31 *Russian Conservation News* 2 (1995), 4.

32 The term originally referred to fortified ramparts protected by sharpened stakes with points facing outwards to prevent assailants from mounting the walls. Adopted and adapted by Russia on a grand scale, the concept came to include modification of forests through selective felling and afforestation to increase impenetrability and continuity of the defence line. The point to be made here is that immense manipulations of nature have long been a feature of Russian landscapes, yet continue to be viewed in the West as environmentally unsound "Communist" aberrations.

33 Ponomarenko, "The Green Wall of Russia." For example, Kerzhenski Zapovednik in the Nizhegorodskaya Oblast, established in 1993, consists of a village, fields, degraded woodlands, copses of older trees along a riverbank, and, as a sop to biodiversity, "some sort of unusual rodent." Reforestation, environmental education, and restoration of the local economy have been declared the site's prioritized projects (Melissa Levy, personal communication, October 1995).

34 For instance, British Columbia's Ministry of Environment variants, charged with nature protection, and the Forest Ministry with its emphasis on timber extraction.

35 Popova, "United Policy Management in the *Zapovedniki* and National Parks of Russia."

36 Maleshin, "A Cloud over the Protected Areas,"2.

37 Ibid., 3.

38 Stepanitsky, "Why I Left the Russian Ministry of Natural Resources."

39 Gordon, "Civil Society, Environmental Organizations and Putin," 18.

40 Maleshin, "The Farcical Third All-Russian Congress of Nature Conservation," 2–3.

41 To quote the catastrophic chain of events: "Dec. 5 telegram to all national parks and *zapovedniki* regarding the inexpediency of their future existence and demanding documents and budgets to justify their continuation. Dec. 8 second telegram from the same deputy minister stating the first had been sent mistakenly and those who made the error will be reprimanded. Dec. 15 Order 1107 On the Incorporation of Changes to the staffing of federal national parks and *zapovedniki* incorporating a suite of five deputy directors on each site." See Williams, Shvarts, and Maleshin, "A Long Dark Month for Russia's Protected Areas," 4.

42 Maleshin, "As 2003 Closes, No Reassurance for Protected Area Managers," 7.

43 "Speaking at a government meeting dedicated to the development of Russia's preserved natural territories, Putin said a total of 21 national parks will appear in Russia and 11 sites will be significantly enlarged." *R.I.A. Novosti* on National Geographic website: https://www.national geographic.com. Accessed 29 October 2018.

44 "Concept for the Development of the System of Specially Protected Territories of Federal Importance to 2020." Government resolution No. 2322-r 22/Dec 2011.

45 An occurrence not confined to Russian national parks. In 1968 at the height of the US environmental movement, Redwood National Park was established along the northern coast of California. It marked the first instance, still singular in its rarity, where preservation of a known valuable natural resource formed the basis for site designation.

46 Anyusky National Park in Khabarovsk Krai, though ostensibly founded in 1999 previous to the Putin era, was thereafter reconfigured to exclude potential gold mining operations. (Personal observation.)

47 Guess, "Arctic National Parks – Establishing National Sovereignty or Genuine Promotion of Tourism."

48 In Russia, without a "roof" (sponsor/protector/legitimizer), one can only be an intruder. This perspective operates at all societal levels, with the government as the ultimate arbiter of acceptance. Organizations disregarding the need of government oversight, much less resistant to it and/or its dictates, as with many international NGOs that arose in Russia in the 1990s, were tolerated yet conceptually incomprehensible. Conversely, even as cold war rhetoric re-enters the international dialogue, areas of government-approved cooperation continue to thrive, including in the sphere of nature protection, converging perceptually as the study and application of environmental best-use strategies.

49 In theory the zoning system provides an integrated approach by which the territories of a national park are classified according to ecosystem and cultural resource protection requirements and the site's capability to provide sustainable visitor experiences. Zones range from strict protection (1) and wilderness (2), through natural environment (3), outdoor recreation (4), and park services (5). As a planning mechanism, the ability of the system to ameliorate preservation/conservation/economic development conflicts has gained it a wide range of adherents, despite the frequent shortcomings of its on-ground efficacy.

50 Walsh, "Putin Diverts New Oil Pipeline from Lake Baikal after Protests." To set the decision in its immediate context, Putin at the time was meeting in the central Siberian city of Tomsk with Angela Merkel and being

pressured by UNESCO to change the route or have Lake Baikal possibly lose its prestigious World Heritage Site status – the right occasion for a "good news" story?

51 Complaints that it and other similar sites are not being sufficiently federally funded overlook the fact that they carry the stigma of their "illicit" beginnings. Roe, "The Forest in the Metropolis." Elk Island's proximity to Moscow makes it especially susceptible to development pressures. An October 2019 petition with 250,000 signatures against such intrusions attests both to the site's vulnerability and to the viability of its supporter base: https://zona.media/news.2019/05/28 losiny_ostrov.

52 All Primorski site descriptions, except for Zov Tigra, note as one of their roles the preservation of Udeghe and Nanai native cultures.

53 Williams, "Reflections on the Beginning of March for Parks." Exemplifying the rapidity of change in the early post-Soviet years, Williams relates how she read of March for Parks in the National Parks Conservation Association publication and within a year had equivalent programs running in Russia. By 1997 nearly all protected areas in the country were participating.

REFERENCES

Albright, H.M. *The Birth of the National Park Service*. Salt Lake City, UT: Howe Brothers, 1985.

Anderson, David G. "'*Etnos*-Thinking' in 1917 and Today." In *Revolutionary Aftereffects: Material, Social, and Cultural Legacies of 1917 in Russia Today*, edited by Megan Swift, 140–55. Toronto: University of Toronto Press, 2022.

Belt, D. "Russia's Lake Baikal: The World's Great Lake." *National Geographic* 181, 6 (1992): 2–39.

Chappell, J.E., Jr. "The Ecological Dimension: Russian and American Views." *Annals of the Association of American Geographers* 65, 2 (1975): 144–62.

Conant, E. "Look Inside Russia's Wildest Nature Reserves – Now Turning 100." *National Geographic*, 10 June 2017.

"Concept for the Development of the System of Specially Protected Territories of Federal Importance to 2020." Government resolution No. 2322-r 22/Dec. 2011.

Danilov, G. *Novaya Zemlya*, April 2010.

Dinerstein, E. "An Emergency Strategy to Rescue Russia's Biological Diversity." *Conservation Biology* 8, 4 (1994): 934–42.

Feshbach, M., and A. Friendly, Jr. *Ecocide in the USSR: Health under Siege*. New York: Basic Books, 1992.

Fondahl, G.A. "Native Economy and Northern Development: Reindeer Husbandry in Transbaykali." PhD diss., Department of Geography, University of California, Berkeley, CA, 1989.
– "First Nation Rights to Land and Resources: An Evaluation of Russian Legislative Approaches and Their Implications in Southeastern Siberia." Paper presented at the Russian-American Working Seminar on Problems of the Peoples of the North, Ministry of Nationality Affairs and Regional Policy, Moscow, May 1995.
– *Freezing the Frontier? Territories of Traditional Nature Use in the Russian North.* Unpublished draft manuscript, Faculty of Natural Resources and Environmental Studies, University of Northern British Columbia, Prince George, BC, 1995.
Forsyth, J. *A History of the Peoples of Siberia: Russia's North Asian Colony, 1581–1990.* New York: Cambridge University Press, 1992.
Fox, S. *The American Conservation Movement.* Madison: University of Wisconsin Press, 1985.
Galazy, G.I. *Baikal: Questions and Answers.* Irkutsk: East Siberian Book Publications, 1987.
Gavva, I.A., V.V. Krinitsky, and Y.P. Yazan. "Development of Nature Reserves and National Parks in the USSR." In *National Parks, Conservation, and Development: The Role of Protected Areas in Sustaining Society,* edited by J.A. McNeely and K.R. Miller, 463–5. Washington, DC: Smithsonian Institution Press, 1984.
Getches, D.H. "Managing the Public Lands: The Authority of the Executive to Withdraw Lands." *Natural Resources Journal* 4, 22 (1982): 279–335.
Gordon, D. "Civil Society, Environmental Organizations and Putin." *Russian Conservation News* 39 (2005): 17–18.
Grigoriew, P., and N. Lopoukhine. "Russian Protected Areas Assistance Project." Report prepared for the World Bank by the Canadian Department of External Affairs and Parks Canada. Ottawa: October 1993.
Guess, Anneliese. "Arctic National Parks – Establishing National Sovereignty or Genuine Promotion of Tourism." 17 September 2011: https://www.thearcticinstitute.org/arctic-national-parks-sovereignty. Accessed 4 January 2019.
Guseva, T., and V. Tseveliov. "Management of Protected Landscapes in Russia." Workshop paper presented at Hatfield Polytechnic Institute, England, February 1992.
IUCN – The World Conservation Union. "Action Plan for Central and Eastern Europe--Losiny Ostrov." Report presented at the Second Pan-European Conference, Strasbourg, 26–7 November 1992: 240–51.
Krever, V., E. Dinerstein, D. Olson, and L. Williams, eds. *Conserving Russia's Biological Diversity: An Analytical Framework and Initial Investment Portfolio.* Washington, DC: World Wildlife Fund, 1994.

Maleshin, N. "A Cloud over the Protected Areas." *Russian Conservation News* 28 (Winter 2002–Spring 2003): 2.

– "The Farcical Third All-Russian Congress of Nature Conservation." *Russian Conservation News* 34 (2003–4): 2–3.

– "As 2003 Closes, No Reassurance for Protected Area Managers." *Russian Conservation News* 34 (2003–4): 7–8.

Marsh, G.P. *Man and Nature, or Physical Geography as Modified by Human Action.* Cambridge, MA: Belknap Press, 1965. (Original work published 1864.)

Marx, K. *Capital: A Critique of Political Economy.* Translated by S. Moore and E. Aveling. New York: Random House, 1906. (Original work published 1867.)

Matthiessen, P. *Baikal: Sacred Sea of Siberia.* San Francisco: Sierra Club Books, 1992.

Meinig, D. "The Interpretation of Ordinary Landscapes." *Geographical Journal* 147, 1 (1981): 109–19.

Micklin, P.P. "The Baykal Controversy: A Resource Use Conflict in the U.S.S.R." *National Resources Journal* 7, 3 (1967): 485–98.

Mote, V.L. "BAM after the Fanfare." In *Soviet Natural Resources in the World Economy,* edited by T. Shabat and A.W. Wright, 40–56. Chicago: University of Chicago Press, 1983.

– "BAM, Boom, or Bust: Analysis of a Railway's Past, Present, and Future." *Soviet Geography* 31 (1990): 321–31.

Nash, R. *Wilderness and the American Mind.* 3rd ed. New Haven, CT: Yale University Press, 1982.

Nikolaevski, A.G. *National Parks.* Moscow: Agropromizdat, 1985.

Oldfield, J.D. *Russian Nature: Exploring the Environmental Consequences of Societal Change.* London: Routledge, 2005.

Polyan, P.M. "Geography and the Inspiration of Nature." *Soviet Geography* 26 (1985): 229–38.

Ponomarenko, S. "The Green Wall of Russia." *Russian Conservation News* (October 1994): 12–13.

Popova, S. "United Policy Management in the Zapovedniki and National Parks of Russia." *Zapovedny Vestnik* in *Russian Conservation News* 31 (2000:) 11–13.

Prishvin, M. *Nature's Diary.* Translated by Lev Navrosov. New York: Penguin Books, 1987. (Original work published 1925.)

Pryde, P.R. "The First Soviet National Park." *National Parks Magazine* 41, 4 (1967): 20–3.

– *Environmental Resources and Constraints in the Former Soviet Republics.* Boulder, CO: Westview Press, 1995.

Rasputin, Valentin. (1981) "Baikal." In *Siberia on Fire: Stories and Essays,* translated by Gerald Mikkelson and Margaret Winchell. DeKalb, IL: Northern Illinois University Press, 1989.

Reimers, N.F., and F.R. Shtil'mark. *Osobo okhraniaemye prirodnye territorii* [Specially Protected Natural Territories]. Moscow: Mysl', 1978.

Roe, A. "The Forest in the Metropolis: Elk Island (Losinyi Ostrov) National Park and the Disappointment of the Russian National Park Movement." *Soviet and Post-Soviet Review* 45, 3 (2018): 287–312.

Runte, A. *National Parks: The American Experience.* 2nd ed. Lincoln: University of Nebraska Press, 1987.

Ryzhikov, A.I. "Regional Differences in Expenditures on Maintenance of Nature Reserves." *Soviet Geography* 31 (1990): 375–82.

Sakharov, A. *The Wonders and Problems of Lake Baikal.* Moscow: Novosti Press, 1989.

– *Irkutsk and Lake Baikal.* Moscow: Planeta Publishers, 1990.

– *Memoirs.* New York: Alfred A. Knopf, 1990.

Stepanitsky, V. "Why I Left the Russian Ministry of Natural Resources" *Russian Conservation News* 28 (2003): 3.

Supreme Soviet of the USSR. *Projected Principles for Legislation in the USSR and the Republics for Specially Protected Nature Areas.* Moscow: 7 July 1991.

Tripp, Michael. "The Emergence of National Parks in Russia with Studies of Pribaikalski and Zabaikalski National Parks in the Lake Baikal Region of South Central Siberia." PhD diss., University of Victoria, 1998.

Volkov, A.E., ed. *Strict Nature Reserves (Aapovedniki) of Russia: Collection of "Chronicle of Nature" Data for 1991–1992.* Moscow: Sabashnikov Publishers, 1996.

Vorob'yev, V.V., and A.V. Martynov. "Protected Areas of the Lake Baykal Basin." *Soviet Geography* 30 (1989): 359–70.

Walsh, N. "Putin Diverts New Oil Pipeline from Lake Baikal after Protests." *The Guardian,* 27 April 2006.

Weiner, D.R. *Models of Nature.* Bloomington, IN: University of Indiana Press, 1988.

– *A Little Corner of Freedom: Russian Nature Protection from Stalin to Gorbachev.* Berkeley: University of California Press, 1999.

Williams, M. "Reflections on the Beginning of March for Parks." *Russian Conservation News* 39 (2005): 2–3.

Williams, M., E. Shvarts, and N. Maleshin. "A Long Dark Month for Russia's Protected Areas." *Russian Conservation News* 34 (2004): 4–5.

PART III

Artistic and Conceptual Aftereffects

7 The Hero and the Revolution in the Works of Boris Akunin and Akunin-Chkhartishvili

ELENA V. BARABAN

The Centennial of the Revolution and the Heroes of Our Time

The centennial of the October Revolution sparked anew a debate about the significance of this "most consequential event of the 20th century."[1] The anniversary inspired a new cycle of scholarly discussions as well as many popular representations of the revolution. Apart from the festivities organized by Russia's communist parties, there were no large-scale public celebrations of the event of the kind that used to be prepared by the Soviet government.[2] The absence of government-sponsored celebrations in 2017 caused a number of commentators to note that the centennial was a source of anxiety or even embarrassment for the present-day power in Russia.[3] Even if it may be groundless, such critical assessment of the Russian authorities' incoherence with regard to the revolution is nonetheless important in revealing a certain longing for guidance on the issue. Indeed, the shifts in the public perception of the February and the October Revolutions of 1917 continue to take place, and, unlike in the Soviet period, there is no definitive recommendation as to how the revolution is to be assessed.[4] However, might there be something positive in the public controversy surrounding the anniversary of the October Revolution and, in general, the idea of a revolution as a way of social transformation? Could the coexistence of celebratory, appreciative, negative, and mixed responses to the revolution indicate society's willingness to engage in a mature discussion of its history and its socially significant events?[5]

The collapse of the Soviet state initiated a series of radical recodifications of the causes, course, and outcomes of the revolution. Established in 1918, the tradition to celebrate the October Revolution with a public demonstration and, starting from 1922, a military parade on Red Square (as well as demonstrations and parades in other cities and towns across the Soviet Union) was abandoned in 1991.[6] In 1995, the military parade on 7 November in celebration of the revolution was replaced for the first time by a re-enactment of the 1941 parade of the defenders of Moscow, a high point in rallying the Soviet people during the Great Patriotic War. This substitution signalled a shift in emphasis, from celebrating the revolution to celebrating Soviet patriotism during the Second World War.[7] The whole point of the 1941 parade, namely a demonstration to the entire world that the Soviet state, itself a symbol of the triumphant revolution, was alive, was no longer highlighted. The re-enactments of the parade on 7 November 1941 have taken place every year since 2000. In turn, the parade and other events in celebration of the revolution were dropped. Still a statutory holiday, from 1996 until 2004, 7 November was "celebrated" as the Day of Agreement and Reconciliation (Den' soglasiia i primireniia). In 2005, this holiday was abandoned, and 7 November became a regular working day. To compensate for the loss of a day off, a new statutory holiday was established – the Day of People's Unity (Den' narodnogo edinstva) – to be celebrated on 4 November. Formally, it refers to the events that took place during the Time of Troubles when, at the end of the Polish-Russian War (1605–18), Kuzma Minin and Prince Dmitrii Pozharsky formed an army to protect Moscow. Markedly atraumatic for today's Russians and decidedly irrelevant for either re-evaluating the Soviet past or making sense of the post-Soviet decades, this holiday nonetheless suggests the idea of unity. Unity sounds simultaneously less demanding and less pessimistic than the reconciliation that was previously suggested as a replacement for the celebrations of the revolution. At the same time, this ephemeral unity, suddenly catapulted from the seventeenth century, is a kind of simulacrum (in Jean Baudrillard's understanding of the term) – that is, a reference with no referent, a pseudo-unity that substitutes, through simulation, for something that disappeared in the 1990s.[8]

The Soviet framework for telling a story about the revolution, whereby the historical truth (istoricheskaia pravda) was on the side of the Bolsheviks (the Reds), collapsed in the Yeltsin era.[9] Post-Soviet narratives about the revolution and the civil war have reversed Soviet-era interpretations of these events. They show them from a point of view that had not been adequately represented during the Soviet period, most notably from the point of view of the Whites.[10] According to Stephen M. Norris, even when they reverse Soviet-era narratives, the recent films about the revolution and the civil war reaffirm their significance as defining events in Russian history and help to connect the past and the present in the Russian consciousness.[11] By contrast, while examining the same kind of popular post-Soviet narratives about the revolution, Mark Lipovetsky states that recent productions convey the public's indifference to the topic.[12] The scholars essentially disagree about whether post-Soviet depictions of the revolutionary past suggest society's real engagement with it or are merely simulacra, a front that conceals a vacuum.

Instead of debating which of the above assessments is viable, I propose to examine characterization in depictions of the revolution – an indispensable component of so-called genre narratives, adventure stories, or melodramas.[13] To be specific, characterization makes the story vivid and believable for the reader or viewer. Consideration of characterization in representations of the revolution is also important for another reason. Underlying the attempts to drop the idea of celebrating the revolution from recent re-enactments of the military parade on 7 November 1941 and instead to make the victory over Nazism in the Second World War into a central unifying moment in Russian history is the longing for national heroes. The latter help Russians identify themselves as heirs to a great past. In the 1990s the revolution ceased to be a suitable setting for a heroic narrative. No representations of the revolution and the civil war today can offer heroic narratives that would be acceptable for the majority of Russians and that could contribute to Russia's patriotic drive.

To be sure, the recent depictions of these events are not mere inversions of the traditional Soviet narrative. Indeed, the positive rendering of the Whites in post-Soviet films does not mean the Whites become "true heroes," the role models for the younger generation. In fact, these characters are depicted as victims of the revolution. Having misunderstood the causes of the revolution, they could not offer Russia anything but a return to an imperfect past.[14] They were either killed or eventually ceased their struggle and accepted an inglorious exile.

Whereas some present-day narratives show the Whites with sympathy but ultimately as losers, other narratives redefine the revolution's leaders. They strip them of the status of heroes. By doing so and offering no substitutes for these formerly positive images, they leave a gap in the semantic field once occupied by Bolshevik leaders. Such are, for example, the two television mini-series released for the centennial, *Trotsky* (*Trotskii*, 2017), directed by Aleksandr Kott and Sergei Statskii, and *The Demon of the Revolution* (*Demon revolutsii*, 2017), directed by Vladimir Khotinenko.[15] Both TV series portray Leon Trotsky, Vladimir Lenin, Alexander Parvus, and other top revolutionaries as highly ambitious, self-serving, greedy, immoral, or even psychopathic individuals who relied on support from foreign intelligence in order to prepare the revolution in Russia. Xenophobic and anti-Semitic in their ideology, these narratives present the leaders of the revolution as essentially traitors, while the revolution itself is viewed as a Western import.

On the one hand, by featuring Trotsky and Parvus as well as the revolution's leaders of the second order (such as, for example, Grigorii Zinoviev, Carl Radek, and Inessa Armand), both television mini-series fill in "the gap" in the viewers' knowledge of Russia's history by providing a detailed portrayal of historical figures who have been "forgotten" in Soviet popular histories. On the other hand, by filling in the information gap, these representations still leave the narrative about the revolution and the civil war devoid of any heroic component. Certainly not as postmodernist in their simulation of a heroic portrayal of the revolution and the civil war as, for example, Victor Pelevin's novel *Buddha's Little Finger* (*Chapaev i pustota*, 1996), these depictions are not mere "reversals" of the heroic narrative about the revolution, which were typical of the Soviet period.[16] Soon after Lenin's death and for almost the entire Soviet period, Trotsky did not "exist" as a positive hero. Moreover, following the Stalin era he practically did not exist as a character in Russian popular narratives at all. Post-Soviet representations of the revolution began to detail his image, but they did not make Trotsky a hero. The same is true of Alexander Parvus. Never even featured in the Soviet Union as a force behind the revolution, Parvus is resurrected from oblivion to highlight the idea that Lenin manipulated his sponsors and fellow revolutionaries to become the revolution's leader. In Khotinenko's film, Lenin tells Parvus that the revolution must be done with "clean hands," which means Parvus is not morally fit to become part of the Bolshevik government after the revolution. However, the scene itself (with Lenin essentially out-cheating Parvus) underscores how unscrupulous Lenin was in his drive for power.[17] The "cleanliness" of his hands, as the TV series depicts, is more than questionable.

In both TV series released for the centennial of the revolution, the defenders of the tsarist regime are portrayed as victims of the revolution and therefore as lacking the vital qualities of true heroes. They abandon their struggle by either failing or leaving their posts.[18] Both narratives thus contribute to a complete destruction of the heroic narrative about the revolution and the civil war. They further dismantle the myth that revolutions are times of heroes. Although perhaps no less inaccurate than Soviet narratives, such portrayals of this period in Russian history are culturally significant, for they reinforce the view of the revolution as a tragedy.

The Writer and the Revolution: Chkhartishvili, Akunin, and Akunin-Chkhartishvili

In this article I trace the formation of a non-heroic narrative about the revolution and the civil war in the novels by Grigorii Chkhartishvili, the most famous of living Russian authors.[19] Mostly known under the pen name Boris Akunin, Chkhartishvili has published more than seventy books, both in series and individually. Editions of his bestsellers reach up to half a million copies.[20] The writer's celebrity status has been reinforced by his political activism.[21] His depiction of the revolution and the civil war is important not only because of the writer's popularity but also because of the novelty of his approach in depicting these events. Their non-heroic depiction by Chkhartishvili resonates well with Russian readers. According to polls conducted on the occasion of the centennial, 92 per cent of the population considers that a revolution is unacceptable (*nedopustima*).[22] Chkhartishvili grounds his characters' non-heroic response to the revolution in the position of individualism. The writer demonstrates that instead of producing heroes, the revolution and the civil war effectively killed them. Unlike many melodramatically depicted White officers in recent films, Akunin's characters understand the reasons that led to the revolution and therefore refuse to defend tsarism. At the same time, they do not (quite) accept the new regime. Instead of taking sides in a social dispute and thus representing *a collective*, they act on individualistic impulses.

In my analysis, I refer to Akunin's novels from his best-selling detective series starring Erast Fandorin, a secret agent in the service of the tsarist police, and to the series *The Family Album* (*Semeinyi al'bom*), published under the pen name Akunin-Chkhartishvili.[23] *The Family Album* so far comprises four novels: *Aristonomy* (*Aristonomiia*, 2012), *The Other Path* (*Drugoi put'*, 2015), *Happy Russia* (*Schastlivaia Rossiia*, 2017), and *Treasury* (*Trezorium*, 2019).[24] The novel *Not Saying Goodbye* (*Ne proshchaius'*, 2018), the last one in the Erast Fandorin series, and *Aristonomy*, the first novel in *The Family Album*, are the only narratives set during the revolution and the civil war. However, other novels from the Fandorin series and *The Family Album* are also important for understanding the author's view of the revolution. Despite the fact that the Fandorin series is in a light genre, described by Akunin as *belles-lettres*, and *The Family Album* is marketed as "serious" literature, both illustrate the same kind of approach to depicting the revolution as crushing the hero. Contrary to the depictions of revolutions as the time of heroes (inspired by the works of Thomas Carlyle and his followers), Akunin shows that the revolution, the civil war, and Stalinist Russia effectively killed heroes.[25]

Live Fast and Die Young: The Last Novel about the Last Hero

In February 2018, Akunin killed Erast Fandorin, a detective who had fascinated readers since 1998 with his courage, intelligence, patriotism, cosmopolitanism, knowledge of foreign languages, mastery of martial arts, and – simply – his elegance and good looks. Immediately upon the release of *Not Saying Goodbye*, readers complained that there was "not enough Fandorin" in the novel and expressed the hope that Fandorin could come back to life.[26] Indeed, the title of the novel as well as the depiction of Fandorin's death leave the reader hoping that, should the author wish, he could resurrect his hero. Furthermore, the narrative technique used in the second-last chapter, titled, like the novel itself, "Not Saying Goodbye," helps to sustain this hope.[27] Fandorin here is the narrator. He describes to his wife, Mona, the circumstances surrounding his death. There is, however, no depiction of the hero's dead body or the burial. Fandorin (who is presumably already in heaven) simply tells his wife that he is "being called" and that he is "not saying goodbye."[28] Moreover, the reader's hope that Fandorin might come back to life could also be nurtured by examples. The ending of *The Black City* (*Chernyi gorod*, 2013), the second-last novel in the Erast Fandorin series, leaves the reader in suspense. It ends with a scene when the revolutionaries in Baku execute the famous detective with a gunshot to his head. The readers assume that this is not the end of their favourite hero because Fandorin is not declared dead and also because of the author's promise that there would be one more novel in the series. In *Not Saying Goodbye*, the reader learns that back in 1914 Fandorin was wounded and fell into a coma. Thanks to the self-sacrificial efforts of his devoted Japanese companion, Masa, Fandorin awakens from his "deep sleep" in 1918. Seeing no sense (*pravda* [truth]) in post-revolutionary Russia, the hero refuses to side with the Whites, the Reds, or the Black and the Green anarchists. Fandorin and Masa decide to leave Russia via the Crimea in order to continue their pursuit of spiritual and physical perfection. In the summer of 1919, on his way to Sevastopol, Fandorin falls in love. He marries Mona Turusova, the daughter of Varvara Suvorova, a woman whom Fandorin had protected during the Russo-Turkish War (1877–8).[29] Fandorin, Mona, and Masa are stuck for some time in Kharkov, occupied by the Whites. While waiting for the moment when his pregnant wife feels well enough to leave for the Crimea, Fandorin helps with investigations of crimes in which innocent people were killed.

He does not care for the Whites' "historical mission," but he cannot be indifferent when innocent orphaned children die as the novel's villain attempts to kill a commander of the White army. Fandorin solves the crime but fails to remove the perpetrator, who, in turn, sets up a bomb that kills Fandorin. In the last chapter, which is set two years after Fandorin's death, the reader learns that Fandorin's son is being raised in Switzerland and that Masa has avenged his master's death.

On the one hand, even though Akunin insists that *Not Saying Goodbye* is his "farewell" to the series, the conventions of the adventure novel could easily allow a sequel to this novel.[30] Such a sequel could explain how Fandorin managed to survive the explosion on his motor-powered draisine. On the other hand, given the historical circumstances in which Akunin kills Fandorin, the hero's death is logical and therefore inevitable. The chronological setting of this novel – the civil war – is crucial for completing the series. Even if Fandorin miraculously survives the explosion and emigrates from Russia, there is nothing left for him to do as a hero. In a sense, by sending Fandorin into a coma for almost three years between 1914 and 1918, Akunin has already prepared his readers for the removal of this hero. A relatively short chronological gap of three years between the events described in *The Black City* and *Not Saying Goodbye* is different from longer chronological gaps between earlier stories about Fandorin. This short stretch of time that Fandorin "misses" seals his fate. His coma frees him of the responsibility to prevent the revolution. This, however, was his mission. In *The Black City* the revolutionaries decide to kill Fandorin not only because he was hunting one of their leaders but also, and primarily, because Fandorin was assigned a new secret mission: to go to Europe in order to prevent the First World War from taking place. As presented in *The Black City*, the Russian tsarist authorities realize that should the First World War take place, it would bring about the demise of the Habsburgs and also destabilize Russia. The revolutionaries in turn need the war as a catalyst for the revolution. By 1918, the time when the narration in *Not Saying Goodbye* begins, the worst has already happened. Not only has Fandorin not fulfilled his mission; he has also been left without a new one. He cannot turn back the tide of history and cannot be a hero. Under the new conditions, there is no political force whose mission he could validate by making it his own.

It is not accidental in this regard that in the opening chapter of *Not Saying Goodbye*, Fandorin is a comical figure. Masa's fellow-travellers on the Samara–Moscow train initially think that the huge package that "the Asian man" (*aziat*) takes with him to the train compartment contains *manufaktura*, some fabric to be sold in Moscow.[31] Then, when Masa uncovers Fandorin's face, the co-travellers worry that they are sharing their train ride with a corpse. Masa's explanation that his master has been *sleeping* since 1914 elicits "an envious" comment from a fellow-traveller: "What a lucky person! I would also have gladly fallen asleep in 1914. I'd ask, 'Please wake me up, my dear friends, when life comes back to normal.' Isn't it great? People beat, slaughter, and rob each other, and this one does nothing but snores about."[32] Although Masa cuts short the woman's disrespectful remark by asserting that if Fandorin had not "fallen asleep" he would not have allowed the First World War and the revolution to take place, overall this scene takes the hero off his pedestal.[33] He is no better than a common person who wishes she could have been relieved of the burden of living through the First World War and the revolution. Even if Masa emphasizes that his master did not fear the responsibility of saving the world from a catastrophe, the truth is that his mission has remained unaccomplished.

This opening of *Not Saying Goodbye* is in sharp contrast with the description of Fandorin in the introductory chapter of *The Death of Achilles* (*Smert' Akhillesa*, 1998), which is also set at the railway station, following the hero's six-year absence from Russia:

> The morning train from St. Petersburg [...] had scarcely slowed to a halt at the platform of Nikolaevsky Station [...] when a young man attired in quite remarkable style leapt out of one of the first-class carriages. He seemed to have sprung straight out of some picture in a Parisian magazine devoted to the glories of the 1882 summer-season fashion: a light suit of sandy-colored wild silk, a wide-brimmed hat of Italian straw, shoes with pointed toes, white spats with silver press-studs, and in his hand an elegant walking cane with a knob that was also silver. However, it was not so much the passenger's foppish attire that attracted attention as his physique, which was quite imposing, one might almost say spectacular. The young man was tall, with a trim figure and wide shoulders. He regarded the world through clear blue eyes, and his slim mustache with curled ends sat quite extraordinarily well with his regular features, which included one distinctive peculiarity – the neatly combed black hair shaded intriguingly into silver-gray at the temples.[34]

The contrast between the young, strong, elegant, and attractive Fandorin in 1882 and the half-dead body that Masa carries around in a bag in 1918 is further underscored by the reversal of the original roles of Fandorin and Masa. In 1882, Masa, who then appears in the Fandorin series for the first time, is introduced as part of Fandorin's luggage: "In addition to suitcases and traveling bags, [the porters] carried out onto the platform a folding tricycle, a set of gymnastic weights, and bundles of books in various languages. Last of all there emerged from the carriage a short, bandy-legged oriental gentleman with a compact physique and an extremely solemn face and fat cheeks."[35] In *Not Saying Goodbye*, Fandorin is Masa's "luggage." Although Fandorin regains his physical and intellectual strength as the novel unfolds and also his "still" good looks, the narrator has to engage himself in the comments about the hero's aging in order to make him suitable for the novel's adventure story and the love sub-plot.

According to Margery Hourihan, in adventure narratives "heroes are young. In most versions of the myth there is no recognition of a future in which they will grow old. [...] Where images of old heroes do occur, they are depicted as dissatisfied, dreaming of the past."[36] This observation is relevant for understanding the characterization of Fandorin. The action of *Not Saying Goodbye* starts when Fandorin is sixty-two and has been "sleeping" for the last three years. At the age when Hercule Poirot already felt bored and bitter after he had retired from crime investigations, Fandorin was not even thinking of retirement. He dies in 1919 at the age of sixty-three, which is past the "retirement" age of Sherlock Holmes, for example, and which is considerably past the active years of James Bond, who, along with Holmes, inspired the image of Akunin's super detective.[37] Yet it is Russian history itself that retires the otherwise agile detective.

To fit the bill of a true hero, Fandorin must be young. At the age of sixty-two he is described as being in excellent physical and intellectual shape. The love story between Fandorin and Mona, who is almost thirty years his junior, abounds in praise for the hero's physical, mental, and emotional state. The narrator asserts that Fandorin feels stronger than when he was younger. He looks forward to becoming a father. Mona sees in Fandorin "a man capable of eliciting a very strong [...] passion." For her he is a "handsome (perhaps even too handsome), elegant middle-aged man whose hair has gone grey early and in an attractive way."[38] Fandorin also describes himself as being in fact "too young." According to the Japanese wisdom that he follows, he has not yet achieved "the age of maturity" that occurs when a man turns sixty-four, the age that represents the pinnacle of a man's "physical and intellectual perfection." Old age, according to Fandorin, will come when he turns eighty-eight.[39] In other words, at the age of sixty-two he could still be a successful adventure-story hero. In *Not Saying Goodbye*, however, he is hardly a dashing hero.

Besides the comical depiction of Fandorin in a coma, there are other indicators in the novel that Fandorin is close to death. He begins his first crime investigation in post-revolutionary Moscow when he is still recovering and goes about in a wheelchair. Later in the novel, his wife Mona makes a wax sculpture of his head, with the hero's eyes closed and the wax head resting on a platter. It evokes associations with a severed head like that of St John the Baptist, who was executed on Herod's order. The wax sculpture is so "realistic" that it inspires awe in the couple's visitors and is later used by Masa to fake Fandorin's death. Another sign that Fandorin is no longer a viable hero is that half of *Not Saying Goodbye* is not about Fandorin. Instead, much of the book relates instead the adventures of Alexei Romanov, a character featured in one of Akunin's less successful novels from the *Kinoroman* series, *Brotherhood with Death*. By allowing a different character to usurp the narrative space, Akunin further highlights that the civil war is not Fandorin's war. Despite the burgeoning crime that the First World War and the revolutions brought about, his hero has no battles to fight. He has turned into a private individual concerned with family matters. Given that, as Akunin himself said, Fandorin is emotionally handicapped and has no luck with women, he is not really a character whose psychology is meant to be explored. [40] In other words, he does not quite know how to be a private individual. He is, therefore, ultimately removed from the scene and dies along with the empire that he had served.

Erast Fandorin as "A Hero of a Different Time"[41]

Fandorin was born in 1856, the year when Alexander II, who became tsar only the year before, acknowledged Russia's defeat in the Crimean War (1853–6) and began preparing the reforms that would change the Russian empire. The more relaxed atmosphere in society that had prevailed under Nicholas I made an impact on Fandorin. His formative years fell during the reforms, the most important of which was the abolition of serfdom in 1861. While for part of Russia's liberal intelligentsia these reforms were not sufficient, Fandorin believed in the evolutionary way of social development. Between 1876 and 1914, he did his best to prevent a revolution in Russia. Understandably, having served the tsars for a long time, he perceives the time following the revolution as being out of joint. Since he does not believe in revolutions, during the civil war he is a "hero of a different time" who no longer can help his country.[42]

Before 2012 (practically fifteen years into his career as a *belles-lettres* author), Chkhartishvili avoided setting his novels in the time of the revolution and the civil war. His books about Erast Fandorin and Fandorin's heirs or family members (the book series *Adventures of Nicholas*

Fandorin (*Prikliucheniia magistra*) and *The Spy Novel* (*Shpionskii roman*) were set before 1917 or in the late 1930s or else in post-Soviet Russia. This was a noticeable gap, a result of the author's deliberate choice.[43] Despite this gap, with only the last novel in the Fandorin series set immediately after the October Revolution, Fandorin's distaste for revolutions and revolutionaries is clear from the start of the series.[44] Some revolutionary (rebel) characters depicted in the series are removed by the regime (for example, General Sobolev in *The Death of Achilles*); some are hunted down by Fandorin.[45] Already in *The Winter Queen* (*Azazel*, 1998), the first novel in the series, set in 1876 when Fandorin is only eighteen years old, the narrator makes critical remarks about revolutions. In other novels, too, the revolutionary movement and revolutionary ideas are mocked or are perceived as a threat by Akunin's narrators and positive characters. Especially important in this regard are *The Turkish Gambit* (*Turetskii gambit*, 1998), *The State Counsellor* (*Statskii sovetnik*, 1999), *The Diamond Chariot* (*Almaznaia kolesnitsa*, 2003), *The Black City* (*Chernyi gorod*, 2012), and *Not Saying Goodbye*.

According to Lady Astair (the villain in *The Winter Queen*), who organizes an international conspiracy in order to control the path of mankind, her system of boarding schools for gifted children is "a genuine world revolution." It is "essential" in her view to maintain her system, for otherwise, "the unjust order of society will produce a different, bloody revolution that will set mankind back by several centuries."[46] Fandorin destroys this "revolutionary" plot. In *The Turkish Gambit*, set during the Russo-Turkish War (1877–8), Anwar Effendi, a French spy of Turkish descent who has infiltrated Russian headquarters, discusses a future Russian revolution with Varvara Suvorova, a young progressive woman, who, as Effendi perceptively notes, is "inclined to view revolutionary ideas sympathetically."[47] He says: "[I]n your Russia, the revolutionaries have already started shooting occasionally. But soon a genuine clandestine war will begin [...]. Idealistic young men and women will start bombing palaces, trains, and carriages."[48] Ironically, although Fandorin and Effendi are enemies, both "see salvation not in revolution, but in evolution" and would agree that "the forces of reason and tolerance must be helped to prevail" in order to prevent "serious and needless convulsions" that threaten the world.[49] The problem is, of course, that while Effendi views Russia as a source of trouble for the civilized world, Fandorin is a Russian patriot ready to defend his country despite its imperfections.

The period of revolutionary terrorism in Russia began on 4 April 1866 with the first attempt to assassinate Alexander II.[50] Although the reign of Alexander III was a less dramatic period for political terrorism,

Akunin depicts Russian revolutionaries' terrorist tactics in the novel *The State Counsellor,* which is set during the reign of Alexander III, following the assassination of Alexander II.[51] In this novel, revolutionaries are fanatics who "sacrifice their own lives" for the "well-being of millions" and who therefore believe that they "have the right to demand sacrifices from others."[52] As Alexander Lobin perceptively notes, in the Fandorin series the revolutionaries become less morally scrupulous in the decades preceding the revolution. As a result, the number of innocent victims killed by revolutionaries grows from novel to novel.[53]

Lobin supports this observation by references to *The Diamond Chariot* and *The Black City.* In *The Diamond Chariot,* set during the Russo-Japanese War (1904–5), Fandorin battles Japanese spies who rely on help from Russian revolutionaries.[54] In this novel, the revolutionary movement is compared to "a deadly tumour" that grows inside the body of a "seriously ill" Russia. Whereas Russia is described here as "a dinosaur" that "had outlived its time on earth," Japan is compared to an "agile predator" that ruthlessly attacks this sickly "behemoth."[55] Although Fandorin "did not know how to heal" his country, he was convinced that a revolution would destroy it.[56] In *The Black City,* set in 1914 in Baku, the social crisis in Russia deepens. Here Fandorin deals with the assassination of the chief of the tsar's guards by revolutionaries, the taking of hostages, a workers' strike, and acts of sabotage and provocation. Whereas revolutionaries were still loners in the Fandorin novels set in the nineteenth century, in *The Black City* oil magnates, revolutionaries, criminals, and foreign intelligence agents form a united front that is determined to crush Russia.[57] Fandorin barely succeeds in postponing the revolution. Because it did not start in Baku in 1914, the revolutionaries resolve that the country will have then to go through a world war, which means that "millions of lives" will be sacrificed "to ignite the revolution."[58]

Despite the fact that Fandorin sees the problems in his country, unlike "progressive" freedom-minded characters in nineteenth-century Russian literature who criticized the tsarist regime and ended up either as superfluous persons or rebels, he continues to serve the tsars. Fandorin, like "progressive" heroes of nineteenth-century literature, is cosmopolitan. Yet, unlike them, he is conservative. He regrets the flaws of tsarism and nonetheless defends it.[59] In making Fandorin a conservative patriot in the service of the tsarist (secret) police, Akunin breaks with the tradition of "great Russian literature" that favoured active or passive critics of the regime, including Decembrists, Onegin, Pechorin, Oblomov, Bazarov, "new persons" from Nikolai Chernyshevsky's novels, and so on.

A master of martial arts and a conservative, Fandorin reminds one of American film and comic book super-heroes. The latter, according to Hourihan, represent a particular "response to the fear of democracy" and "take upon themselves the responsibilities of moral judgment and the maintenance of order, that is: of the capitalist establishment."[60] Hourihan writes that the presence of super-heroes

> is a promise that order exists, that moral chaos and social uncertainty are not fundamental to the human condition. At the same time, however, these super-heroes are rabid individualists who operate outside the formal structures of social control and their appeal is partly to the suppressed anarchic longings of modern audiences [...], who dream of freedom from the innumerable constraints which modern society imposes. Superman and his kind owe no formal allegiance to anyone, nor does anyone have power over them. Therefore they are potentially wild and rebellious figures, but they voluntarily serve the interests of the establishment, appearing at moments of crisis to defeat evil doers and restore order. They are embodiments of an abstract ideal of social control, and they are profoundly conservative, opposing any agents of change, who are always defined by the stories as criminals or dangerous malcontents.[61]

The qualities of a superhero as outlined by Hourihan are relevant for understanding the character of Erast Fandorin, even though he does not possess supernatural powers.

Akunin's narrators depict the second half of the nineteenth century and the beginning of the twentieth century as the period during which there was a potential to avoid the tragic developments of 1917 but which, nonetheless, also was a time when the revolutionary movement gained momentum. In *Not Saying Goodbye*, chaos reigns in every corner of the former Russian empire, regardless of whether that part is controlled by the Reds, the Whites, or the anarchists. Fandorin is ultimately defeated by the forces of evil. By representing revolutionaries as agents of chaos and by exposing them as unscrupulous fanatics who disregard fundamental social values, Akunin's detective novels contribute to the destruction of the Soviet myth of the revolution as the time of heroes.

Fandorin and the Unavoidable Revolution

Given the critical representation of the Bolshevik Revolution and revolutionaries, why, following the collapse of the Russian empire, can Fandorin not find his place in Russia? Since he had served the empire for so many years, why would Fandorin not support the Whites? While the answer to these questions is provided in almost each novel in the Fandorin series, Fandorin's response is also relevant for understanding why post-Soviet depictions of the White movement have failed to produce a heroic narrative of the revolution capable of replacing the Soviet one.

In the 1990s and the early 2000s the majority of the publications about the revolution depicted it as a break with Russia's wonderful past. Since fourteen out of fifteen books about Erast Fandorin are set before the revolution and of these most are set in the nineteenth century, it may seem that Akunin's narrators view imperial Russia nostalgically. Perhaps to add to such a view, a note on the dustjackets of the original editions of the nine first novels of the series reads, "To the memory of the nineteenth century when literature was great, the belief in progress was infinite and crime as well as its investigation showed both elegance and taste."[62] However, this teaser is somewhat misleading, for, while depicting the nineteenth century as a rather prosperous and stable period in Russia, Akunin's narrators nonetheless never idealize it. After all, the "elegance" in the above-mentioned blurb is assigned to crimes as well as to their investigations. Indeed, unlike popular post-Soviet narratives about the tsarist family, the revolution, and the civil war that essentially dismantled the Soviet view on these topics, Akunin's portrayal of the pre-revolutionary era incorporates a critical view of appalling social inequality, injustice, and corruption.[63] Fandorin observes how these flaws in the tsarist system are exacerbated over the last decades of the nineteenth century and in the early twentieth century.

Already in 1891, Fandorin sees that tsarism is a rotten social system. The main villain in *The State Counsellor* is Prince Pozharsky, who was to supervise the fight against the revolutionaries but instead helped them to organize their activity. Pozharsky presumably intended to crush them afterwards, supposedly for the benefit of the state but also for his own benefit. For the sake of "saving Russia,"[64] Pozharsky sacrificed innocent lives. Observing the corruption among Russian officials, Fandorin feels sympathy towards revolutionaries. It depresses him that in Russia "everything [...] is topsy-turvy. Good is defended by fools and scoundrels, evil is served by martyrs and heroes."[65] Disillusioned, Fandorin resigns from government service, leaves for abroad, and returns to Russia only as a private detective, on requests from the Russian government.

As depicted in *The Diamond Chariot* and *The Black City*, the scale of corruption in the government and among the revolutionaries increases in the early twentieth century.[66] In *The Black City*, the country is described as "an old dying elephant."[67] After the revolution, the moral degradation of Russian society leads to chaos. Skukin, the main villain in *Not Saying Goodbye*, is a family member of one of the White Army military commanders.[68] He switches sides between the Reds and the Whites several times. He is only interested in finding the "collective" that would ensure that he is in a position of power. He commits abominable crimes that lead to the death of many innocent people. He also arranges for Fandorin to die in an accident. By depicting Skukin as an influential figure in the Whites' headquarters and later in the Bolshevik secret police, Akunin exposes both main sides in the civil war as corrupt and unworthy of having power in Russia.

In *Not Saying Goodbye*, four parts are titled "The Black Truth," "The Red Truth," "The Green Truth," and "The White Truth," according to the political forces that competed for power in Russia during the civil war: the anarchists in Moscow, the Bolsheviks, the anarchists in Ukraine (led by Nestor Makhno), and the White Army. None of these "truths" is convincing and clear-cut. As Fandorin demonstrates, the borders between these "truths" are blurred, and confused individuals switch political camps out of selfish or arbitrary considerations rather than shrewd analysis and moral considerations. Fandorin "explores" the camps of the anarchists and the Whites and rejects both. He is not shown "exploring" the Bolshevik camp. The Reds are represented in the novel through the character of Alexei Romanov, a former White officer who has switched to the Bolsheviks. The critical perception of the main political groups by Akunin's protagonist justifies for him individualism as the only possible alternative to siding with any particular camp in a situation of social, moral, and political chaos. Fandorin becomes a private individual and looks for a new turf (outside of Russia) where he can exercise the best of his qualities.

As Aleksandr Lobin notes, Akunin's historical and philosophical concept implies that the world can become better only thanks to the moral development of the individual, not through a revolution. The ideal society is founded on law and order and respect for the rights of individual citizens and social groups.[69] This philosophical position, which has been expressed indirectly through the narrator's comments and the details in the story lines throughout the Fandorin series, is summed up in *Aristonomy* (2012), the first novel in the series *The Family Album*. Anton Klobukov, the protagonist in *Aristonomy*, may be viewed as the opposite of Erast Fandorin. Yet, his characterization is based upon the same principles that are important for creating the image of Fandorin. Moreover, Klobukov's response to the 1917 revolutions and the civil war illuminates why in the last novel in the Fandorin series the hero dies.

A "Serious" Novel about the Revolution

In 2012, Akunin announced that, feeling tired of writing popular detective novels, he had decided to publish his first "serious" book.[70] To indicate how serious this project was he published it under the double-barrelled pen name Akunin-Chkhartishvili (no first name given).[71] Aside from communicating the idea that this book was different from the books that Akunin published as *belles-lettres*, the double pen name is also suitable for a novel that has a twofold structure. *Aristonomy* encompasses two narratives. One is a philosophical tract about *aristonomy*, the ability of an individual to develop his or her dignity. An *aristonom* is an aristocrat of spirit, a responsible, respectful, and compassionate person who is committed to self-enhancement and, like children educated in Lady Astair's boarding schools (*The Winter Queen*), has discovered his or her gift and therefore can do something better than others. The more *aristonoms* there are, the better society becomes. The concept of *aristonomy* is predicated on the idea of evolution – gradual improvement of beneficial qualities in the individual or in the community. Setting a story about an *aristonom* in the time of a revolution allows the author to contrast evolution and revolution by demonstrating that revolutions destroy heroes. A survivor is a non-heroic personality who is able to adapt to the aftermath of the revolution by withdrawing into his or her private life.

The philosophical thread in *Aristonomy* is split into several sections, each of which serves as a "theoretical" introduction to fictional sections that essentially form an adventure novel about Anton Klobukov, a young man who manages to develop *aristonomic* qualities during the catastrophic events of the revolutions in 1917 and the civil war. Although the novel does not specify who has written the philosophical treatise, by the end of the book, the impression is that these are the protagonist's personal notes. The narrative begins in St Petersburg, a month before the February Revolution. To shorten his agony of dying from consumption, Anton's father, Mark Klobukov, a former university professor of law, commits suicide. As his loyal comrade, his wife also commits suicide.[72] The death of Anton's parents is symbolic: the Russian idealist liberal intelligentsia, the heir to the Decembrists, has prepared a revolution but dies melodramatically before it occurs, thus avoiding responsibility for the chaos that the revolution triggers.[73]

The former students of Mark Klobukov help Anton survive throughout the February Revolution, the October Revolution, and the civil war. They represent various factions of Russia's intelligentsia, including constitutional democrats, liberals, and Bolsheviks. At different life junctions, each of these characters becomes a father figure to Anton. While helping him out of respect for his father, each naively assumes that Anton shares his views. Anton, however, never commits to any of the ideological camps. He eventually abandons all his "fathers," nonetheless without betraying them.[74] In the meantime, the "fathers" are one by one destroyed by the historical forces unleashed by the revolutions.[75] Rather than being depicted with sympathy, the idealist father figures representing different ideologies within the Russian intelligentsia are portrayed as fanatics and are thus exposed as false "heroes." While their convictions eventually lead to their demise, Anton's wishy-washiness ensures his survival.

Anton's position of pragmatic individualism and his dedication to working on improving his self rather than attempting to reform society form the basis for the Soviet intelligentsia, famous for its internal exile and withdrawal from the public sphere.[76] Unlike famous characters in Mikhail Bulgakov's *The White Guard*, Alexei Tolstoy's *Ordeal*, Boris Pasternak's *Doctor Zhivago*, or Mikhail Sholokhov's *The Quiet Don*, Anton does not quite take sides during the revolution and the civil war. For him (and the narrator of *Aristonomy*), the Whites and the Reds are caricatures, although the proletarians look especially ridiculous.[77] By criticizing the radical left and right, *Aristonomy* justifies the intellectual's withdrawal from social activism. Like the characters in the novels by Sholokhov, Pasternak, and Tolstoy, Anton tries to survive under any regime.[78] However, unlike these characters, he regards historical events as a game of sorts. He uses social and political circumstances pragmatically, as a means for exploring his self.

As a depiction of the decline of the intelligentsia, Akunin-Chkhartishvili's novel immediately evokes Pasternak's *Doctor Zhivago*, which also focused on the tragic fate of the intelligentsia. In Akunin's novel, the old intelligentsia is dead. As a social type, Klobukov announces the birth of a new intellectual, someone who attempts to stay humane in the midst of chaos. Klobukov, like Yuri Zhivago, tries to be apolitical but fails. Against his will (like Zhivago) he is forced to serve the Reds and the Whites. Also like Pasternak's protagonist, Klobukov manages to get through the civil war without killing anyone. Instead, as a medic (although Akunin's protagonist never formally completed his medical degree), he saves lives. The fact that the completion of *Aristonomy* was inspired by the peaceful protests against Vladimir Putin's decision to run for the presidency again in 2012 is important for understanding the novel's ethos. Akunin, who was an active participant in the protests in 2011–12, reworks Pasternak's plot to demonstrate what happens to the country when the intellectually and ethically most capable members of society become apolitical. Their wishy-washiness leads to tragedy. In offering historical parallels to the social and political crisis of 2011–12 through *Aristonomy*, Akunin allies himself with "Zhivago's children," as Vladislav Zubok calls some of the last generations of Soviet intelligentsia.[79]

Klobukov is the opposite of a popular action hero. According to Hourihan, "The hero is a man of action and it is in action that he expresses his nature – skill, courage, dominance and determination. He is neither contemplative nor creative. He marches onward, and when he encounters [...] a difficulty he deals with it."[80] For such characters, "action involving an extreme level of skill or great danger" provides "extraordinary fulfilment akin to that of a mystical experience."[81] Anton hardly fits this mandate. He is contemplative and creative, and he can barely resolve any difficulty in his life without help from the outside.

Anton is a pacifist who would not take up a weapon or harm another human being. To ensure that he can live through the civil war while switching from the White Guard to the Red cavalry, the narrator endows Anton with "peaceful" tasks such as writing a plan of how a future Russian republic in the Crimea might look under Baron von Wrangel or serving as a medic in the Red cavalry. In *The Other Path*, a sequel to *Aristonomy*, Anton describes himself as having feminine characteristics. He explains to his future wife that he "lacks the masculinity to be a surgeon" and that his "life credo certainly has something effeminate," for he hesitates to resolve any pain-giving problems (*bol'nykh problem*) and limits his involvement by "pacifying the suffering that these problems have caused."[82] When in the middle of the 1920s his girlfriend expresses nostalgia for the heroic time of the civil war, Klobukov disagrees. For him it is much better to hear the petty squabbles of his neighbours over rubber shoes than to live during a time when people "heroically" kill each other using machine guns.[83] The word "evolution" is repeated many times in both *Aristonomy* and *The Other Path*. The descriptions of the horrors of the revolution and the civil war serve to convince the reader that evolution is the only possible path for the individual's and mankind's progress. Akunin-Chkhartishvili's answer to the crisis of the revolution is an escape into elitism and individualism.

The Death Planned Ahead

Six years before the publication of Akunin's *Not Saying Goodbye*, the novel *Aristonomy* by Akunin-Chkhartishvili provided a theoretical explanation for the removal of Erast Fandorin. The novelty of Akunin's and Akunin-Chkhartishvili's approach in depicting the revolution and the civil war as a time that crushed heroes lies in the fact that both protagonists, Anton Klobukov and Erast Fandorin, ultimately see a possibility for personal growth (evolution) regardless of the historical and political circumstances in which they find themselves. The philosophical treatise on *aristonomy* helps the reader to view Anton not simply as a survivor after a catastrophe or a member of a particular society but also as an individual who strives to become a better person. Like Fandorin, Anton perceives revolutions as regressive events that wreak social havoc. His fascination with the 1917 February Revolution, as described in *Aristonomy*, is short-lived.[84] In the months when the Bolsheviks prepare to take power, the euphoric feeling of freedom disappears.[85] Whereas Fandorin looks conservative when he works on preventing the revolution at the time when people like Anton Klobukov's "father figures" work for the revolution to take place, the individualistic response to the revolution by Anton endorses Fandorin's view of history. Like Fandorin, Anton craves evolution. Outside his professional life as a specialist in anaesthiology, Anton is an avid photographer. He is a witness to events. He takes pictures of those who take sides, perform "surgeries," and perish in the cruel world.

Both characters, the non-heroic Anton Klobukov and the heroic Erast Fandorin, regard the revolution from the position of individualism. While both characters understand the injustice of the tsarist system as the cause of the revolution, they do not glorify the revolution. For them it is the time of chaos that crushes heroes. Heroic personalities like Fandorin perish. Non-heroic ones like Klobukov have a chance to survive. Klobukov, unlike Fandorin, is flexible enough to carve out for himself a niche in Soviet society that allows him to live his private life and be the best in his profession, anaesthesiology, which, symbolically, is needed in a highly traumatized society. Fandorin, on the contrary, is too much a hero, and therefore the revolution removes him.

As the above analysis demonstrates, Akunin and Akunin-Chkhartishvili avoid black-and-white portrayals of the revolution and the civil war. On the one hand, the interpretations of these events by Akunin (and Akunin-Chkhartishvili), namely the vision of the revolution as the time that kills heroes, echo a sense of anxiety that the centennial of the revolution revealed. On the other hand, neither the Erast Fandorin series nor the novels that make up the *Family Album* series, reject the revolution. Conversely, both series depict the revolution and the civil war as having crucial significance for changing Russia. The works that have been examined in this article assert the value of the individual who maintains his or her dignity despite the chaos of social and political upheavals. Rather, in the works of Akunin and Akunin-Chkhartishvili, these disturbances become an opportunity for personal growth – and perhaps propose a vision of the revolution that transcends the contradictory interpretations it has been assigned in post-Soviet Russia.

NOTES

1 Smith, *The Russian Revolution*, 1.
2 Anonymous, "Ot kommunistov do 'Iabloka.'" See also Anonymous, "V Moskve nachalas' demostratsiia v chest' stoletiia Oktiabr'skoi revolutsii."
3 See Lipovetsky, "Screening the Revolution," in this volume. See also Kalinin, "The Spectre of the Revolution"; and Dobrenko, "Vse, chto vy khoteli znat' o revoliiutsii," 184.
4 The opinion polls conducted around the ninetieth anniversary of the Russian Revolution revealed that while about 36 per cent of the Russian population still celebrate 7 November, 49 per cent of the respondents view the revolution negatively as an event that destroyed "the great empire and brought discord" and suffering; 15 per cent of the Russian people are indifferent to celebrating or condemning the revolution. Anonymous, "Tret' rossiian schitaet Den' Oktiabr'skoi revolutsii prazdnikom – opros." In turn, Ilya Kalinin notes that there is much more public consensus regarding the (negative) evaluation of the 1990s than regarding the assessment of the revolution and its aftermath. See Kalinin, "Patriotizm eklektiki, ili postsovetskii pishetsia slitno."
5 Nikita Mikhalkov explains the fear of revolution as, possibly, the Russian response to the latest revolution in Ukraine and also, possibly, as a manifestation of the public's mature attitude toward Russian history. In other words, the Russian public has now learned the lessons of the past: the revolutions of 1917 resulted in a series of tragedies not to be repeated. See Mikhalkov, "Stoletie revoliutsii, rasstavliaem tochki nad 'i.'"
6 On 7 November 1925 the military parade was cancelled because of public mourning for Mikhail Frunze, a hero of the civil war and a Soviet military commander. See more in Anonymous, "Voennye parady na Krasnoi ploshchadi."
7 Maria Snegovaia argues that in the 1970s, instead of the revolution, the Second World War became viewed as the main historical event in Russia. See Snegovaia, "Kuda i pochemu ischezla Oktiabr'skaia revoliutsiia iz pamiati naroda?"
8 See Baudrillard, *Simulacra and Simulation*; see also Mankovskaia, *Estetika postmoderna*, 60.

9 This concerns even more or less psychologically complex narratives from the 1970s and 1980s, which featured some sympathetic White officers. See Lipovetsky, "Screening the Revolution," in this volume.

10 Stephen Norris examines Oleg Fomin's *Gentleman Officers: Save the Emperor* (*Gospoda ofitsery: spasti imperatora*, 2008), Andrei Kravchuk's television mini-series *Admiral* (*Admiral*, 2008), and Nikita Mikhalkov's *Sunstroke* (*Solnechnyi udar*, 2014). Norris, "Revising History, Remaking Heroes."

11 Ibid., 216.

12 See Lipovetsky, "Screening the Revolution," in this volume.

13 See, for example, Joshua Gass, "Moll Flanders and the Bastard Birth of Realist Character"; and Rimmon-Kenan, *Narrative Fiction*, 60–71.

14 On the assessment of why the Bolsheviks won the civil war, see, for example Suny, "Why the Bolsheviks Won the Civil War."

15 The alternative title of the TV series is *Parvus's Memorandum* (*Memorandum Parvusa*). The TV series was released on the *Rossiia* TV channel; *Trotsky* appeared on *Pervyi kanal* (First channel). See an examination of these TV series in Baraban, "Lenin, Trotsky, and Parvus in the Battle for Russian Unity."

16 On Pelevin's novel, see Mørch, "Reality as Myth"; Polotovskiĭ and Kozak, *Pelevin i pokolenie pustoty*; and Noordenbos, "Shocking Histories and Missing Memories."

17 The figure of Parvus has never received much attention in scholarly literature. One exception is Zeman and Scharlau, *The Merchant of Revolution*.

18 A similar narrative logic is proposed in Nikita Mikhalkov's melodrama *Solnechnyi udar* (*Sunstroke*, 2014), which depicts White officers as giving up their struggle. They are not heroes who die on the battlefield; they surrender in hope that the Bolsheviks will allow them to emigrate from Russia.

19 A former literary scholar, translator from Japanese and English, and a journal editor, who began writing historical detective novels in the 1990s.

20 Norris, "Boris Akunin," 327. Akunin's individual books often sell 200,000 copies in their first week of release.

21 In August 2008, he criticized Russia's military campaign against Georgia. See, for example, Kseniia Larina, "Rossiia i Gruziia." In 2012 he became one of the founders of the League of Voters that organized opposition protests against Putin's re-election. The writer's reputation as "a powerful voice in his country's opposition movement" has been solidified in numerous interviews with the writer. See Clover, "Russia's Protest Movement Gets Organised." See Navalny and Akunin, "The Akunin-Navalny Interviews." See also McGrane, "Boris Akunin: Russia's Dissident

Detective Novelist." A teaser in the *Financial Times*, for example, reads: "Russia's dissident detective novelist talks about oligarchs, angering the Kremlin and why even peaceful revolution could lead to Russia's collapse." See Thornhill, "Lunch with the FT: Boris Akunin." Feeling disappointed with the Russian public, Akunin moved to western Europe in 2013 with no plans to return to Russia unless the atmosphere there changes so that the majority of Russians stop supporting Putin. Akunin's Interview to Russian Service BBC.

22 The polling was conducted by VTSIOM (All-Union Center for the Study of Public Opinion), the most reputable of the public opinion research centres. See minute 1' in Mikhalkov, "Stoletie revoliutsii, rasstavliaem tochki nad 'i.'"

23 *Azazel* (*The Winter Queen*) alone, the first novel in the Erast Fandorin series, has sold about 15 million copies.

24 A better translation of the title of the last novel could be *Sunny Russia* or *Serendipitous Russia*, since the first letters of the title words can suggest the abbreviation SR (socialist revolutionaries), which is significant for the novel's storyline.

25 Especially influential have been Thomas Carlyle's *The French Revolution: A History* (1837) and *On Heroes, Hero-Worship, and the Heroic in History* (1841). Many historians and politicians as well as theoreticians of socialist revolution, including Karl Marx, Friedrich Engels, and Vladimir Lenin, engaged in discussions of Carlyle's ideas on the role of the "great man" in history.

26 About half of it is about Alexei Romanov, a Russian counterintelligence officer who appears in the novella *Strannyi chelovek. Grom pobedy, razdavaisia*, the fourth book in Akunin's rather unsuccessful series *Brotherhood with Death. Our Favourite Films* (*Smert' na brudershaft. Liubimye fil'my*), known also as *The Cinematic Novel* (*Kinoroman*) was published by AST in 2009. See more than sixty readers' reviews of Akunin's *Not Saying Goodbye* on Labyrinth (Labirint): Anonymous, "Retsenzii i otzyvy na knigu *Ne proshchaius'*."

27 Akunin, *Ne proshchaius'*, 396–403.

28 Ibid., 402–3. Fandorin is presumably "called" by God's messenger. A similar transition from life to death as well as the narration of one's death from the "I" perspective is used in *Tam... (Over There...*, 2012) by Anna Borisova, one of the pen names of Grigorii Chkhartishvili. Only in the original publication of the novel was the identity of the author hidden under this pen name. In subsequent editions, the book cover included the name Boris Akunin and featured *Over There...* as a book in Akunin's new literary project *Avtory* (Authors), while the name "Anna Borisova"

appeared in brackets. See, for example: [Anna Borisova], *Tam...* Moscow: AST, 2017 – (Boris Akunin: proekt "Avtory").

29 The story of Varvara Suvorova and Fandorin is part of the novel *The Turkish Gambit.*

30 See the first minute of the interview with Akunin: Boris Akunin and RTVI, "Boris Akunin o poslednem romane pro Fandorina."

31 Akunin, *Ne proshchaius'*, 13.

32 Ibid., 16.

33 Ibid.

34 Akunin, *The Death of Achilles*, 3.

35 Ibid., 3–4.

36 Margery Hourihan, *Deconstructing the Hero*, 71–2.

37 It is believed that Sherlock Holmes (one of the inspirations for the image of Fandorin) was born on 6 January 1854. Holmes finally "retires" from his investigating practice in 1903 at the age of forty-nine. In 1912–14 he briefly returns to his intelligence activities (he is then sixty years old). Klinger, "The World of Sherlock Holmes," xli–xliii.

38 Akunin, *Ne proshchaius'*, 251.

39 Akunin, *Ne proshchaius'*, 256.

40 Akunin, "Boris Akunin ob obraze Erasta Fandorina."

41 *A Hero of a Different Time* [*Geroi inogo vremeni*] is a novel that Grigorii Chkhartishvili published under the pen name Anatolii Brusnikin as part of his *Avtory* (Authors) project in 2013.

42 The title of one of Chkhartishvili's novels released under the pen name Anatolii Brusnikin.

43 See Baraban, "A Country Resembling Russia."

44 See more about the depiction of revolutionaries in this novel in Lobin, "Istoriia i revoliutsiia v tvorchestve B. Akunina."

45 In *The Death of Achilles*, General Sobolev is removed. In the novel *The Black City* Fandorin tries to hunt down the revolutionary whose *nom de guerre* is Odysseus.

46 Akunin, *The Winter Queen*, 213.

47 In *Not Saying Goodbye*, the reader learns that this woman, Varvara Suvorova, later became the mother of Fandorin's third wife, Mona. Akunin, *Ne proshchaius'*, 264–5.

48 Akunin, *The Turkish Gambit*, 201.

49 Ibid., 201.

50 It ended in 1911 with the assassination of Petr Stolypin.

51 Under the conservative rule of Alexander III, the terrorists' activities were not as pronounced as under Alexander II or Nicholas II.

52 Akunin, *The State Counsellor*, 186.

53 Lobin, "Istoriia i revoliutsiia ..." E-copy, no page numbers.
54 Akunin, "Book 1: Dragonfly-Catcher," in Akunin, *The Diamond Chariot*, 3–118.
55 Akunin, *The Diamond Chariot*, 36. For the same quotation in the original see Akunin, *Almaznaia kolesnitsa*, 52.
56 Akunin, *The Diamond Chariot*, 36.
57 Akunin, *Chernyi gorod*, 36. See more in Lobin, "Istoriia i revoliutsiia ..." E-copy, no page numbers.
58 Akunin, *Chernyi gorod*, 343. See more in Lobin, "Istoriia i revoliutsiia ..." E-copy, no page numbers.
59 Fandorin's conservative patriotism had seemed to be a poor match for Akunin's political activism. In the character of Fandorin, Akunin has popularized qualities that could be used by Vladimir Putin's image-makers. Both Fandorin and Putin champion physical fitness, both know several foreign languages, both worked as secret agents, both guard their privacy, and both are conservative and patriotic. In his conversation with the writer Liudmila Ulitskaia, Boris Akunin admits that especially outside Russia he has been frequently asked if his character Erast Fandorin has qualities that Akunin sees in Vladimir Putin. See minutes 31'–33' in Otkrytka, "Liudmila Ulitskaia i Grigorii Ckhartishvili. Podslushivaem pisatel'skie razgovory." (Last accessed 12 July 2018.)
60 Hourihan, *Deconstructing the Hero*, 65.
61 Ibid., 65–6.
62 There are nine such novels: *The Winter Queen, Turkish Gambit, Leviathan, Special Assignments, State Counsellor, Death of Achilles, Coronation, She Lover of Death, He Lover of Death*. This note was no longer part of the back cover design in the *Diamond Chariot* (*Almaznaia kolesnitsa*) set during the Russo-Japanese War.
63 Nostalgic narratives about tsarist Russia include, for example, Edvard Radzinsky, *The Last Tsar: The Life and Death of Nicholas II* (London: Doubleday, 1992); Edvard Radzinsky, *Alexander II: The Last Great Tsar* (New York: Free Press, 2005); Stanislav Govorukhin's documentary film *Rossiia, kotoruiu my poteriali* (1992); and Gleb Panfilov's feature film *Romanovy. Ventsenosnaia semia* (2000), among others.
64 Akunin, *The State Counsellor*, 287.
65 Ibid., 188.
66 Lobin, "Istoriia i revoliutsiia ..." E-copy, no page numbers.
67 Ibid., 84, 323.
68 Phonetically, this last name reminds one of the derogatory "*sukin*" as in the expression "*sukin syn*" (son of a bitch).
69 Lobin, "Istoriia i revoliutsiia ..." E-copy, no page numbers.
70 The book is longer than any of the previous volumes by Akunin. One edition is 811 pages. Its original print-run was 79,000 copies, which is

considerably lower than the print runs of any one of Akunin's adventure novels and yet is still high by contemporary publishing standards.

71 Zakharov Publishers released the novel in hard cover, but the book appeared also in other formats. In some, the original double pen-name Akunin-Chkhartishvili was split into two, with both first names given: "Boris Akunin, Grigorii Chkhartishvili."

72 In their commitment to the ideals of social justice, Anton's parents remind the reader of the characters in Chernyshevsky's novel *What Is to Be Done?* or the populists who admired Chernyshevsky and his work.

73 Mark Klobukov's father (Anton's grandfather) was one of the Decembrists who spent many years in hard labour in Siberia. See Akunin-Chkhartishvili, *Aristonomiia*, 26.

74 The last name, "Klobukov," phonetically reminds one of Kolobok, an adventurous character of a Russian folk-tale, who escapes, one after another, a series of animals threatening to swallow him. First, one of the disciples of Anton's father helps Anton to become a government employee under the Provisional Government. After the October Revolution, Anton is a victim of the Red Terror. From a Bolshevik jail he is saved by Bolshevik Rogachov, one of his father's former students. Then Petr Berdyshev, an ideologist of the White Guard and also a former student of Mark Klobukov, helps Anton to emigrate to Switzerland. There Anton studies medicine, focusing on anaesthesiology. However, like Klim Samgin from Gorkii's eponymous novel, Anton is bored abroad. On an impulse he returns to Russia. He arrives in the Crimea, where Berdyshev attempts to realize the plan that was proposed in Vasilii Aksenov's novel *The Island of Crimea* (Ostrov Krym, 1979). Berdyshev suggests that the White Guard must temporarily abandon plans to reconquer all of Russia from the Bolsheviks and instead focus on creating a democratic Russia in the Crimea. Anton is appalled by the White Terror. He meets Bolshevik Rogachov again and switches sides, not so much out of conviction but almost accidentally.

75 Rogachov, Anton's Bolshevik "father figure," outlives the others by more than a decade and perishes in the Great Purge.

76 On internal exile, see, for example, Etkind, *Internal Colonization: Russia's Imperial Experience.*

77 Some depictions of proletarians are allusions to characters mocked in Bulgakov's *Heart of a Dog*. Anton's civic wife Pasha is a former maid in his parents' house. Soon after the October Revolution Pasha becomes an activist in one of the women's departments. She is inspired by the ideas of women's liberation (the section is a parody of Alexandra Kollontai's theory of free love). Although Pasha visits Anton after he is seized and thrown into a jail by Bolsheviks, she does not feel obliged to be loyal to him.

She picks up a different civic husband, Comrade Shmakov. The latter's description (associated with the topic of bathroom hygiene) and even his last name are reminiscent of Bulgakov's *Heart of a Dog*. Akunin-Chkhartishvili, *Aristonomiia*, 217–22.

It is noteworthy that another brutal proletarian in *Aristonomy* also has a last name starting with "sh": Khariton Shurygin. Akunin-Chkhartishvili, *Aristonomiia*, 475–7; 487–8; 515–20; 526–7; 530–3.

78 Some of the characters in the famous narratives about the revolution (Vadim Roshchin in Alexey Tolstoy's *Ordeal*, for example) could be unconvincing, but they were not switching sides only out of boredom.

79 See Zubok, *Zhivago's Children*.

80 Hourihan, *Deconstructing the Hero*, 95.

81 Ibid.

82 Akunin-Chkhartishvili, *Drugoi put'*, 97. Klobukov also explains that when he was little, he disliked "boys'" games and liked to watch how the girls played. See Akunin-Chkhartishvili, *Drugoi put'*, 101. By making Anton a specialist medic, Akunin-Chkhartishvili compares him to Dr Zhivago from Pasternak's novel. Furthermore, while for Zhivago poetry becomes more important than medicine, for Anton philosophy becomes a way of escaping from society's pressures. Klobukov, like Zhivago, initially admires the February Revolution and then experiences horror when living through the violence and chaos that it left.

83 Ibid., 149–51.

84 Akunin-Chkhartishvili, *Aristonomiia*, 93–5.

85 Ibid., 114–20.

REFERENCES

Akunin, Boris. *Almaznaia kolesnitsa*. Moscow: Zakharov, 2003.
– *The Winter Queen: A Fandorin Mystery*. Translated by Andrew Bromfield. New York: Random House Trade Paperbacks, 2004.
– *The Death of Achilles: A Fandorin Mystery*. Translated by Andrew Bromfield. New York: Random House Trade Paperbacks, 2006.
– *The Turkish Gambit: A Fandorin Mystery*. Translated by Andrew Bromfield. New York: Random House Trade Paperbacks, 2006.
– *The State Counsellor: The Further Adventures of Fandorin*. Translated by Andrew Bromfield. London: Phoenix, 2008.
– *The Diamond Chariot: The Further Adventures of Erast Fandorin*. Translated By Andrew Bromfield. London: George Weidenfeld and Nicholson, 2011.
– *Chernyi gorod*. Moscow: Zakharov, 2012.

– "Boris Akunin ob obraze Erasta Fandorina." Youtube channel *OlegMenshikov .Ru*, 9 July 2014: https://www.youtube.com/watch?v=5MGlISGV2zM. (Last accessed 18 July 2018.)

– *Ne proshchaius'*. Moscow: Zakharov, 2018.

Akunin, Boris, and RTVI. "Boris Akunin o poslednem romane pro Fandorina, ekranizatsiiakh svoikh knig i prezidentskikh vyborakh." Video interview in *Skvoznoi efir*, RTVI. 8 February 2018. https://www.youtube.com /watch?v=IxE5g1PT1fE. (Last accessed 12 July 2018.)

Akunin-Chkhartishvili (no first name given). *Aristonomiia*. Moscow: Zakharov, 2012.

– *Drugoi put'*. Moscow: Zakharov, 2015.

Anonymous. "Tret' rossiian schitaet Den' Oktiabr'skoi revolutsiii prazdnikom – opros." *RIA Novosti: Rossiia segodnia*. 7 November 2008: https://ria.ru/society/20081107/154584116.html. (Last accessed 12 July 2018.)

– "Ot kommunistov do 'Iabloka': V den' stoletiia Oktiabr'skoi revolutsii po vsei Rossii proshli mitingi i demonstratsii." *Nastoiashchee Vremia*. 7 November 2017: https://www.currenttime.tv/a/28840001.html. (Last accessed 12 July 2018.)

– "V Moskve nachalas' demostratsiia v chest' stoletiia Oktiabr'skoi revolutsii." *RIA Novosti. Rossiia segodna*. 7 November 2017. https://ria.ru/society /20171107/1508328868.html. (Last accessed 12 July 2018.)

– "Retsenzii i otzyvy na knigu *Ne proshchaius'. Prikliucheniia Erasta Fandorina v XX veke. Chast' vtoraia* Borisa Akunina." *Labirint*. https://www.labirint.ru /reviews/goods/616706/. (Last accessed 12 July 2018.)

– "Voennye parady na Krasnoi ploshchadi." Wikipedia. https://ru.wikipedia .org/wiki/%D0%92%D0%BE%D0%B5%D0%BD%D0%BD%D1%8B%D0 %B5_%D0%BF%D0%B0%D1%80%D0%B0%D0%B4%D1%8B_%D0%BD %D0%B0_%D0%9A%D1%80%D0%B0%D1%81%D0%BD%D0%BE%D0 %B9_%D0%BF%D0%BB%D0%BE%D1%89%D0%B0%D0%B4%D0%B8. (Last accessed 12 July 2018.)

Baraban, Elena V. "A Country Resembling Russia: The Use of History in Boris Akunin's Detective Novels." *SEEJ* Forum: *Innovation through Reiteration: Post-Soviet Popular Culture. Slavic and East European Journal. SEEJ* 48, 3 (2004): 396–420.

– "Lenin, Trotsky, and Parvus in the Battle for Russian Unity." *Warsaw East European Review. WEER* 10 (2020): 51–69.

Baudrillard, Jean. *Simulacra and Simulation*. Ann Arbor: University of Michigan Press, 1994.

Clover, Charles. "Russia's Protest Movement Gets Organised." *Financial Times*, 18 January 2012: https://www.ft.com/content/f482927e-41f8-11e1-9506 -00144feab49a?mhq5j=e5. (Last accessed 15 July 2018.)

Dobrenko, Evgeny. "Vse, chto vy khoteli znat' o revoliiutsii, no boialis' sprosit' u Iiuriia Trifonova, ili Ochen' dlinnyi kurs istorii VKP(b)." *Novyi mir* 12 (2017): 183–9.

Etkind, Alexander. *Internal Colonization: Russia's Imperial Experience.* Cambridge: Polity Press, 2011.

Gass, Joshua. "Moll Flanders and the Bastard Birth of Realist Character." *New Literary History* 45, 1 (2014): 111–30.

Hourihan, Margery. *Deconstructing the Hero: Literary Theory and Children's Literature.* London and New York: Routledge, 1997.

Kalinin, Ilya. "Patriotizm eklektiki, ili postsovetskii pishetsia slitno." *Ab Imperio* 1 (2011): 274–83.

– "The Spectre of the Revolution." *The Times Literary Supplement,* 15 February 2017: https://www.the-tls.co.uk/articles/private/spectre-russian -revolution/. (Last accessed 12 July 2018.)

Klinger, Leslie S. "The World of Sherlock Holmes." In Sir Arthur Conan Doyle, *The New Annotated Sherlock Holmes. The Complete Short Stories: The Adventures of Sherlock Holmes and The Memoirs of Sherlock Holmes,* edited with a preface and notes by Leslie S. Klinger, Vol. 1, xvii–lxvii. New York: Norton, 2005.

Larina, Kseniia. "Rossiia i Gruziia: Esli u nas obshchee budushchee?" *Ekho Moskvy,* 16 August 2008: www.echo.msk.ru/programs/kulshok/534013 -echo.phtml.

Lipovetsky, Mark. "Screening the Revolution: Transformations of the Revolutionary Narrative in Russian Film since the 1960s." In this volume, 216–48.

Lobin, Aleksandr Mikhailovich. "Istoriia i revoliutsiia v tvorchestve B. Akunina (na materiale tsikla romanov 'Prikliucheniia Erasta Fandorina')." In *Vestnik Viatskogo gorudarstvennogo gumanitarnogo universiteta,* 10 (2014): 148–54: https://cyberleninka.ru/article/n/istoriya -i-revolyutsiya-v-tvorchestve-b-akunina-na-materiale-tsikla-romanov -priklyucheniya-erasta-fandorina. (Last accessed 18 June 2018.)

Mankovskaia, N.B. *Estetika postmoderna.* St Petersburg: Aleteia, 2000.

McGrane, Sally. "Boris Akunin: Russia's Dissident Detective Novelist." *The New Yorker,* 27 July 2012: https://www.newyorker.com/books/page -turner/boris-akunin-russias-dissident-detective-novelist. (Last accessed 15 July 2018.)

Mikhalkov, Nikita. "Stoletie revoliutsii, rasstavliaem tochki nad 'i.'" Interview on the channel *Politika Rossii i Ukrainy*: 19 October 2017: https://www .youtube.com/watch?v=qGYG-NnOWGY. (Last accessed 12 July 2018.)

Mørch, Audun J. "Reality as Myth: Pelevin's *Čapaev i Pustota*." *Scando-Slavica* 51, 1 (1 September 2005): 61–79.

Navalny, Alexei, and Boris Akunin. "The Akunin-Navalny Interviews."
11 January 2012: https://www.opendemocracy.net/od-russia/alexei
-navalny-boris-akunin/akunin-navalny-interviews-part-i. (Last accessed
15 July 2018.)

Noordenbos, Boris. "Shocking Histories and Missing Memories: Trauma in
Viktor Pelevin's *Čapaev i Pustota.*" *Russian Literature* 85 (1 October 2016):
43–68.

Norris, Steven M. "Boris Akunin (Grigorii Shalvovich Chkhartishvili, 1956–)."
In *Russia's People of Empire: Life Stories from Eurasia, 1500 to the Present,*
edited by Willard Sunderland, 327–37. Bloomington: Indiana University
Press, 2012. ProQuest Ebook Central: http://ebookcentral.proquest.com
/lib/umanitoba/detail.action?docID=816836. (Last accessed 15 July 2018.)

– "Revising History, Remaking Heroes: Soviet-Russian Cinema and the Civil
War." In *Ruptures and Continuities in Soviet/Russian Cinema: Styles, Characters
and Genres before and after the Collapse of the USSR,* edited by Birgit Beumers
and Eugene Zvonkine, 200–18. London and New York: Routledge, 2017.

Otkrytka. "Liudmila Ulitskaia i Grigorii Ckhartishvili. Podslushivaem
pisatel'skie razgovory." *Otkrytaia Rossiia
Club.* Youtube.com Channel *Otkrytka,* 11 May 2017: https://www.youtube.com
/watch?v=NChl1yIGzMk. (Last accessed 12 July 2018.)

Polotovskiĭ, Sergeĭ, and Roman Kozak. *Pelevin i pokolenie pustoty.* Moscow:
Mann, Ivanov i Ferber, 2012.

Rimmon-Kenan, Shlomith. *Narrative Fiction: Contemporary Poetics.* 2nd ed.
London and New York: Routledge, 2002.

Smith, S.A. *The Russian Revolution: A Very Short Introduction.* Oxford: Oxford
University Press, 2002.

Snegovaia, Maria. "Kuda i pochemu ischezla Oktiabr'skaia revoliutsiia
iz pamiati naroda?" *Colta.ru,* 11 November 2017: http://www.colta.ru
/articles/society/16626. (Last accessed 15 July 2018.)

Suny, Ronald Gregor. "Socialism and Civil War." In *The Soviet Experiment:
Russia, the USSR, and the Successor States,* 2nd ed., 56–95. Oxford: Oxford
University Press, 2010.

Thornhill, John. "Lunch with the FT: Boris Akunin." *Financial Times,* 1 March
2013: https://www.ft.com/content/77f7ca96-80d4-11e2-9c5b-00144feabdc0
?mhq5j=e5. (Last accessed 15 July 2018.)

Zeman, Z.A.B., and W.B. Scharlau. *The Merchant of Revolution: The Life of
Alexander Israel Helphand (Parvus) 1867–1924.* London, New York, and
Toronto: Oxford University Press, 1965.

Zubok, V.M. *Zhivago's Children: The Last Russian Intelligentsia.* Cambridge, MA:
Harvard University Press, 2009.

8 Screening the Revolution: Transformations of the Revolutionary Narrative in Russian Film since the 1960s

MARK LIPOVETSKY

Many commentators noticed the obvious resistance and anxiety of Russian authorities in the run-up to the celebration of the centennial of the 1917 revolution in Russia. In Ilya Kalinin's words, "The common past is used as a screen on which to project the fears of those who are currently in power." In his opinion, today Russian authorities seek to create "a national historical narrative that denies revolution altogether."[1] Looking at the emphatic lack of interest in the centennial of the revolution among Russian authorities and the "masses" alike, Evgeny Dobrenko recalls Baudrillard's words about the 200-year celebration of the French Revolution: "remembering signifies the absence" of the revolution itself.[2] Dobrenko adds: "One might say the same about the Russian Revolution in the Soviet epoch. Its annual celebrations served as an endless funeral. However, today something opposite has happened: the space of celebration, remembering, and ritual became empty. This means that the Revolution remains a living trauma of post-Soviet Russia, it belongs to today: debates about the sanctity of the last Russian tsar or about monuments to executioners and victims of Stalinism symptomize this trauma, which remains uncured even under the layers of history."[3]

Russian political scientist Maria Snegovaia, in an article under the illuminating title "Where and Why Did the October Revolution Disappear from the Popular Memory?," reminds us that "a fundamental substitution of the revolution as the starting point [of modern Russian history] for the victory in the war [the Second World War] happened in the Brezhnev period. And as in many aspects of Russian politics, it resulted from an intentional policy of the Kremlin rather than a change of public moods. It is the Brezhnev epoch in which Putin's system has its sources."[4] I will continue this approach and will try to show how a paradoxical narrative about the revolution and civil war that would diminish and, eventually, erase the revolution completely has been created throughout the entire late Soviet period by the efforts of the predominantly liberal intelligentsia. Further, I will outline the main phases of this process, focusing on its beginnings in the 1960s and early 1970s and briefly touching on its conclusions in the 2010s. I will focus especially on those films and TV productions in which transformations of the revolutionary narrative highlight associations (or dissociations) of the revolution with violence.[5] My analysis will be mainly based on the typology of discourses of violence that Birgit Beumers and I have introduced in the book *Performing Violence: Literary and Theatrical Experiments of New Russian Drama* and which I will briefly outline here.[6]

Discourses of Violence in Soviet Culture

A discourse of revolutionary violence was adopted by the Soviet state immediately after its inception and chiefly functioned as a staging device for power. In conformity with Michel Foucault's description of executions in pre-modern culture, the Soviet state created a special theatre of terror, thus demonstrating absolute power over its subjects. At the same time, as modern historians have shown, violence of this type is represented in Soviet culture as a process of modernity based on the "scientific" regulation of society by means of the elimination, persecution, or marginalization of entire categories of the population that are actually or potentially dangerous for the proletariat and therefore do not fit in with the utopian model of the new society.[7] This logic unites the discourse of revolutionary violence with the discourses of modern control over the course of history, a stance typical for many ideocratic states, including the Soviet one. During the Soviet era this practice typically was accompanied by a "medical" rhetoric of "social prevention," "hygiene," and "cleansing" and relied on statistics that determined the "planned economy" of terror. Evgeny Dobrenko, in his exploration of socialist realism, has revealed a symbolic "pedagogy of terror" that connected literature and art with the Gulag.[8]

Revolutionary violence penetrates the entire spectrum of revolutionary discourses: above all, the Bolshevik rhetoric of radical modernization proposed by the party ideologists. The revolutionary discourse of violence is, in its early stages, also articulated not only by such outstanding authors of the 1920s and 1930s as Vladimir Mayakovsky and Sergei Eisenstein but also by the less talented yet no less active authors of *Cement* (1925), *The Rout* (*Razgrom*, 1927), and *Chapaev* (1923), the Proletkult poets and the "Smithies" (*Kuznitsa*), as well as the "Komsomol" poets. From 1934 this discourse was also absorbed by a canonical socialist realism that merged the revolutionary justifications of violence with the glorification of the Soviet state as the sacred goal of violence, as well as the sacred supreme executioner.

The complexity of the modernizing discourse of revolutionary violence is closely connected to the dual role of the Russian intelligentsia as a major agent of modernization – the first victim of revolutionary violence, and at the same time the scapegoat for modernization's failures. Thus, the revolutionary discourses of violence (merged with state violence) in the 1920s develop alongside the intelligentsia's discourse of historical trauma, shaped by the guardians of the Westernized version of Russian culture who experience the revolution as a global catastrophe. This is articulated in the work of Osip Mandelstam, Konstantin Vaginov, Anna Akhmatova, Maximilian Voloshin, Mikhail Bulgakov, and many other outstanding writers of the first half of the twentieth century.[9] This is why, as Nancy Ries remarks, the litany of suffering and victimization is extremely important for the symbolical identification of the Soviet intelligentsia.[10] Not without reason were the two main loci of the sacred in post-Stalinist culture simultaneously chronotopes of violence and suffering: the Second World War in official culture, and the Gulag in the unofficial sphere.

Both the discourse of revolutionary violence and the intelligentsia's discourse of trauma (a flip side of violence) confronted a third discourse – of communal violence, or in other words, causeless violence or "Little Terror," to use Tatiana Tolstaya's catchphrase.[11] This power-ideological "total war" characterizes the daily relations of submission on a horizontal level and is most acutely represented by the violence of the mob (revolutionary or not), languages of criminal subcultures, discourses of everyday xenophobia, everyday wars in the *komunalka* (communal apartment) setting, and so on. To a certain extent this discourse represents the cultural staging of biological aggression, although it should not be reduced to a mere reflection of biological factors, since aggression is here created as one of the forms of self-identification and self-realization of collective, communal bodies. The arbitrariness in the definition of the Other – the target of violence – transforms this type of violence into a form of social communication that is destructive and self-destructive at the same time. Because of a focus on bodies, communal discourses of violence are often articulated not just verbally but performatively, and frequently recall archaic rites.

Early attempts to depict and analyse the discourse of communal violence in Russian culture can be seen in Anton Chekhov's stories "Peasants" ("*Muzhiki*," 1897) and "In the Ravine" ("*V ovrage*," 1899); Maxim Gorky's works, such as, for example, the cycle *Through Russia* (*Po Rusi*, 1912–13); but especially in post-revolutionary literature – including but not limited to Boris Pil'niak's early prose, Evgeny Zamiatin's short stories of the 1920s, and Isaak Babel's *Red Cavalry* ("*Konarmiia*," 1923–5). Especially notable in this respect are the "poems in prose" about the peasants' and Cossacks' uprisings during the civil war – such as "Humus" ("*Peregnoi*," 1922) and "*Vireneia*" (1924) by Lydia Seifullina; *Russia Washed in Blood* (*Rossiia krov'iu umytaia*, 1929–32) by Artem Veselyi; *The Volga Uprising* (*Povol'niki*, 1922) by Alexander Yakovlev; or *Vataga* (*Gang*, 1924) by Viacheslav Shishkov, among others.[12] Sholokhov's *The Quiet Don* (first book published in 1928) also belongs to this lineage. Of course, each of these writers created his or her own version of the discourse of communal violence, and each of them justified or criticized it from different perspectives. The fear of the peasantry in Gorky contrasts to the excitement of the revolution's bloody carnival in Seifullina and ambivalent attitudes to it in Veselyi. Pil'niak explains the mass violence by Russia's "eternal metaphysics." Zamiatin builds on this foundation a vision of rapid de-modernization, and Babel's hero simultaneously desires and appals the fusion of his subjectivity with the "collective body" of thugs and murderers. Sholokhov inscribes the communal violence of the Cossacks' uprising into the panorama of similar violent manifestations of confronting ideological forces (the Reds, the Whites, fighters for the Cossacks' independence, etc.). Probably the most multifaceted representation of the discourse of communal violence can be found in the works of Mikhail Zoshchenko, who situates communal violence in the setting of a "normal" communal apartment, thus proving that the civil war has shaped the everyday life of ordinary Soviet people.

Socialist realism in general and Soviet films of the 1930s to 1950s about the revolution and civil war, in particular, formalized these discourses by assigning each of them (in a radically simplified way) to a particular political force – namely, to the Reds (always positive), Whites, and "Greens" (both also represented as negative). By this means, socialist realist classics provided a very schematic and at the same time highly idiomatic formula for each of the discourses associated with violence in Soviet culture. Most significantly, these idioms were performative rather than verbal, and their strength was inseparable from the filmic representation of violence or, more frequently, its brutal effects.

For example, the Vasiliev "brothers" famous *Chapaev* (1934) – a model for imitations and an object for polemics for many subsequent Soviet films about the revolution and civil war – most prominently represents the connection between violence and the intelligentsia. The Whites are depicted as the force performing defence of its cultural values through violence: Colonel Borozdin plays Beethoven but doesn't spare a brother of his devoted orderly Petrovich from a torturous death. The "psychic attack" of the Kappel officer unit marching under the flag with skulls and bones (complete fiction) is accompanied by a comment from the Reds: "Krasivo idut – Intellikhentsiia!" (They're marching beautifully! – Intellikhentsia!).

The Reds' discourse of revolutionary violence appears not only through Chapaev's famous charge of the Whites but also in the shooting of Chapaev's associate for marauding, which is demanded by Furmanov and eventually authorized by Chapaev. The ideological justification for revolutionary violence is provided by a pipe-smoking commissar who embodies state power and tames Chapaev's anarchic freedom with disciplinary measures. Furmanov's disciplinary violence echoes the White general's disciplinary measures against deserters – which include the beating to death of Petrovich's brother. While Furmanov's violence is depicted as necessary and justifiable, the general's refusal to excuse the deserter is displayed as highly immoral. This crucial difference between seemingly mirroring discourses of violence is associated in *Chapaev* with the emancipatory pathos of the revolution – lacking in the general's idea of discipline and highlighted in Furmanov's.

Through the analysis of Furmanov's novel *Chapaev*, Katerina Clark coined a famous formula of the socialist realist narrative as the transformation of spontaneity into consciousness.[13] Chapaev's violent rage against the regiment's medics who refuse to certify his relative as a doctor as well as his Cossacks' violence against peasants stand not only for spontaneity, in Clark's terminology, but also for communal violence. In many other films of the 1930s to the 1950s, communal violence will also be manifested by the "Greens," such as Makhno's anarchists and Petliura's peasant armies, as well as by smaller units with an unclear or non-existent political orientation, typically called gangs (*bandy*). In the Vasiliev brothers' film, this formula also includes the cooptation of a communal violence by a revolutionary one. Chapaev's death in the film's finale represents a tragic sacrifice for the victory of revolution, a sacrifice that obviously sanctifies this fusion.

Such a distribution of discourses of violence between warring political forces can also be detected in such socialist realist classics as *My iz Kronshtadta* (*We Are from Kronstadt*, directed by Efim Dzigan, 1936); *Shchors* (directed by Aleksandr Dovzhenko, 1939); *Aleksandr Parkhomenko* (directed by Leonid Lukov, 1942); *Shkola muzhestva* (*The School of Courage*, directed by Vladimir Basov and Mikhail Korchagin, 1954); and *Optimisticheskaia tragediia* (*The Optimistic Tragedy*, Samson Samsonov's film of 1963 based on Vsevolod Vishnevsky's 1932 play).[14]

However, in the 1960s, this disposition undergoes a radical change.

A Paradigm Shift

Certainly, in the literature of the 1920s the relations between discourses of violence and forces participating in the revolutionary war were depicted in a much more complex way than in socialist realist films of the 1930s. Two films released in 1956 – Sergei Gerasimov's *The Quiet Don* and Grigorii Chukhrai's *The Forty First* – utilize the subversive potential of early Soviet literature protected by the political clout of their authors – Mikhail Sholokhov and Boris Lavrenev. By 1956 both became acknowledged classics of socialist realism. However, both films are based on pre- or even anti-socialist realist texts created mainly in the 1920s.[15] One may say that these films were the first to materialize the spirit of the Thaw and, thus, in many ways defined further representations of the revolution in Soviet cinema.

Gerasimov's *The Quiet Don*, following the literary source, destabilizes the socialist realist triad by depicting both pre-revolutionary and post-revolutionary violence as *equally brutal and inhuman*; the violence of the Cossacks' peaceful lifestyle (e.g., Stepan's routinized beating of Aksinia) and the violence of the First World War; revolutionary violence coming from the Reds and the counter-revolutionary violence of their opponents, the Whites and Cossacks fighting for the Don's freedom from the Soviets – bandits in Soviet lingo. Scenes of executions performed by actors on all sides of the conflict match each other in their cruelty. However, the typology of violence remains intact. The Reds and Whites mirror each other in their class fascism, serving as the justification for discrimination and plain brutality toward those Cossacks whose class origins and economic standing don't fit ideological expectations. Communal violence is represented in *The Quiet Don* as the source feeding both the Reds and the Whites and, at the same time, as an independent force during the Cossacks' uprising against the Reds and Whites alike.

Grigory Melekhov, the protagonist of this saga, takes different sides in the course of the revolutionary war, and each of his affiliations leads him to a crisis point when he cannot perpetrate violence anymore. His acute sense of personal dignity pushes him away from each side of the confrontation – the Reds, the Whites, and the Cossacks' uprising alike. He is neither accepted by the new social order nor able to accept the revolution with its regime of normalized violence. Although the film contains numerous scenes and heroes that resonate with the socialist realist canon, the "outcast" and anti-hero Grigory in the memorable performance of Petr Glebov is represented in *The Quiet Don* with an obvious authorial compassion, which surely is conveyed to the film's viewers; consequently, his discontent appears as a radical vindication

Figure 8.1. Govorukha-Otrok and Mariutka as a new Adam and Eve on an uninhabited island

of the revolution. For Grigory the revolution did not bring any expected emancipation but only turned his life into an endless tragedy.

In *The Forty First*, the debut of director Grigory Chukhrai, Chukhrai joined forces with one of the most conceptual cameramen of the Soviet cinema – Sergei Urusevsky. As Denise Youngblood remarks, "Chukhrai was certainly aware that [Yakov] Protazanov's [1927] version had sparked a firestorm of criticism in the late 1920s for its sympathetic portrayal of the class enemy."[16] Authors of the 1956 version created an explicitly romantic and expressive visual language to tell the story of love between a semi-literate Red Army female soldier Mariutka (Izolda Izvitskaia) and a captive White officer and former student of literature Govorukha-Otrok (Oleg Strizhenov), who are stranded together on an uninhabited island in the Aral Sea (figure 8.1).

Strizhenov, probably the most romantic actor in the Thaw cinema, plays Govorukha as an incredibly lovable character; while Izvitskaya doubles the lustre coming from her partner by displaying Mariutka's rapid emotional education – albeit along a patriarchal scenario – under the influence of her newly found love for a recent class enemy. Lavrenev's novella of 1924 problematized the class ideology, although later interpretations emphasized the necessity to sacrifice love (i.e., humanity) for the sake of class struggle. According to this logic, Mariutka's killing of Govorukha in the finale, when he rushes to greet the Whites approaching the island on a boat, was lauded by Soviet critics as the neoclassical sacrifice of feelings for the sake of the class duty. The romantic aura of Chukhrai/Urusevsky's film completely and unambiguously dispels this logic: the revolution appears in this film as the systematic destruction of humanity by various forms of violence always posing as right and necessary. Once again, in this film, the Reds' and the Whites' class justifications of violence are depicted as mirroring each other. Therefore, Mariutka's final shooting kills not only Govorukha but herself as well; it also destroys any hope for the preservation of humanity in a larger world beyond the utopian space of a secluded island.

New Representations of Violence and New Discursive Alliances

A new surge in the cinematic interpretations of the revolution falls in the period from 1967 to 1971. Films that appear at this time seek ways to move beyond socialist realist language and logic, and simultaneously to *reconceptualize the revolution* in order to preserve its significance, but in new terms. A few factors came together to produce this new surge in the reworking of the revolutionary narrative. The fiftieth anniversary of the revolution in 1967 was a reason for commissioning "historical-revolutionary" films from the directors of the new generation (all born no later than the early 1930s), who had already absorbed the limited but nevertheless inspiring liberties of the Thaw, as well as the artistic lessons of the European New Wave in cinema. The anniversary also coincided with a profound ideological crisis caused by the failure of Khrushchev's Thaw, which the intelligentsia of this generation interpreted as an anti-Stalinist revolution – thus justifying a new interest in the 1920s. The generation of the sixties perceived people of the revolutionary era as victims of Stalinism that had destroyed the revolution while hijacking its rhetoric. The Thaw's attempt to separate revolutionary discourses from Stalinism obviously failed; therefore, revolution had to be reinvented to serve the emancipation of the new generation from the fetters of Stalinism.

In these films the Reds' violence typically is not represented visually or through scenes of interrogations and executions. However, it is represented by its discourse, which unmistakably reads as Stalinist. In *V ogne broda net* (*No Path through Fire*, 1967) by Gleb Panfilov, *Sluzhili dva tovarishcha* (*Two Friends Served in the Army*, 1968) by Evgeny Karelov, and *Svoi sredi chuzhikh, chuzhoi sredi svoikh* (*At Home among Strangers, a Stranger among His Own*, 1974) by Nikita Mikhalkov, important ideological debates appear between characters belonging to the Reds: on the one side, proto-Stalinist dogmatists propagating merciless violence against all those who don't fit the Bolshevik vision of the "class-clean society," and on the other characters trying to defend values of "abstract humanism," suggesting trust in a person rather than in the person's class origin and other ideas typical of the anti-Stalinist discourse of the Thaw. Nevertheless, the Whites' and the "Greens'" violence is represented quite graphically in these movies.

Notably, the Whites' violence in these films centres on the counter-intelligence officers' propensity for torturing and executing anybody who expresses even mild dissent. In this respect, the Whites' brutality serves as an Aesopian substitute for the Red Terror in the 1920s and the Great Terror in the 1930s. For example, each of the five episodes of the 1970 mini-series *Aide-de-camp of His Excellency* opens with a dedication to "the first Chekists" accompanied by an iconic profile of Dzerzhinsky. However, within the film the profile of the Whites' counter-intelligence head, Colonel Shchukin (performed by Vladimir Kozel), displays a striking similarity to Dzerzhinsky (figures 8.2 and 8.3).

The parallelism between the Whites and the Reds in these films also develops in a different, I would say more positive, direction. *Aide-de-camp of His Excellency* is especially revealing in this respect. In the first episode of the film, a group of Whites find themselves captured by the gang of "bat'ka Angel" (father Angel). In the cellar where they are thrown, they find two Red commanders. One of the White officers is wounded, and the Red commander tears off the sleeves of his tunic to bandage the lieutenant's wound. Then both the Whites and the Reds unite forces and manage to escape from the bandits. In a memorable scene, after the escape, they debate who controls the territory where they are resting after the chase – and having not reached a conclusion, peacefully and respectfully part ways in opposite directions. Later, one of the Red commanders – Emelyanov, who is also the Chekist – is captured by the Whites, and the lieutenant, who now serves in counter-intelligence, recognizes him and his still sleeveless tunic. As

Figures 8.2. and 8.3. Dzerzhinsky's profile on the film's dedication to
"The First Chekists," and Vladimir Kozel as Shchukin, the head of the Whites'
counter-espionage

a gesture of gratitude, he records Emelyanov as an ordinary soldier and not as a Red commander, thus saving his life. In the next episode, the lieutenant releases the captive under the false premise that he is a railroad worker.

There are numerous episodes like this in the mini-series. Taken together, they re-conceptualize the civil war as a struggle between moral people, who can be found among both the Reds and the Whites (but not among the "bandits"), and their immoral opponents, who also can be found in either camp.[17] The film depicts as persons of high morals not only another Red commander who helps the lost son of the White colonel but also the commander of a White army, General Kovalevsky (Vladislav Strzhel'chik), and a former imperial officer serving as the head of the Red headquarters who is wrongfully accused of being the Whites' mole.

A central character, Lt Pavel Kol'tsov (performed by Yurii Solomin), is shown as the epitome of moral fibre and a model of tact and sophistication (figure 8.4). Although as a spy he constantly deceives and lies, he never loses his dignity, honour, and gentleman's elegance. He offers an odd synthesis of the Reds and the Whites: while serving the Reds, in his demeanour and behaviour he nevertheless exemplifies the positive image of a White officer, with whom the viewer would want to identify. Kol'tsov in many ways appears as a predecessor of Shtirlitz – the heroic and dignified role model for the late Soviet intelligentsia. However, he also opens a gallery of attractive and honourable White officers in Soviet cinema. In his central monologue, in which he responds to a teenager's question – "Pavel Andreevich, vy shpion?" ("Pavel Andreevich, are you a spy?") – Kol'tsov in a sincere and honest manner, without revolutionary slogans and demagoguery, defends the emancipatory meaning of the revolution, which, in his interpretation boils down to a respect for human dignity independent of a person's social status and class origin. Paradoxically, Kol'tsov while wearing the White officer's uniform, persistently displays this set of values, thus dissociating them from the Red cause.

Tashkov's mini-series echoes Aleksandr Askol'dov's film The Commissar (1967), in which moral solidarity also prevails over conflicting ideological interpretations of revolutionary violence. Notably, this film was banned by the Soviet censorship despite or rather because of its most pronounced emancipatory message – a commissar Vavilova (Nonna Mordiukova) leaves her child with a Jewish family and returns to the frontlines in order to defend the Jews from impending calamities, including the future Holocaust. The depiction of the civil war as a battle between moral and immoral forces, where the borders of

Figure 8.4. General Kovalevsky and Lt Kol'tsov as examples of refinement and elegance

morality do not coincide with the frontlines between the Reds and the Whites, is also detectable in Evgeny Karelov's *Two Friends Served in the Army* (1968), featuring the unforgettably tragic figure of Lieutenant Brusentsov, played by Vladimir Vysotsky (figure 8.5).

This approach can be seen most forcefully in filmic versions of Mikhail Bulgakov's plays – first and foremost *Flight* (1970) by directors Aleksandr Alov and Vladimir Naumov, and *Days of the Turbins* (1976) by Vladimir Basov, who himself played Myshlaevsky. In these films, the best actors of the period, Vladislav Dvorzhetsky, Mikhail Ulianov, Oleg Efremov, Aleksey Batalov, and Andrei Miagkov, portray White officers as complex and tragic human beings; they are not ideal but are able to experience moral pain and preserve their honour and human dignity in the midst of the historical tragedy. The Reds in these films are completely removed from the picture, appearing only as a faceless force of the historical catastrophe.

Flight presents the Whites' violence through the figure of general Khludov (Vladislav Dvorzhetsky), whom Alov and Naumov depict as a proto-Pontius Pilate from Bulgakov's *The Master and Margarita*; his moral self-torture removes his crimes from the ideological context, paradoxically representing him, the murderer, as a symbol of moral judgment and the superiority of moral criteria over any political

Figure 8.5. Vladimir Vysotsky as Lt Brusentsov in Evgeny Karelov's *Two Friends Served in the Army*

justifications. Khludov's counterpart, General Charnota, in the eccentric performance of Mikhail Ulianov, appears as an outlandish and hapless trickster who, despite his numerous transgressions, is more moral than the cynical businessman Korzukhin (Evgeny Evstigneev), whose train carts filled with stolen furs Khludov orders burnt back in Crimea.

Similarly, in *Days of the Turbins*, the decision of the Turbins and their friends not to fight against the Reds is presented as an inevitable choice dictated by the fact that all the other forces of revolutionary history prove to be equally immoral. Acceptance of the Bolsheviks allows the Turbins, at least, to preserve their home as the epitome of love and family honour (illusory, of course). The next step in the development of this narrative will occur in numerous films that depict White officers and members of the intelligentsia as joining the ranks of the Bolsheviks. Moral values in films like *The Red Square* (*Krasnaia ploshchad'*, 1970) by Vasilii Ordynskii will be replaced by the idea of the Russian state's power, which stands up as an "eternally" superior value that unites the patriotic Whites and the non-dogmatic Reds. Notably, in this version of the narrative, the emancipatory idea will be pushed aside: the Whites and the Reds appear here as allies caring equally about the greatness of the Russian state but divided by incompatible ideological dogmas, neither of which has any validity today.

In this context, it is not surprising that the most brutal violence in films of the late 1960s and early 1970s is associated with the "Greens" or "bandits," who are invariably depicted as an agglomerate of déclassé elements united by greed, immorality, and contempt for human life and dignity. In other words, "destructive elements" driven by egotistic interests rather than by concern for the Russian state and its future appear almost solely responsible for the violence of the revolution and civil war. This rewriting of the revolutionary narrative appears first in such innovative films as Andrei Smirnov's *Angel* (1967, banned by censorship), but becomes especially noticeable in the films that seemingly represent the revolution in a de-ideologized light, using its events merely as a background for adventurous, Western-like plots. Among the large number of such films, the most remarkable are the saga *Imperceptible Avengers* (*Neulovimye mstiteli*, 1967–71) by Edmond Keosaian, *White Sun of the Desert* (*Beloe solntse pustyni*, 1970) by Vladimir Motyl', *Bumbarash* (1971) by Nikolai Rasheev and Abram Naroditsky, and *At Home among Strangers, a Stranger among His Own* (*Svoi sredi chuzhikh, chuzhoi sredi svoikh*, 1974) by Nikita Mikhalkov. Notably, critics responded very positively to the use of formerly sanctimonious plots of the civil war as the material for dynamic action movies full of quotations from Western films.[18]

Especially illuminating in this respect is *White Sun of the Desert* – a movie that enjoyed a cult reputation throughout the entire late Soviet period, and beyond. At first glance, the adventures of the Red soldier Sukhov (Anatolii Kuznetsov) in Central Asia, and his struggle with Black Abdulla (Kakhi Kavsadze) and his gang has the goal of saving women from Abdulla's harem. However, unlike, for example, Andrey Konchalovsky in *The First Teacher* (*Pervyi uchitel'*, 1965) and Irina Poplavskaya and Sergei Yutkevich in *Dzhamilia* (1972), Vladimir Motyl' treats the theme of the emancipation of women from patriarchal oppression ironically, as an irrelevant and self-defeating utopian ideal. Sukhov's imaginary adoption of the entire harem, along with his beloved Katerina Matveevna, visually solidifies such a perception by radically downplaying the emancipatory meaning of the revolution and reducing it to lip service at best (figure 8.6).

The friendship between Sukhov and a former imperial customs officer, Vereshchagin (Pavel Luspekaev), presents a much more serious undertone. Vereshchagin's motto, "Ia mzdu ne beru, mne za derzhavu obidno" ("I don't take bribes, I take an insult for the state"), lays the foundation for an alliance between the Red Army soldier and the imperial officer, since both of them selflessly defend state interests against selfish and greedy gangsters, who predictably appear as the main

Figure 8.6. Sukhov's dream about the "adoption" of Abdulla's harem

source of violence. However, the fact that both Sukhov and Veresh-chagin are ethnic Russians, while their opponents – "bandits" – are predominantly non-Slavic, transforms Sukhov's and Vereshchagin's battle with Abdulla into a war for the *restoration of imperial power and imperial order*. Vereshchagin's tragic death fulfils the same function as Chapaev's death at the end of the Vasilievs' film: it sanctifies the values for which the hero dies. Thus, the revolution in one of the most popular films of the 1970s finds its ultimate meaning and justification in the restoration of the imperial order – in other words, the revolutionary narrative imperceptibly transforms into its own opposite.

It would be valid to say that these films' reconceptualization of the revolution suggested that anti-Stalinist forces in the late socialist USSR continued the legacy of morally solid representatives of *both* proponents *and* opponents of the revolution, and that they together had been defending Russia's greatness against the self-serving and brutal masses. This revisionist narrative reflected the quest of post-Stalinist cultural and political elites for new cultural and historical self-justifications, invariably located outside of Soviet ideological doctrine. It also suggested a radical shift in the cultural imaginary in which White officers' epaulets stood for lost but rediscovered symbols of dignity, honour, and moral truth; while Soviet shabby uniforms were becoming less and less distinguishable from the bandits' colourful outfits. Nevertheless, despite these shifts, the *positive* association between state power and violence – initially solidified by socialist realism – remained intact, only violence was now represented by a hybrid of the revolutionary and the intelligentsia's formerly warring discourses.

This new hybrid discourse of violence rejected class origin as a basis for political – and moral – judgment but highlighted state interests as a valid excuse for violence. Service to the state's interests, eventually, also appeared as the ultimate criterion of *moral* legitimacy, the one and only solid foundation. Certainly, in this formula the nature of the Russian state would be imagined as basically unchangeable despite all revolutions, and its stability was construed as founded on that of its elites. An imaginary continuity between pre-revolutionary and post-revolutionary elites, between the Whites and the Reds, was crucial for the finalization of this version of the revolutionary narrative. In short, the state's greatness based on its morally dignified elites replaced the emancipatory meaning of the revolution, thus making the revolution virtually irrelevant for the late Soviet intelligentsia's self-identification.

Art and/as the Revolution

There is another path in the evolution of this narrative that complicates its straightforward logic. I mean those films that represent the revolution as a condition for and the essence of the new art – first of all, *No Path through Fire* (*V ogne broda net*, 1967) by Gleb Panfilov, *Shine, Shine, My Star* (*Gori, gori, moia zvezda*, 1969) by Alexander Mitta, and *The Intervention* (*Interventsiia*, 1967) by Gennadii Poloka. These films attempt to dissociate the revolution from violence altogether, connecting it instead with avant-garde art as the purest embodiment of a revolutionary striving for freedom. In late Soviet culture the avant-garde still was under suspicion as "degenerate art," so its interpretation as the vehicle for true revolutionary emancipation remained a risky business smelling of subversion. The risk, however, appeared to be associated with the fact that the avant-garde legacy seemed to be too emancipatory from the authorities' standpoint.

No Path through Fire is undoubtedly a groundbreaking work in this context. Contemporary critics (Igor Gulin, Pavel Arseniev) see in it the freshness of Italian neorealism fused with a novel understanding of the meaning of the revolution.[19] In no way does the film gloss over the destruction and suffering brought about by the revolution. Among

Figure 8.7. One of Tanya's pictures in *No Path through Fire* (actual artist –
Marksen Gaukhman-Sverdlov)

the film's characters appears a peasant who speaks with stunning candour about the hunger and devastation instigated by the Reds' raids on
the village. "I want the world revolution sooner," says the film's protagonist, Tanya Tyotkina (Inna Churikova). "People are suffering too
much." Naively, she believes that people's suffering, caused by the Russian Revolution, will end as soon as the revolution becomes global, and
the film's authors do not hide their ironic stance towards her naivety.

   Nevertheless, the film is filled with joy – joy derived from Tanya's
first love and her self-discovery as an artist of the revolution. Tanya's
paintings (figure 8.7) appear as dividers between the film's chapters –
they seemingly illustrate the plot of the film. Created in a neoprimitivist
style reminiscent of both Pirosmani and Pavel Filonov, they represent a
higher, even *transcendental*, plane in relation to the mundane life of the
medical and propaganda train that the film portrays. In other words,
they seek to function as icons. Yet they rise to this meaning only in the
film's finale, which connects Tanya's art with her life, or rather with her
death.

   In the film's finale, Tanya together with a dogmatic communist, Petrovich (Mikhail Gluzskii), is captured by the Whites. The White officer,

whom Evgeny Lebedev plays with an uncanny power, after learning that Tanya wants to become an artist, first tests her artistic intuition – Tanya correctly identifies, on a wall covered by a dozen icons, one that is truly valuable. This gesture connects Tanya's art with the conversation between her and the colonel (figure 8.8), in which the meaning of the revolution is interpreted in religious terms, which in turn signifies a radical transformation of the revolutionary narrative.

> COLONEL: ... You see, we both love Russia. But what's going on in our Russia?
> TANYA: Revolution.
> COLONEL: And what is it for, did you ask yourself? [...]
> TANYA: To get rid of all those who make people suffer (*chtoby vsekh muchtelei pogubit'*). [...]
> COLONEL: So you believe that the time will come when people would stop torturing other people.
> TANYA: I do.
> COLONEL: So you believe in universal harmony?
> TANYA: What?
> COLONEL: You believe in the Rapture?
> TANYA: What? I don't understand you ...
> COLONEL: When everybody will be happy.
> TANYA: Yes, I do believe in this.
> COLONEL: And for this let the brother kill his brother, the Russian kill another Russian, is it so?
> TANYA: There is no path in through fire. [...]
> COLONEL: So, you have this faith.
> TANYA: Yes, I do.
> COLONEL: Such a faith ... But for faith one has to suffer. Are you ready to suffer?

This conversation not only completely avoids the issue of revolutionary violence, it effectively circumvents the revolution itself. After translating Tanya's rhetoric into religious terms (universal harmony, the Rapture) reminiscent of Russian religious philosophy of the turn of the century, the colonel comes to a radical conclusion: What seems to be a civil war is indeed a religious war! It's not about the revolution, it's about faith! Perhaps it's the greatest religious war in Russian history, but it has nothing to do with Marxism or a communist utopia. It's about world harmony, as religious wars have always been.

Certainly, such an interpretation devalues any ideological differences between the Reds and the Whites, between revolutionary violence and

Figure 8.8. A dialogue about faith between Tanya and the White colonel

its counterparts. If the civil war is a religious battle between competing faith systems, then those whose faith is stronger would defeat
those who are less fanatical. The content of faith means less than the
ardour of believers. Tanya's seemingly senseless self-sacrifice clearly
demonstrates that the Bolsheviks' faith is stronger, which is why the
Bolsheviks win. Tanya's pictures that appear after the end of the film's
narrative directly manifest this vision. They are accompanied by the
singing of verses from Alexander Blok's *The Twelve*. The chorus vocal-
izes the famous line "Mirovoi pozhar v krovi" ("The global fire in
blood") but stops short of the next line: "Gospodi, blagoslovi" ("God
bless you!") It's the viewer who is supposed to finish the sequence in
his/her own mind. In this context, Tanya's pictures suddenly change
their meaning – Red Army trumpeters now look like angels glorifying
a newly ascended martyr. Ironically, from this perspective, it's not surprising that thirty-three years later the same Gleb Panfilov would make
an icon-like film about the Romanovs – *Romanovy, ventsenosnaia sem'ia*
(*The Romanovs, a Crowned Family*, 2009). If faith and martyrdom are all
that matter, the object of veneration is indeed replaceable: while in 1967
this was the Russian Revolution, in 2009 it's the Russian monarchy.

However, it is important that in *No Path through Fire* it is the neoprimitivist art of a fictional Tanya Tyotkina that preserves the revolutionary faith and thus justifies both suffering and violence alike. After the
Great Terror and the disappointments of the Thaw, revolutionary art
arises as the sole uncorrupted symbol of the revolution, as its magic

essence. Connections between Tanya's art and the avant-garde are not clearly drawn, but the distinction between her works and the socialist realist canon is obvious. In Aleksandr Mitta's *Shine, Shine, My Star*, an enthusiastic wandering actor and theatre director Iskremas – the name standing for "Art for revolutionary masses" – played by young Oleg Tabakov, dreams about a new theatre that engages the entire town through his large-scale performance about Joan of Arc. An avant-gardist genealogy of Iskremas's artistic vision is demonstrative, albeit presented with a touch of irony. He directly refers to Meyerhold as his authority, but his own vision of theatre is more reminiscent of Nikolai Evreinov's productions of early Soviet mass shows. Iskremas's avant-gardism is contrasted to the conformism of the movie theatre's director (Evgeny Leonov).

Iskremas's ally appears in the form of Fedor (Oleg Efremov), a self-made painter and sculptor working in the expressionist manner. If Fedor is nonchalantly executed by a White soldier, the movie theatre's director invariably enjoys both popularity among the townsfolk and the support of every administration in the town, thanks to his ability to change the commentary to his "drama at the seashore" according to the ruling ideology of the moment. However, despite Iskremas's devotion to the revolution, the Red authorities are no more supportive of his projects than the Whites. Tellingly, the White officers are played in this film by famous directors from the generation of the sixties – Vladimir Naumov and Marlen Khutsiev – thus appearing as cultural rather than political authorities. These officers, after a short and unsuccessful attempt to tame Iskremas, torture the artist by shooting at him blindfolded – the so-called cuckoo game. Taken together, these and similar plot details suggest the interpretation of Mitta's film as a parable about the marginalization and persecution of truly revolutionary art by *any* form of power – this art is too countercultural by default, and therefore is suspicious to Reds and Whites alike.

However, as usual with the films of this period, neither the Whites nor the Reds but the "bandits" represent true evil in this film. In the movie's culmination, Iskremas sacrifices his production in order to destroy the plans of the local "bandits," who are trying to take control of the town; in retaliation, he is killed by one of the surviving members of the gang in the film's finale. Iskremas's sacrificial offering suggests that avant-garde art reaches its highest point when it destroys theatre's fourth wall, not for the sake of shock but in a desperate gesture against violence. Indeed, this is a sweetened version of an avant-garde art that, as we know, not infrequently did orchestrate revolutionary violence. But this redaction may not seem too saccharine if, once again, the viewer can accept the implicit equation between an imaginary avant-garde art and the lost and forgotten spirit of the revolution – humanistic rather than violent. The film's authors present this spirit as reconstructed, but in fact it is created anew in front of the viewers' eyes along with Iskremas's production.

Despite their authors' positive presentation of the avant-garde, neither *No Path through Fire* nor *Shine, Shine, My Star* is avant-gardist in its own right. Gennadii Poloka, however, does take this logical step in his film *Intervention* (1968). The plot of this film centres on the adventures of the leader of the Red underground in Odessa, which is controlled by the Whites and by French forces. The hero, "a Jew, a Communist, and a trickster" (Ilya Kukulin),[20] not only has the provocative last name "Brodsky" but also is performed by Vladimir Vysotsky. Yet, this plot serves only as a frame for a playful production that revives experiments of the Meyerhold and Brecht theatres, including buffoonish masks, carnival grotesques, and cabaret-like songs. Naturally, if avant-garde art preserves the emancipatory and defamiliarizing power of the revolution, its historical forms should be retrieved from oblivion. Despite its heroic plot, the film was shelved for its alleged "formalism." The official letter from the head of the committee for cinematography to the Party's Central Committee explained the ban in the following words: "Film director Poloka was shooting his film in a genre of political farce and grotesque buffonade. An eccentric stream of masks subdued the revolutionary theme ... Selected stylistics came into conflict with the concept of the film and play."[21] This means that the authorities refused to recognize the revolutionary semantics of the film's form, or rather they did recognize it but ruled it out as incompatible with the *proper* style of a revolutionary narrative, which they imagined as much more traditionalist and, in any case, non-avantgardist. There was an explicit order to destroy *The Intervention* and recycle the film used for its production. However, Poloka managed to save one copy, which he secretly screened until its deshelving in 1987.

A similar fate awaited the film *Pervorossiiane* (*First Russians*, 1967). It was based on Olga Berggoltz's long poem *Pervorossiisk* and directed by the nonconformist artist Evgeny Shiffers in collaboration with, or rather under the protection of, an official film director, Aleksandr Ivanov. *Pervorossiiane* synthesizes a religious interpretation of the revolution that is reminiscent of Panfilov's film, with an even more radical visual avant-gardism than in Poloka's film. The prohibition against avant-gardist films about the revolution clearly demonstrated the incompatibility between the revolutionary energy "frozen" in avant-gardist artistic devices and the new version of the revolutionary narratives that gravitated to conservatism in ideology and aesthetics alike.

No Way Out, or Conclusion(s)?

How did the cine-narrative on the Russian Revolution transform in the 2000s, when the ideology of the state as the ultimate value came to be adopted by the cultural and ideological mainstream? Nowadays, one can trace this ideology in the cinematic representation of any historical period – from the medieval Rus' (*Viking, Sofia*) to Brezhnev's times (*Optimists, Our Happy Tomorrow*, etc.). The revolutionary period depicted from this viewpoint appears in the TV series *The Death of Empire* (2005) by the director Vladimir Khotinenko; a pro-state and pro-Orthodox faith rewriting of the socialist realist *Chapaev* in the TV series *Passions for Chapai* (2012) by Sergei Scherbin and in the monarchist remake of the *Imperceptible Avengers – Gentlemen Officers: To Save the Emperor* (*Gospoda ofitsery: Spasti imperatora*, 2004) – although this film reveals more similarities with the *Magnificent Seven*. The same Andrei Kravchuk in 2008 would create a reversal of the socialist realist portrayal of the revolutionary hero in his biopic *Admiral* (2008), about the leader of the White movement, Admiral Kolchak. As Andrei Arkhangelsky, an authoritative critic, wrote about *Admiral*, "This film is good specifically because it is openly anti-Bolshevist. An intentional idealization of the Whites is better than a preposterous directorial effort to combine 'Soviet' and 'pre-Soviet.' At least, the viewer gets a chance to disagree with the position of the film's author – by this means, we could trigger in the society a discussion about moral and other values."[22] The discussion did not follow, and the idealized image of Kolchak was accepted by society as calmly as the new TV version of *The Road to Calvary* (2017) by Alexei Tolstoi directed by Konstantin Khudiakov, in which the socialist realist story of the reforging of four pre-revolutionary *intelligenty* into supporters of the new regime is transformed into the story of fighting for family values that transcend any political and ideological affiliations.

Notably, all these films either minimize or glamorize violence associated with the revolution and civil war. Symptomatically, one of the few films to address these issues with true artistic courage remains virtually unknown and marginalized – I mean the first film by Aleksandr Rogozhkin, *Chekist* (1991), based on the novella *Shchepka* (*Sliver*) written by Vladimir Zazubrin (1895–1937) in 1923 and published only in 1989. Both the literary text and the film depict from the inside the "mechanics" of the Red Terror. This film fills a lacuna in the Soviet visual vocabulary by creating an iconography of the Red violence, supposedly inspired by revolutionary faith. In this film, Rogozhkin creates a naturalistic and at the same time highly symbolic image of violence – with naked bodies mechanically loaded into trucks, with the shooting of naked people next to doors (to the next world? to the kingdom of communism?), a process that is repeated so many times that it becomes a ritual (figure 8.9). Naturally, this ritual drives everyone crazy who is involved in the mechanical process of murdering people captured by the net of terror for anything – for serving in the imperial army, for befriending another victim, for making jokes. The characters who are performing this massacre are depicted almost as idealists who are willing to sacrifice their idealism, along with their friends and relatives, feelings, and sanity for the sake of the revolution. Notably, this film also contains (in full agreement with Zazubrin's text), a personified image of the revolution as a cynical and unappealing Cheka cleaning lady, played by Nina Usatova.

However, in the 2010s, the most influential and resonant films about the revolution did not avoid the theme of violence. Especially important in this respect were *The Life of One Woman* (*Zhila-byla odna baba*, 2011) by Andrei Smirnov; *Sunstroke* (*Solnechnyi udar*, 2014) by Nikita Mikhalkov; and *Angels of Revolution* (*Angely revoliutsii*, 2014) by Aleksei Fedorchenko. Each of these films adopts the perspective of one of three forces shaping the cinematic narrative of the revolution and civil war since the 1930s – the Whites (Mikhalkov), the Reds (Fedorchenko), and the "bandits" (Smirnov).

Smirnov (b. 1941) and Mikhalkov (b. 1945) belong to the same generation of the late 1960s (even their biographies are somewhat similar – both had famous Soviet writers as their fathers, and therefore belonged to the top Soviet elite from childhood); however, their political positions in today's spectrum are opposites: while Mikhalkov is the loudest and most ecstatic supporter of Putin and his neonationalist agenda, Smirnov in his interviews and other statements invariably shows solidarity with liberal critics of the regime. Despite their ideological differences, their filmic representations of the revolution display similar transformations of their shared "canvas" – the revolutionary cine-narrative of the 1960s and 1970s.

Both Smirnov and Mikhalkov reduce the triad of the Whites/ Reds/"bandits" to a binary opposition, thus simplifying the pre-existing narrative. Smirnov depicts the Bolsheviks' warfare against peasants (later participants of Antonov's uprising, whom Soviet propaganda typically labelled as "bandits"); while Mikhalkov focuses on the classical Reds-versus-Whites confrontation. However, both portray the

Figure 8.9. Revolution in Rogozhkin's *Chekist* resonates both with medieval images of hell and photographs of the Holocaust

Reds as solely responsible for the civil war's violence and foreign to the "organically Russian" way of life. Smirnov does this more subtly – his Reds do not belong to the peasant world and appear as alien invaders in the village. Mikhalkov with alt-right candour emphasizes the Jewishness of Rozalia Zemliachka, while depicting her partner in crime, a Hungarian Bolshevik, Mate Zalka, as unable to pronounce even one Russian word. The only ethnic Russian character responsible for the execution of thousands of White officers is portrayed by Mikhalkov as a former nice boy who had been shocked by Darwin's theory of evolution, lost his faith in God, and became Bolshevik. Not too subtle either.

Smirnov tells the story of the revolution and civil war from the standpoint of an illiterate and much-suffering peasant woman from the Tambov region – Darya (played by Darya Ekamasova). She is the victim of the patriarchal repression in her husband's family before the revolution; this violence, which includes Darya's rape by a husband and her father-in-law, emerges in Smirnov's film as the epitome of communal violence but not as a justification for the revolution. Darya's life becomes even worse when she remains alone with a child after the First World War and borders on catastrophe after the revolution. Her sufferings and the sufferings of the people around her, especially of her secret lover Lebeda (Aleksei Serebrennikov), sometimes are caused by their neighbours, but most frequently they come from the Reds, whose violence is depicted graphically and as lacking any moral justification. The film's culmination comes with the formation of the Antonov Rebel Army, which supposedly purifies the communal violence of the peasants' world by transforming it into a retaliatory and just violence of a peasants' defensive war against brutal foreign invaders – the Bolsheviks. Notably, unlike the Reds' crimes, the violence performed by the Antonov's army is only mentioned in the film but not depicted visibly.

Sunstroke is not the first of Mikhalkov's films about the revolutionary epoch – but in both *At Home among Strangers, a Stranger among His Own* (1974) and *The Slave of Love* (1975) he depicted Bolsheviks as the epitome of morality and their political opponents as cynics, sadists, and opportunists. In *Sunstroke* Mikhalkov completely turns this binary upside down: not only do Bolsheviks appear as moral freaks, but the entire film's narrative circles around the juxtaposition of an idyllic pre-revolutionary love story (loosely based on Bunin's "Sunstroke") and the bleak scenes of the concentration camp for thousands of White officers in Crimea, after the defeat of Vrangel's army. Mikhalkov intentionally blurs geographic coordinates; in one scene future victims of the Red Terror are taking a group photograph at the steps of the would-be Potemkin staircase; in another, he obviously mocks Eisenstein's carriage scene. His logic is clear – avant-garde art, exemplified by *Battleship Potemkin*, appears in *Sunstroke* as the accomplice of the Red Terror. The Whites, on the contrary, are depicted only and exclusively as innocent victims. Their innocence is even more pronounced than that of Smirnov's peasants: they voluntarily gave up and subjugated themselves to the Reds, who promised them life but instead sank the boat with officers locked inside. Tragic victims of this evil scheme, they die without resistance and violence – like Boris and Gleb, famous Russian martyr saints, multiplied a thousand times. The film critic Anton Dolin called *Sunstroke* "our *Titanic*," arguing that the motif of the ship connects the pre-revolutionary love story and the final scene of massacre.[23] The meaning of the ship as a metaphor of the state is too obvious to require any additional comments. However, these metaphors do not outweigh the oversimplifications in Mikhalkov's narrative, which uses only two colours: black versus white, sunstroke versus darkness.

Alexei Fedorchenko (b. 1966) belongs to the "last Soviet generation" (to use Alexei Yurchak's expression) – one that is obviously quite distant from that of Smirnov and Mikhalkov. A winner of numerous international and national awards, he is famous for an interest both in the cultural archaeology of the 1930s (*Pervye na Lune / First on the*

Moon, 2005) and in the archaic and invented cultural traditions of Russia's national minorities (*Ovsianki / Silent Souls,* 2010; *Nebesnye zheny lugovykh mari / Celestial Wives of the Meadow Mari,* 2012). *Angels of Revolution* fuses together two interests of the director and his frequent scriptwriter, Denis Osokin: the film tells a story of the Kazym Cultural Base (*Kazymskaia kul'tbaza,* 1930) whose undertakings served as a trigger for the Kazym Uprising (1931–4) of the Khanty and Nentsy against the Soviet colonization that also included collectivization. However, at the same time the film is a reflection on the Soviet avant-garde and its historical meaning. The historical character Polina Schneider, played by Darya Ekamasova, the star of Smirnov's epic, gathers around herself for the Kazym expedition brilliant representatives of the avant-garde, among whom one may recognize Eisenstein (who is making a film about the Mexican uprising) or Arseny Avraamov, a composer of symphonies made from industrial noises. The film's form is also a tribute to the avant-garde legacy: Fedorchenko depicts the world of artists in a dreamy and grotesque manner, and the entire revolutionary discourse appears to be a form of fairy tale akin to the Khanty's myths and tales.

One of the opening scenes underscores the fairy-tale origins of avant-gardist projects: Polina receives a new assignment at the Commissariat of Nationalities. This commissariat Fedorchenko situates in a peculiar house (actually located near Neviansk, in the Sverdlovsk region) that is decorated to almost baroque excess with Soviet symbolism, producing the effect of a fairy-tale *teremok* of the Soviet era. It is no wonder that one of the film's characters, Ivan the composer, delivers a passionate monologue about "our Commissariats" as sources of poetry. This *teremok* indeed functions as a source of poetic and radical avant-gardist projects, which, at the same time, affect the life of real people and even whole nationalities.

While obviously admiring his avant-gardists, Fedorchenko methodically highlights links between each of the avant-gardists' inventions and violence. Polina takes hold of Termenvox after shooting its inventor, who turns out to be a class enemy (a fully fictional motif); a film director Petr uses real people sentenced to death in the scene of execution in his Mexican movie; Nikolai, an inventor of new Soviet burial rites (figure 8.10), meets Polina while "recruiting" her (among others) to his partisan unit by means of torture; an artist, Zakhar, while erecting a monument to Judas (a famous legend), destroys the life of his model, a monk, who not only wrecked the monument but also hanged himself on its ruin ...

Figure 8.10. New Soviet coffins in *The Angels of Revolution*

Most importantly, while depicting the cultural mission of avant-gardists in Kazym, Fedorchenko does not hide its colonialist meaning – along with a hospital and school, they impose alien cultural models and without mercy desecrate the Khanty's sacred lake, for which the insulted Khanty kill all avant-gardists. The film doesn't show the blood-shed of the uprising – we only see the dead bodies of Polina and artists lying with ropes on their necks on the floor; violence is replaced either by a Khanty ritual or a childlike fighting between traditional wooden figurines.

Fedorchenko offers three versions of the finale in *Angels of Revolution* – each adding a new angle to the image of the revolution and its mean-ing. In the first finale, the faces of killed avant-gardists appear on the screen of smoke, which in a previous scene they themselves used for showing the movie about the Khanty goddess they made on a sacred island. The meaning of this finale is obvious: the avant-garde merges with traditional culture, and avant-garde artists are interchangeable with ancient gods and spirits – they also create new worlds, in which they themselves live and die as humans.

The second finale depicts a Soviet punitive operation against the Khanty's uprising. Notably, Polina's lover, the composer Ivan (Oleg

Iagodin), commands a military unit sent to punish the rebels. We see him ordering the eyelids of its leader – Kniaz' (Prince) – to be cut. After this a camera follows a long train of deer-led sledges loaded with dead bodies of Khanty on them, concluding with the roped body of Kniaz' with bloody circles around his eyes. Obviously, not avant-gardists but Khanty are sacrificed here in this rite of the new world's formation. However, in the next scene Ivan kills himself while hiding in the basket of a deflated blimp made of deer skins – a clear symbol of the avant-gardist dream's failure. An inspired avant-gardist flight to the sky proves to be incompatible with the Soviet terror and functions of a torturer and executioner.

The third finale is non-fictional – it shows a Khanty woman, who indeed was the first child born in the maternity ward created by Polina Schneider. A celebration of her birth is shown in the movie, but here she appears as an old and crippled woman in the sterile interior of a contemporary apartment that bears no signs of the national Khanty culture. She crosses an apartment with her walker while singing "A Song of the Troubled Youth" ("*Pesnia o trevozhnoi molodosti*") by Lev Oshanin and Alexandra Pakhmutova from the 1958 film about the civil war *Po tu storonu* (*On the Other Side*, dir. Fedor Filippov). This song, typical of the late Soviet revolutionary narrative, sounds like an epitaph both for the avant-gardist revolutionary imagination and the national culture that was destroyed in the process of Soviet colonization.

Fedorchenko's film, especially in comparison to Mikhalkov's and Smirnov's attempts at epic, appears as the only successful version of a reworking of the late Soviet revolutionary narrative. Fedorchenko obviously continues the line that begins with *No Path through Fire, Shine, Shine, My Star,* and *Intervention*. At the same time, *Angels of Revolution* is almost unique as a film in deviating from the dominant narrative on the revolution.

While adopting the viewpoint of his heroes, Fedorchenko does not try to whitewash their responsibility for historical tragedies; neither does he try to present them as pure victims of history. On the contrary, he emphasizes the connections between avant-garde art and revolutionary violence – a motif absent or muffled in late Soviet films. Moreover, *Angels of Revolution* widens the spectrum of revolutionary violence by including in it a discourse of colonialism, which in late Soviet films (such as *White Sun of the Desert*) had been presented predominately in a positive way. Fedorchenko avoids both ascribing violence to "them" as opposed to "us" as well as wholesale justification of "our" violence as necessary or even sacred. "Our" responsibility for violence appears here as the basic condition for the recovery of revolution's striving for freedom. In this respect, *Angels of Revolution* contains the seed of an entirely new narrative, or several narratives, on the revolution.

Since the 1920s the narrative of the revolution and civil war had been sacred territory in Soviet culture, where even little changes could have had tremendous resonance. In post-Stalinist culture, this narrative became one of the main tools for the revision of the foundation of the Soviet political and ideological model. As we see, the main vector of these revisions considered the official justifications of the revolutionary violence while at the same seeking to formulate different discursive connections between the late Soviet elites and political forces involved in revolutionary conflicts. To sum up, our brief survey of transformations of the revolutionary narrative in films of the 1960s and 1970s reveals the following dominant tendencies:

- The mirroring of the discourse of violence and forces that traditionally embody them in Soviet culture (as in *The Quiet Don*) allows the possibility of various alliances between the Reds and the Whites, who appear united either by the concept of moral dignity or by the state interests of Great Russia or even, in particular cases (*White Sun of the Desert*), the interests of the Russian empire.
- "The Greens"/"bandits" – who traditionally signify the masses – are not only excluded from all these alliances but also rise as the main source of violence and revolutionary chaos.
- Discourses of violence associated with the Reds and the Whites are either minimized or – by different means – associated with Stalinism and the Great Terror. As a result of these transformations, the emancipatory idea of the revolution fades away and is reduced to mere rhetorical gestures.
- Simultaneous attempts to preserve the revolution's emancipatory meaning through the filmic representation of avant-garde art were inconsistent because of the official resistance towards avant-gardist aesthetics, as well as viewers' unpreparedness for it.

While routinely turning upside down established Soviet discourses on the revolution, the civil war, and its heroes, post-Soviet film mainly preserves this discursive condition, testifying to the fact that the revolution still constitutes a foundational trauma for contemporary elites, cultural and political alike. The late Soviet interpretations of the Russian Revolution, as we can see, symbolically justified a mutually beneficial consensus between political and cultural elites; this consensus grew on the fundamental fear of the "masses" as destructive anti-state as well as anti-cultural anarchic forces. Although this consensus apparently broke in the years of perestroika, in the 2000s it gradually returned and apparently continues to be relevant in today's cultural and political atmosphere, where both the authorities and the mainstream of the oppositional intelligentsia remain afraid of the masses. This fear obviously contradicts the oppositional intelligentsia's dreams about emancipation from a corrupt and nationalist regime. The quest for the resolution of this contradiction will inevitably require new revisions of the discourse on the revolution, first and foremost in cinema as the art form with the broadest public appeal. *Angels of Revolution* is only a first step in this direction.

NOTES

This chapter is a much-expanded and revised version of the article "Za chto borolis'? Revoliutsionnyi narrative v sovetskikh i postsovetskikh fil'makh o Grazhdanskoi voine," which appeared in *Neprikosnovennyi zapas* 2, 118 (2018): 91–111.

1 Kalinin, "The Spectre of the Revolution."
2 Baudrillard, "Revolution and the End of Utopia," 233.
3 Dobrenko, "Vse, chto vy khoteli znat' o revoliiutsii," 184. One of the most prominent debates about the "sanctity of the last Russian tsar" centred on Alexei Uchitel's film *Matilda*, which debuted at the precise moment of the revolution's centenary, on 26 October 2017. Calls to ban this cinematic depiction of Tsar Nicholas II's love affair with ballerina Matilda Kschesinskaia came from Duma deputy Natalia Poklonskaia as well as members of the Russian Orthodox Church. See Kolonitsky and Matskevich, "Idle Memory?"
4 Snegovaia, "Kuda i pochemu ischezla Oktiabr'skaia revoliutsiia iz pamiati naroda?"
5 For a survey of similar film material, yet from a different perspective, see Norris, "Revising History, Remaking Heroes."
6 See Beumers and Lipovetsky, *Performing Violence*, 49–67.
7 This approach was described in 1995 by Zygmunt Bauman as "political gardening," or "creative destruction": "What we learned in this century is that modernity is not only about producing more and travelling faster, getting richer and moving around more freely. *It is also about – it has been about – fast and efficient killing, scientifically designed and administered genocide.* [...] [The] destruction [of people who did not fit the model of a perfect universe] was a *creative* destruction, much as the the removal of weeds is a creative act in pursuit of a designed garden beauty. In the case of Hitler,

the design was a race-clean society. In the case of Lenin, the design was a class-clean society. In both cases, at stake was an aesthetically satisfying, transparent, homogeneous universe free from agonizing uncertainties, ambivalence, contingency – and therefore, from the carrier of lesser value, the backward, the unteachable and untouchable. But this was, was it not, precisely the kind of universe dreamed up and promised by the philosophers of Enlightenment, to be pursued by the despots whom they sought to enlighten." Zygmunt Bauman. "The Century of Camps," in Beilharz, ed., *The Bauman Reader*, 269, 272; emphasis in the original.

8 See, for example, Dobrenko, *Political Economy of Socialist Realism*, 208–64, 307–32.

9 For a detailed analysis of the discourse of historical trauma in the Mandelshtam's *Egyptian Stamp* see Lipovetskii, "Allegoriia istorii: *Egipetskaia marka* Osipa Mandel'shtama."

10 See Ries, *Russian Talk*, esp. 83–125.

11 From Tolstaya, "The Great Terror and the Little Terror (1991)."

12 See Leiderman, "Krovavyi karnaval. 'Poemy v prize' 1920-kh godov."

13 See Clark, *The Soviet Novel*, 83–9.

14 See about some of these films: Vaisfel'd, "Pravda kharakterov"; Zorkaia, "V poiskakh pravdy"; Salynskii, "Printipial'naia udacha iskusstva"; Youngblood, *Russian War Films*, 37–50.

15 Although *The Quiet Don* received the Stalin Prize in 1941, its first two volumes appeared in 1928, while the second part was completed by 1932 and only published in 1940 (after the publication of *Virgin Land Upturned*). Boris Lavrenev was awarded the Stalin Prize twice – in 1945 and 1950 for shamelessly ideological works, but his *Forty First* written in 1924 and already turned by Yakov Protazanov into a silent film in 1927, albeit quite different from his later writings, was regularly reprinted in his numerous volumes.

16 Youngblood, *Russian War Films*, 115.

17 Curiously, this message of *Aide-de-camp of His Excellency* has been reproduced and even enhanced in the recent novel by Boris Akunin *Ne proshchaius'* (*Not Saying Goodbye*, 2018). While openly replaying themes and situations of Tashkov's mini-series, Akunin makes his perennial protagonist, the Great Detective Erast Fandorin, pontificate a moral position very similar to that of Kol'tsov: "He said that his enemies are neither the Reds, nor the Greens, nor the Violets, but bastards of any kind who can be coloured differently. As well as the enemies of the motherland. Who to consider enemies of the motherland in the current circumstances – is not too obvious. He personally thinks that anybody participating in this damn massacre is guilty." Akunin, *Ne proshchaius*. Ebook, no pagination.

18 See, for example, very positive reviews of Keosaian's films: Shcherbakov, "Vozvrashchenie zhanra"; Smolianitskii, "Prodolzhenie sleduet."
19 Arsen'ev and Gulin, "Tragediia i fars sovetskogo iazyka (o lingvopragmatike fil'mov Gleba Panfilova)."
20 Kukulin, *Mashiny zashumevshego vremeni*, 415. See also 415–18 for the analysis of Poloka's film.
21 Fomin, ed., *Kinematograf Ottepeli*, 169.
22 Arkhangel'skii, "Byl poriadok."
23 "Anton Dolin o 'Solnechnom udare' Mikhalkova." https://kuzmaabrikosov .wordpress.com/2014/10/15/dolin-udar/.

REFERENCES

Akunin, Boris. *Ne proshchaius'*. Litres, 2018. Ebook.
"Anton Dolin o 'Solnechnom udare' Mikhalkova." https://kuzmaabrikosov .wordpress.com/2014/10/15/dolin-udar/.
Arkhangel'skii, Andrei. "Byl poriadok." *Kommersant*, 19 October 2008. https:// www.kommersant.ru/doc/2301567.
Arsen'ev, Pavel, and Igor' Gulin. "Tragediia i fars sovetskogo iazyka (o lingvopragmatike fil'mov Gleba Panfilova)." *Translit* 12 (2014). http://www .trans-lit.info/materialy/12-materialy/tragediya-i-fars-sovetskogo-yazyka -o-lingvopragmatike-filmov-gleba-panfilova.
Baudrillard, Jean. "Revolution and the End of Utopia." In Jean Baudrillard, *The Disappearance of Art and Politics*. New York: St Martin's Press, 1992.
Beilharz, Peter, ed. *The Bauman Reader*. Oxford: Blackwell, 2001.
Beumers, Birgit, and Mark Lipovetsky. *Performing Violence: Literary and Theatrical Experiments of New Russian Drama*. Bristol and Chicago: Intellect, 2008.
Clark, Katerina. *The Soviet Novel: History as Ritual*. Bloomington and Indianapolis: Indiana University Press, 2003.
Dobrenko, Evgeny. *Political Economy of Socialist Realism*. New Haven, CT: Yale University Press, 2007.
– "Vse, chto vy khoteli znat' o revoliiutsii, no boialis' sprosit' u Iiuriia Trifonova, ili Ochen' dlinnyi kurs istorii VKP(b)." *Novyi mir* 12 (2017): 184 [183–9].
Fomin V.I., ed. *Kinematograf Ottepeli: Dokumenty i svidetel'stva*. Moscow: Materik, 1998.
Kalinin, Ilya. "The Spectre of the Revolution." *The Times Literary Supplement*, 15 February 2017. https://www.the-tls.co.uk/articles/private/spectre -russian-revolution/.

Kolonitsky, Boris, and Maria Matskevich. "Idle Memory? The 1917 Anniversary in Russia." In *Circles of the Russian Revolution: Internal and International Consequences of the Year 1917 in Russia,* edited by Łukasz Adamski and Bartłomiej Gajosj, 202–19. London and New York: Routledge, 2019.

Kukulin, Ilya. *Mashiny zashumevshego vremeni: Kak sovetskii montazh stal metodom neofitsial'noi kul'tury.* Moscow: NLO, 2015.

Leiderman, Naum. "Krovavyi karnaval. 'Poemy v proze' 1920-kh godov: Poetika i semantika." *Voprosy literatury* 5 (2008): 241–67.

Lipovetskii, Mark. "Allegoriia istorii: *Egipetskaia marka* Osipa Mandel'shtama." In *Paralogii: Transformatsii russkogo (post)modernistskogo diskursa v russkoi kul'ture 1920-kh-2000-kh godov.* Moscow: Novoe Literaturnoe Obozrenie, 2008, 73–114.

Norris, Steven M. "Revising History, Remaking Heroes: Soviet-Russian Cinema and the Civil War." In *Ruptures and Continuities in Soviet/Russian Cinema: Styles, Characters and Genres before and after the Collapse of the USSR,* edited by Birgit Beumers and Eugene Zvonkine, 200–18. London and New York: Routledge, 2018.

Ries, Nancy. *Russian Talk: Culture and Conversation during Perestroika.* Ithaca, NY: Cornell University Press, 1997.

Salynskii, Afanasii. "Printipial'naia udacha iskusstva." *Iskusstvo kino* 9 (1963): 25–8.

Shcherbakov, Konstantin. "Vozvrashchenie zhanra." *Iskusstvo kino* 6 (1967): 59–61.

Smolianitskii, S. "Prodolzhenie sleduet." *Iskusstvo kino* 1 (1969): 39–44.

Snegovaia, Maria. "Kuda i pochemu ischezla Oktiabr'skaia revoliutsiia iz pamiati naroda?" *Colta.ru,* 11 November 2017. http://www.colta.ru/articles/society/16626.

Tolstaya, Tatiana. "The Great Terror and the Little Terror (1991)." In *Pushkin's Children: Writings on Russia and Russians,* translated by Jamey Gambrell, 14–26. Boston and New York: Mariner Books, 2003.

Vaisfel'd, Iosif. "Pravda kharakterov." *Iskusstvo kino* 7 (1954): 95–102.

Youngblood, Denise J. *Russian War Films: On the Cinema Front, 1914–2005.* Lawrence: University of Kansas Press, 2007.

Zorkaia, Neia. "V poiskakh pravdy." *Iskusstvo kino* 7 (1958): 74–80.

Contributors

Megan Swift is an associate professor of Russian studies at the University of Victoria (British Columbia). She is the author of the award-winning *Picturing the Page: Soviet Illustrated Children's Literature and Reading under Lenin and Stalin* (University of Toronto Press, 2020). Her work has appeared in *Russian Review, Russian Literature,* and *Canadian Slavonic Papers.* She co-edited the Literature section of *The Routledge Encyclopedia of Modernism* (2016).

Maria Silina is an adjunct professor at the Université du Québec à Montréal at the Department of History of Art. They are the author of *History and Ideology: Architectural Sculpture of the 1920s–1930s in the USSR* (in Russian, 2014). Their current book project is dedicated to Soviet museums in the interwar era.

Julie Deschepper is a scientific assistant at the Kunsthistorisches Institut in Florenz–Max-Planck-Institut. Her research focuses on the material culture of socialism, especially architecture, monuments, and objects, and she explores theories of cultural heritage and global iconoclasm as well. She is currently turning her dissertation into a book titled *Entre trace et monument: Une histoire patrimoine soviétique en Russie (1917–2017)* (CNRS Editions, 2023). Her work has also appeared in journals (*International Journal of Heritage Studies; Passés Futurs, 20 & 21: Revue d'histoire*), and she was recently the guest editor of the *Revue Russe.* She is the co-coordinator of the francophone network of the Association of Critical Heritage Studies.

Jennifer Utrata is a professor of sociology in the Sociology and Anthropology Department at the University of Puget Sound in Tacoma, Washington. She is the author of the award-winning *Women without Men:*

Single Mothers and Family Change in the New Russia (Ithaca, NY: Cornell University Press, 2015). She has published articles in *Gender & Society*, *Journal of Marriage & Family*, *Contexts*, and several edited volumes. During 2018–19 she was an ACLS Burkhardt Fellow at the University of Washington. Her second book project examines intensive grandparenting and family inequality in the United States.

David G. Anderson holds the Chair in the Anthropology of the North at the University of Aberdeen. He is the author of *Identity and Ecology in Arctic Siberia* (2000) and editor of several volumes in northern anthropology, the most recent of which is *Life Histories of Etnos Theory in Russia and Beyond* (2019).

Michael W. Tripp is a professor of geography (retired/adjunct) at Vancouver Island University, British Columbia, with research interests and consulting experience since the 1970s in Russian émigré communities and in Russian national parks and protected areas. His most recent publication as contributing author was *A Professor of the Russian Language in Tokyo: Dushan Todorovic and His Early Life*, (Nabuhiro Shiba, 2018). He is currently writing *A Vladivostok Diary, 1918*, based on the memoirs of his great-grandmother.

Elena V. Baraban is an associate professor of Russian at the University of Manitoba. Her publications include *The Akunin Project: The Mysteries and Histories of Russia's Best-Selling Author* (University of Toronto Press, 2021), a volume of articles co-edited with Stephen M. Norris; the volume of essays *Fighting Words and Images: Representing War across the Disciplines* (University of Toronto Press, 2012), co-edited with Stephan Jaeger and Adam Muller; as well as a number of articles on Soviet and post-Soviet popular culture in *Canadian Slavonic Papers*, *Slavic and East European Studies Journal*, *Ab Imperio*, *Iskusstvo kino*, and *Aspasia*. Dr Baraban's current research project is on Stalin-era cinema.

Mark Lipovetsky is a professor of Russian studies at Columbia University (New York). He is the author of ten books and more than a hundred articles on twentieth- and twenty-first-century Russian literature and culture. Among his most recent publications is the co-authored *History of Russian Literature* (Oxford: Oxford University Press, 2018) and a five-volume collected works of Dmitry Prigov, edited with a group of colleagues. In 2019, Lipovetsky was awarded the Andrei Bely Prize for his contribution to Russian literature.

Index

.S.A

LITARY ROAD
ANDA NEW YORK 14150
6) 693–2768
. NO. 98–0013676

FAX 1–800–221–9985

PROOF OF DELIVERY MUST
S OF RECEIPT.
GOODS SENT BY MAIL.
ED IN TRANSIT TO CARRIER.
TERMS IN FORCE AT INVOICE

ET PREUVE DE LIVRAISON
EES DANS LES 15 JOURS DE

R MARCHANDISE EXPEDIÉE

ES EN COURS DE ROUTE AU

UJETTES AUX CONDITIONS
DE FACTURATION.

NDITION: NET 30 JOURS

O THE
RE DE

ORONTO PRESS
DIT DEPT.
RIN STREET
ONTARIO
5T8

PLEASE QUOTE INVOICE NO AND
ACCOUNT WHEN MAKING
ENQUIRIES

*S'IL VOUS–PLAÎT CITER CE NUMÉRO
DE FACTURE ET NO. DE CLIENT
DANS TOUTES CORRESPONDANCES*

INVOICE NO. NO. DE FACTURE
4871069

ACCOUNT NO. NO. DE CLIENT
773005 000

INVOICE DATE DATE DE FACTURE

PAGE NO.
1

8224844 000

Ctl#7497923

MM. RE	✓	LIST PRICE PRIX LISTE	DISC. % ESC. %	PICKED BY *TRIE PAR*
1		75|00		

PACKED BY
EMPAQUETTE PAR

NO. OF CARTONS
NO. DE CAISSES

SHIPPED BY
EXPÉDIÉ PAR

Packing Slip

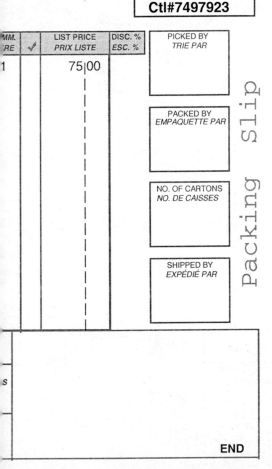

S

END

DISTRIBUTION
UTPDISTRIBUTION.COM

CANADA

5201 DUFFERIN STREET, TORONTO
ONTARIO, CANADA M3H 5T8
TEL.(416) 667-7791 FAX(416) 667-7832
DUNS:251-314-902 SAN 1151134

TOLL FREE NORTH AMERICA TEL. 1-800-565-

ALL CLAIMS INCLU
BE MADE WITHIN 1
NOT RESPONSIBL
REPORT BOOKS D
ALL SALES SUBJE
DATE.
TOUTES RÉCLAMA
DOIVENT ETRE EF
RECEPTION.
PAS RESPONSABI
PAR LA POSTE.
PORTER TOUTES
TRANSPORTEUR.
TOUTES VENTES
EN VIGUEUR À LA

TERMS: NET 30 DA

PAYMENT TO BE
TOUT PAIEMENT

S E H X I P P É E D D I É T À O	SHIPPED TO / EXPÉDIÉ À

HARRIET MURAV
SLAVIC REVIEW
UNIVERSITY OF ILLINOIS
URBANA,IL,U.S.
61801-3716

I F
N A
V C
O T
I U
C R
E É

T À
O

REVIEW COPIES-FREES
6760/203
800 BAY STREET, MEZZANINE
TORONTO, ON
M5S 3A9

UNIVERSITY
ATTN:
5201 D
TOROI

QTY SHIPPED QTÉ EXPÉDIÉE	ISBN-13 BINDING –RELIURE/PUBLISHER-ÉDITEUR	TITLE – TITRE AUTHOR – AUTEUR	ORDER NO ./NOUN ORDRE UTP REF/REF. UTP	O BOJ
1	9781487529567 cloth UTP	REVOLUTIONARY AFTERE SWIFT	SLAVICREV	

SPECIAL MESSAGE/ MESSAGE SPÉCIAL

14 W

TOTAL BO
TOTAL DES

INVOICES MAILED SEPARATELY

SHIPPED BY EXPÉDIÉ PAR	DATE SHIPPED DATE D'EXPÉDITION	WAYBILL NO. NO. DE CONNAISSEMENT	WEIGHT POIDS Kg
*BEST		TRAK#	.4